one thousand gifts

2 in One BOOK & DEVOTIONAL

ANN VOSKAMP

NEW YORK TIMES BESTSELLER

D1319120

ZONDERVAN®

A book destined to become a classic, the sort of book you dog-ear and reread for the sheer joy of cherishing the words and experiencing the depth of the heart that wrote it.

Mary DeMuth

author of *Thin Places: A Memoir*

Where do I begin? Do I tell you that Ann Voskamp writes like a poet with the heart of a mystic? Or do I share with you how *One Thousand Gifts* is so profound that if we internalize this message of lifestyle gratitude and all-pervasive grace, we can know Christ like Adam knew Eve. To write of such beautiful, intimate union requires the pen of a spiritual artist. Open this book, then open your heart.

Lisa Whelchel

actress, speaker, and author of *Creative Correction and Friendship for Grown-Ups*

This book is one that will change the way you see the world.

Marybeth Whalen

author of *The Mailbox* and *She Makes It Look Easy* and director of www.shereads.org

Very rarely in my life have I been given the privilege of sharing about something so exquisite. As I moved from page to page, I became convinced that my life would never be the same. Prepare yourself to leave these pages a changed person. Thank you, Ann—you are the 1001st thing I have on my list today.

Angie Smith

author of *I Will Carry You* and speaker with Women of Faith

As I read *One Thousand Gifts*, I kept thinking of Walt Whitman's haunting phrase, "Finally shall come the poet." It's a rare gift that can render both life's everyday intimacies and the heart's broken rhythms in language at once lucid and lyrical, but Ann does it without seeming to try. And most of all, best of all, she employs that language to tell a story of a life—her own—transformed by the simple act of giving thanks. Finally comes the poet.

Mark Buchanan

author of *The Rest of God* and *Spiritual Rhythm*

Compelling, poetic, and poignant, Ann Voskamp's *One Thousand Gifts* dares us to become grateful in everything. Voskamp is a beautiful narrator, retelling painful, sometimes grief-stricken moments with fearless vulnerability. *One Thousand Gifts* is a masterpiece full of wise hope and light, with simple truths that will inspire you to see God's grace in everyday circumstances, blessings, and hardships.

Matthew Paul Turner
author of *Churched* and *Hear No Evil*

The book itself is the best gift of all — one that stays with you and keeps blessing your life long after you've read the last word.

Holley Gerth
DaySpring editorial director, author, and counselor

To find your deepest heart — to know joy — read your Bible, and this treasure of a book, this portal into the deep goodness of God and of life.

Kelly Monroe Kullberg
author of *Finding God Beyond Harvard*

Ann Voskamp's writing is vibrant, her insights piercing.

Tony Woodlief
World magazine columnist and author of *Somewhere More Holy*

This book is like a treasure hunt. Ann sits beside you and speaks words that will inspire you to open the door into the miracle of holy joy.

Bobbie Wolgemuth
author of *When Morning Gilds the Skies* and compiler of the *NCV Mom's Bible*

One Thousand Gifts reads like a series of prize-winning photographs, bringing the reader to stop and marvel at the depth and detail, the light and shadow, of all those scattered moments in life. Ann Voskamp tells the story behind the image — in memorable, mesmerizing prose.

Allison Pittman
author of *For Time and Eternity* and *Forsaking All Others*

ZONDERVAN

One Thousand Gifts 2 in One Book and Devotional
Copyright © 2013 by Ann Morton Voskamp

One Thousand Gifts
Copyright © 2010 by Ann Morton Voskamp

One Thousand Gifts Devotional
Copyright © 2012 by Ann Morton Voskamp

This title is also available as a Zondervan ebook. Visit www.zondervan.com/ebooks.

This title is also available in a Zondervan audio edition. Visit www.zondervan.fm.

Requests for information should be addressed to:

Zondervan, *Grand Rapids, Michigan 49530*

ISBN 978-0-310-62032-7 (softcover)

Published in association with William K. Jensen Literary Agency, 119 Bampton Court, Eugene, Oregon 97404.

Cover design: Michelle Lenger
Cover photography: Masterfile® , iStockphoto®
Interior design: Beth Shagene

Printed in the United States of America

13 14 15 16 17 18 19 /DCI/ 21 20 19 18 17 16 15 14 13 12 11 10 9 8 7 6 5 4 3 2 1

For the Farmer,
who tended and grew my soul

contents

CHAPTER 1

an emptier, fuller life

Every sin is an attempt to fly from emptiness.
Simone Weil, Gravity and Grace

A glowing sun-orb fills an August sky the day this story begins, the day I am born, the day I begin to live.

And I fill my mother's tearing ring of fire with my body emerging, virgin lungs searing with air of this earth and I enter the world like every person born enters the world: with clenched fists.

From the diameter of her fullness, I empty her out — and she bleeds. Vernix-creased and squalling, I am held to the light.

Then they name me.

Could a name be any shorter? Three letters without even the flourish of an *e*. Ann, a trio of curves and lines.

It means "full of grace."

I haven't been.

What does it mean to live full of grace? *To live fully alive?*

They wash my pasty skin and I breathe and I flail. I flail.

For decades, a life, I continue to flail and strive and come up so seemingly ... *empty*. I haven't lived up to my christening.

Maybe in those first few years my life slowly opened, curled like cupped hands, a receptacle open to the gifts God gives.

But of those years, I have no memories. They say memory jolts awake with trauma's electricity. That would be the year I turned four. The year when blood pooled and my sister died and I, all of us, snapped shut to grace.

⁓

Standing at the side porch window, watching my parents' stunned bending, I wonder if my mother had held me in those natal moments of naming like she held my sister in death.

In November light, I see my mother and father sitting on the back porch step rocking her swaddled body in their arms. I press my face to the kitchen window, the cold glass, and watch them, watch their lips move, not with sleep prayers, but with pleas for waking, whole and miraculous. It does not come. The police do. They fill out reports. Blood seeps through that blanket bound. I see that too, even now.

Memory's surge burns deep.

That staining of her blood scorches me, but less than the blister of seeing her uncovered, lying there. She had only toddled into the farm lane, wandering after a cat, and I can see the delivery truck driver sitting at the kitchen table, his head in his hands, and I remember how he sobbed that he had never seen her. But I still see her, and I cannot forget. Her body, fragile and small, crushed by a truck's load in our farmyard, blood soaking into the thirsty, track-beaten earth. That's the moment the cosmos shifted, shattering any cupping of hands. I can still hear my mother's witnessing-scream, see my father's eyes shot white through.

My parents don't press charges and they are farmers and they keep trying to breathe, keep the body moving to keep the soul from atrophying. Mama cries when she strings out the laundry. She holds my youngest baby sister, a mere three weeks old, to the breast, and I can't imagine how a woman only weeks fragile from the birth of her fourth child witnesses the blood-on-gravel death of her third child and she leaks milk for the babe and she leaks grief for the buried daughter. Dad tells us a thousand times the story after dinner, how her eyes were water-clear and without shores, how she held his neck when she hugged him and held on for dear life. We accept the day of her death as an accident. But an act allowed by God?

For years, my sister flashes through my nights, her body crumpled on gravel. Sometimes in dreams, I cradle her in the quilt Mama made for her, pale green with the hand-embroidered Humpty Dumpty and Little Bo Peep, and she's safely cocooned. I await her unfurling and the rebirth. Instead the earth opens wide and swallows her up.

At the grave's precipice, our feet scuff dirt, and chunks of the firmament fall away. A clod of dirt hits the casket, shatters. Shatters over my little sister with the white-blonde hair, the little sister who teased me and laughed; and the way she'd throw her head back and laugh, her milk-white cheeks dimpled right through with happiness, and I'd scoop close all her belly-giggling life. They lay her gravestone flat into the earth, a black granite slab engraved with no dates, only the five letters of her name. Aimee. It means "loved one." How she was. We had loved her. And with the laying of her gravestone, the closing up of her deathbed, so closed our lives.

Closed to any notion of grace.

Really, when you bury a child — or when you just simply get up every day and live life raw — you murmur the question soundlessly. No one hears. *Can there be a good God?* A God who graces with good gifts when a crib lies empty through long nights, and bugs burrow through coffins? Where is God, *really*? How can He be good when babies die, and marriages implode, and dreams blow away, dust in the wind? Where is grace bestowed when cancer gnaws and loneliness aches and nameless places in us soundlessly die, break off without reason, erode away. Where hides this joy of the Lord, this God who fills the earth with good things, and how do I fully live when life is full of hurt ? How do I wake up to joy and grace and beauty and all that is the fullest life when I must stay numb to losses and crushed dreams and all that empties me out?

My family — my dad, my mama, my brother and youngest sister — for years, we all silently ask these questions. For years, we come up empty. And over the years, we fill again — with estrangement. We live with our hands clenched tight. What God once gave us on a day in November slashed deep. Who risks again?

Years later, I sit at one end of our brown plaid couch, my dad stretched out along its length. Worn from a day driving tractor, the sun beating and the wind blowing, he asks me to stroke his hair. I stroke from that cowlick of his and back, his hair ringed from the line of his cap. He closes his eyes. I ask questions that I never would if looking into them.

"Did you ever used to go to church? Like a long time ago, Dad?" Two neighboring families take turns picking me up, a Bible in hand and a dress ironed straight, for church services on Sunday mornings. Dad works.

"Yeah, as a kid I went. Your grandmother had us go every Sunday, after milking was done. That was important to her."

I keep my eyes on his dark strands of hair running through my fingers. I knead out tangles.

"But it's not important to you now?" The words barely whispered, hang.

He pushes up his plaid sleeves, shifts his head, his eyes still closed. "Oh . . ."

I wait, hands combing, waiting for him to find the words for those feelings that don't fit neatly into the stiff ties, the starched collars, of sentences.

"No, I guess not anymore. When Aimee died, I was done with all of that."

Scenes blast. I close my eyes; reel.

"And, if there really is anybody up there, they sure were asleep at the wheel that day."

I don't say anything. The lump in my throat burns, this ember. I just stroke his hair. I try to sooth his pain. He finds more feelings. He stuffs them into words.

"Why let a beautiful little girl die such a senseless, needless death? And she didn't just die. She was *killed*."

That word twists his face. I want to hold him till it doesn't hurt, make it all go away. His eyes remain closed, but he's shaking his head now, remembering all there was to say no to that hideous November day that branded our lives.

Dad says nothing more. That shake of the head says it all, expresses our closed hands, our bruised, shaking fists. No. No benevolent Being, no grace, no meaning to it all. My dad, a good farmer who loved his daughter the way only eyes can rightly express, he rarely said all that; only sometimes, when he'd close his eyes and ask me to stroke away the day between the fingers. But these aren't things you need to say anyways. Like all beliefs, you simply live them.

We did.

No, God.

No God.

Is this the toxic air of the world, this atmosphere we inhale, burning into our lungs, this *No, God*? *No, God, we won't take what You give. No, God, Your plans are a gutted, bleeding mess and I didn't sign up for this and You really thought I'd go for this? No, God, this is ugly and this is a mess and can't You get anything right and just haul all this pain out of here and I'll take it from here, thanks. And God? Thanks for nothing.* Isn't this the human inheritance, the legacy of the Garden?

I wake and put the feet to the plank floors, and I believe the Serpent's hissing lie, the repeating refrain of his campaign through the ages: God isn't good. It's the cornerstone of his movement. That God withholds good from His children, that God does not genuinely, fully, love us.

Doubting God's goodness, distrusting His intent, discontented with what He's given, we desire ... I *have desired* ... *more*. The fullest life.

I look across farm fields. The rest of the garden simply isn't enough. It will never be enough. God said humanity was not to eat from the Tree of the Knowledge of Good and Evil. And I moan that God has ripped away what I wanted. No, what I *needed*. Though I can hardly whisper it, I live as though He stole what I consider rightly mine: happiest children, marriage of unending bliss, long, content, death-defying days. I look in the mirror, and if I'm fearlessly blunt—what I have, who I am, where I am, how I am, what I've got—this simply isn't enough. That forked tongue darts and daily I live the doubt, look at my reflection, and ask: Does God really love me? If He truly, deeply loves me, why does He withhold that which

I believe will fully nourish me? Why do I live in this sense of rejection, of less than, of pain? Does He not want me to be *happy*?

~

From all of our beginnings, we keep reliving the Garden story.

Satan, he wanted more. More power, more glory. Ultimately, in his essence, Satan is an ingrate. And he sinks his venom into the heart of Eden. Satan's sin becomes the first sin of all humanity: *the sin of ingratitude*. Adam and Eve are, simply, painfully, ungrateful for what God gave.

Isn't that the catalyst of all my sins?

Our fall was, has always been, and always will be, that we aren't satisfied in God and what He gives. We hunger for something more, something other.

Standing before that tree, laden with fruit withheld, we listen to Evil's murmur, "In the day you eat from it your eyes will be opened . . ." (Genesis 3:5 NASB). But in the beginning, our eyes were already open. Our sight was perfect. Our vision let us see a world spilling with goodness. Our eyes fell on nothing but the glory of God. We saw God as He truly is: good. But we were lured by the deception that there was more to a full life, there was more to see. And, true, there was more to see: the ugliness we hadn't beheld, the sinfulness we hadn't witnessed, the loss we hadn't known.

We eat. And, in an instant, we are blind. No longer do we see God as one we can trust. No longer do we perceive Him as wholly good. No longer do we observe all of the remaining paradise.

We eat. And, in an instant, we see. Everywhere we look,

we see a world of lack, a universe of loss, a cosmos of scarcity and injustice.

We are hungry. We eat. We are filled ... and emptied.

And still, we look at the fruit and see only the material means to fill our emptiness. We don't see the material world for what it is meant to be: *as the means to communion with God*.

We look and swell with the ache of a broken, battered planet, what we ascribe as the negligent work of an indifferent Creator (if we even think there is one). Do we ever think of this busted-up place as the result of us ingrates, unsatisfied, we who punctured it all with a bite? The fruit's poison has infected the whole of humanity. *Me*. I say no to what He's given. I thirst for some roborant, some elixir, to relieve the anguish of what I've believed: God isn't good. God doesn't love me.

If I'm ruthlessly honest, I may have said yes to God, yes to Christianity, but really, I have lived the no. I have. Infected by that Eden mouthful, the retina of my soul develops macular holes of blackness. From my own beginning, my sister's death tears a hole in the canvas of the world.

Losses do that. One life-loss can infect the whole of a life. Like a rash that wears through our days, our sight becomes peppered with black voids. Now everywhere we look, we only see all that isn't: holes, lack, deficiency.

In our plain country church on the edge of that hayfield enclosed by an old cedar split-rail fence, once a week on Sunday, my soul's macular holes spontaneously heal. In that church with the wooden cross nailed to the wall facing the country road, there God seems obvious. Close. Bibles lie open. The sanctuary fills with the worship of wives with babies in arms, farmers done with chores early, their hair slicked down.

The Communion table spread with the emblems, that singular cup and loaf, that table that restores relationship. I remember. Here I remember Love and the Cross and a Body, and I am grafted in and held and made whole. All's upright. There, alongside Claude Martin and Ann Van den Boogaard and John Weiler and Marion Schefter and genteel Mrs. Leary, even the likes of me can see.

But the rest of the week, the days I live in the glaring harshness of an abrasive world? Complete loss of central vision. Everywhere, a world pocked with scarcity.

I hunger for filling in a world that is starved.

But from that Garden beginning, God has had a different purpose for us. His intent, since He bent low and breathed His life into the dust of our lungs, since He kissed us into being, has never been to slyly orchestrate our ruin. And yet, I have found it: He does have surprising, secret purposes. I open a Bible, and His plans, startling, lie there barefaced. It's hard to believe it, when I read it, and I have to come back to it many times, feel long across those words, make sure they are real. His love letter forever silences any doubts: "His secret purpose framed from the very beginning [is] to bring us to our full glory" (1 Corinthians 2:7 NEB). He means to rename us — to return us to our true names, our truest selves. He means to heal our soul holes. From the very beginning, that Eden beginning, that has always been and always is, to this day, His secret purpose — our return to *our full glory. Appalling* — that He would! Us, unworthy. And yet since we took a bite out of the fruit and tore into our own souls, that drain hole where joy seeps away, God's had this wild secretive plan. *He means to fill us with glory again.* With glory and grace.

Grace, it means "favor," from the Latin *gratia*. It connotes a free readiness. A free and ready favor. That's grace. It is one thing to choose to take the grace offered at the cross. But to choose to live as one *filling* with His grace? Choosing to *fill* with *all* that He freely gives and fully live—with glory and grace and God?

I know it but I don't want to: it is a choice. Living with losses, I may choose to still say yes. Choose to say yes to what He freely gives. Could I *live* that—the choice to open the hands to freely receive whatever God gives? If I don't, I am still making a choice.

The choice not to.

The day I met my brother-in-law at the back door, looking for his brother, looking like his brother, is the day I see it clear as a full moon rising bright over January snow, that choice, saying yes or no to God's graces, is the linchpin of it all, of everything.

My brother-in-law, he's just marking time, since Farmer Husband's made a quick run to the hardware store. He's talking about soil temperature and weather forecasts. I lean up against the door frame. The dog lies down at my feet.

John shrugs his shoulders, looks out across our wheat field. "Farmers, we think we control so much, do so much right to make a crop. And when you are farming," he turns back toward me, "you are faced with it every day. You control so little. Really. It's God who decides it all. Not us." He slips his big Dutch hands into frayed pockets, smiles easily. "It's all good."

I nod, almost say something about him just leaving that new water tank in the back shed for now instead of waiting any longer for Farmer Husband to show up. But I catch his eyes and I know I have to ask. Tentatively, eyes fixed on his, I venture back into that place I rarely go.

"How do you know that, John? Deep down, how do you *know* that it really is all good? That *God* is good? That you can say yes — to whatever He gives?" I know the story of the man I am asking, and he knows mine. His eyes linger. I know he's remembering the story too.

New Year's Day. He asks us to come. Only if we want. I don't want to think why, but we know. "Already?" I search my husband's face. "Today?" He takes my hand and doesn't let go. Not when we slide into the truck, not when we drive the back roads, not when we climb the empty stairwell to the hospital room lit only by a dim lamp. John meets us at the door. He nods. His eyes smile brave. The singular tear that slips down his cheek carves something out of me.

"Tiff just noticed Dietrich had started breathing a bit heavier this afternoon. And yeah, when we brought him in, they said his lung had collapsed. It will just be a matter of hours. Like it was at the end for Austin." His firstborn, Austin, had died of the same genetic disease only eighteen months prior. He was about to bury his second son in less than two years.

I can't look into that sadness wearing a smile anymore. I look at the floor, polished tiles blurring, running. It had only been a year and six months before that. The peonies had been in full bloom when we had stood in a country cemetery watching a cloud of balloons float up and into clear blue over pastures. All the bobbing, buoyant hopes for Austin — floating away. Austin had hardly been four months old. I had been there on that muggy June afternoon. I had stood by the fan humming in their farm kitchen. The fan stirred a happy-face balloon over Austin's placid body. I remember the blue of his eyes, mirrors of heaven. He never moved. His eyes moved me. I had caressed my nephew's bare little tummy. His chest had heaved for the air. And heaved less ... and less.

How do you keep breathing when the lungs under your fingers are slowly atrophying?

I had stumbled out their back steps, laid down on the grass. I had cried at the sky. It was our wedding anniversary. I always remember the date, his eyes.

And now, New Year's Day, again with John, Tiffany, but now with their second-born son, Dietrich. He's only five months old. He was born to hope and prayers—and the exact same terminal diagnosis as his brother, Austin.

John hands me a Kleenex, and I try to wipe away all this gut-wrenching pain. He tries too, with words soft and steady, "We're just blessed. Up until today Dietrich's had no pain. We have good memories of a happy Christmas. That's more than we had with Austin." All the tiles on the floor run fluid. My chest hurts. "Tiffany's got lots and lots of pictures. And we had five months with him."

I shouldn't, but I do. I look up. Into all his hardly tamed grief. I feel wild. His eyes shimmer tears, this dazed bewilderment, and his stoic smile cuts me right through. I see his chin quiver. In that moment I forget the rules of this Dutch family of reserved emotion. I grab him by the shoulders and I look straight into those eyes, brimming. And in this scratchy half whisper, these ragged words choke—*wail*. "If it were up to me ..." and then the words pound, desperate and hard, *"I'd write this story differently."*

I regret the words as soon as they leave me. They seem so un-Christian, so unaccepting—so *No, God!* I wish I could take them back, comb out their tangled madness, dress them in their calm Sunday best. But there they are, released and naked, raw and real, stripped of any theological cliché, my exposed, serrated howl to the throne room.

"You know ..." John's voice breaks into my memory and his gaze lingers, then turns again toward the waving wheat field. "Well, even with our boys ... I don't know why that all happened." He shrugs again. "But do I have to? ... Who knows? I don't mention it often, but sometimes I think of that story in the Old Testament. Can't remember what book, but you know—when God gave King Hezekiah fifteen more years of life? Because he prayed for it? But if Hezekiah had died when God first intended, Manasseh would never have been born. And what does the Bible say about Manasseh? Something to the effect that Manasseh had led the Israelites to do even more evil than all the heathen nations around Israel. Think of all the evil that would have been avoided if Hezekiah had died earlier, before Manasseh was born. I am not saying anything, either way, about anything."

He's watching that sea of green rolling in winds. Then it comes slow, in a low, quiet voice that I have to strain to hear.

"Just that maybe ... maybe you don't want to change the story, because you don't know what a different ending holds."

The words I choked out that dying, ending day, echo. Pierce. There's a reason I am not writing the story and God is. He knows how it all works out, where it all leads, what it all means.

I don't.

His eyes return, knowing the past I've lived, a bit of my nightmares. "Maybe ... I guess ... it's accepting there are things we simply don't understand. But He does."

And I see. At least a bit more. When we find ourselves groping along, famished for more, we can choose. When we are despairing, we can choose to live as Israelites gathering manna. For forty long years, God's people daily eat manna—a substance whose name literally means "What is it?" Hungry, they choose to gather up that which is baffling. They fill on that which has no meaning. More than 14,600 days they take their daily nourishment from that which they don't comprehend. They find soul-filling in the inexplicable.

They eat the mystery.

They eat the mystery.

And the mystery, that which made no sense, is "like wafers of honey" on the lips.

A pickup drives into the lane. I watch from the window, two brothers meeting, talking, then hand gestures mirroring each other. I think of buried babies and broken, weeping fathers over graves, and a world pocked with pain, and all the mysteries I have refused, *refused*, to let nourish me. If it were my daughter, my son? Would I really choose the manna? I only tremble, wonder. With memories of gravestones, of combing fingers through tangled hair, I wonder too ... if the rent in the canvas of our life backdrop, the losses that puncture our world, our own emptiness, might actually become places to see.

To see through to God.

That that which tears open our souls, those holes that splatter our sight, may actually become the thin, open places to see through the mess of this place to the heart-aching beauty beyond. To Him. To the God whom we endlessly crave.

Maybe so.

But how? How do we choose to allow the holes to become seeing-through-to-God places? To more-God places?

How do I give up resentment for gratitude, gnawing anger for spilling joy? Self-focus for God-communion.

To fully live—to live full of grace and joy and all that is beauty eternal. It is possible, wildly.

I now see and testify.

So this story—my story.

A dare to an emptier, fuller life.

CHAPTER 2

a word to live ...
and die by

Eucharist [thanksgiving] is the state of the perfect man.
Eucharist is the life of paradise. Eucharist is the
only full and real response of man to God's creation,
redemption, and gift of heaven.
Alexander Schmemann

I slam upright, jolt the bed hard, hands gripping the cotton
sheets wild.

There's a halo of light by the door. I breathe, heave breathe.
There are stars.

I can hear the clock in the kitchen, the one over the dining
room table, making time, one loud, sure tick at a time.

My chest pounds the hooves of a thousand stallions running
on and away, and the universe outside the window holds—the
one stuck through with the stars—and I breathe. I breathe.

It was all dream, a mirage of the moon.

I feel my hand across the threads of sheets and there is a bed
sure under the body and there are morning stars all in place
out the window and his bare shoulders rise and fall beside me

in the heavy slumber and the relief courses through my veins, veins draining away the fear blue. It was all a dream.

I fall back to the pillow, lie on relief. I don't close my eyes. I stare out the window and I wonder that there is real breath in these real lungs and that is the real red Antares, Scorpion's beating heart, hanging below that waning crescent moon and I am here to see it. And they were just four nightmares in one night, a silver thread unraveling through black. And for me, she who says she never has dreams.

I lie there and untangle the memory of scenes, the string all twisted, one long strand of nightmares plagiarizing life, the fibers of the neocortex working through my life, all the life most important. I revisit dream scenes and I think about this. The all most important.

It has seemed real, the dream. It was a faceless doctor — just a voice — and it was a pallid room of walls and no windows and it was just the uttering of one word and I can feel it again, how the veins constrict.

That haunting "C" word, the one with gluttonous belly and serrated teeth and the voracious appetite to divide and dominate. *Cancer.*

It's a slam to the gut. I green. And he blandly says the cancer's been invisibly consuming bits and pieces of me while I've birthed the six babies, mopped their muddy prints off the floors, kissed the lips of their father at the door. He says there's nothing to be done. All's been devoured. Just wrap up the last of my living.

Already? No more? The heart hammers and the blood surges, scream of electric blue.

Gasping, grasping, I had tried to struggle free, to emerge up into life. Into the four scone-colored walls, the dim light at

the door, the pure white matelassé bedspread pulled up over
the vows. How I wanted to surface and breathe and keep this
skin on and *live*. But night's noose had tightened, and I'd been
strangled back into this dream script of telling the news of my
impending demise to husband, father, brother. In terrifying
nightmare fashion, they all shrug their shoulders, walk away
blithe. *I want to live. Fully live.* What is the message of dreams?
I remember it, four times escaping up into consciousness only
for the rope burn back into the choked out good-byes and last
anguished touches.

I lie there long staring at ceiling, listening to the beat of my
untamed heart.

This ...

But this ... this waking to the crack of a nightmare, this
violet shock through the veins, even this might be better than
the way I usually wake. Since ... I want to say since after the
six babies, or at least since the third — the first girl and the one
with the dimples — when motherhood began to sag me ...
but really, no, it began years earlier. Since the girl with thick
glasses in Mr. Colquhoun's English class read books to escape
thoughts of her mama sitting up in a psychiatric hospital aching
for the baby that bled through the blankets. Yes, it really has
been all those years since then.

For years of mornings, I have woken wanting to die. Life
itself twists into nightmare. For years, I have pulled the covers
up over my head, dreading to begin another day I'd be bound
to just wreck. Years, I lie listening to the taunt of names ringing
off my interior walls, ones from the past that never drifted far
and away: Loser. Mess. Failure. They are signs nailed overhead,
nailed through me, naming me. The stars are blinking out.

Funny, this. Yesterday morning, the morning before, all

these mornings, I wake to the discontent of life in my skin.
I wake to self-hatred. To the wrestle to get it all done, the
relentless anxiety that I am failing. Always, the failing. I yell
at children, fester with bitterness, forget doctor appointments,
lose library books, live selfishly, skip prayer, complain, go to
bed too late, neglect cleaning the toilets. I live tired. Afraid.
Anxious. Weary. Years, I feel it in the veins, the pulsing of
ruptured hopes. Would I ever be enough, find enough, do
enough? But this morning, I wake wildly wanting to live.
Physically feeling it in the veins trembling, the hard pant of
the lungs, the seeing it in the steady stars, how much I *really*
want to *really* live. How I don't want to die. Is that the message
of nightmares and dreams? To live either *fully* alive ... or in
empty nothingness?

It's the in between that drives us mad.

It's the life in between, the days of walking lifeless, the
years calloused and simply going through the hollow motions,
the self-protecting by self-distracting, the body never waking,
that's lost all capacity to fully feel—this is the life in between
that makes us the wild walking dead.

The sun climbs the horizon. I throw back the covers, take
another breath, and begin. I *get* to. I *get* to live. A lone morning
dove woos from high in the spruce tree. In the kitchen, I
stand over the heat of the stove, slowly stirring the wooden
spoon through the bubbling-up oatmeal, but my eyes are on
the window, on the field. Freshly fallen snow coruscates in
the sun, countless stars across fields, trees in the woods falling
soundlessly, their blue shadows stretching. Down by the lane,
where the gravel curves to the road, where that bulk of a
yellow lab has been digging hard, steam rises slow off the
earth's black loam.

Life has mirages of its own.

The nightmare creeps up the nape of the neck, clamps me in a chokehold of reality.

The end *will* come.

Doctor's warning or not, the end will come, and this life of the bare toes across grass, the sky raining spring down on eyelashes, the skin spread close under sheets, blink of the fireflies on dusky June nights—all this will all end.

I turn off the stove.

I toss in a load of laundry, pull a recipe book out of the cupboard to plan the day's menu, wipe off the counters. I try to breathe and press on. But I'm rattled, upended, undone. I can't quite shake the reality of the dream. The nightmare of my life.

Which road through this brief land? What is all most important? How to live the fullest life here that delivers into the full life ever after?

A child tromps in, boots still on, with a chestful of mail. Between the flyers of a grand opening for a new flooring store in town and a sale on tires lies a letter from my recently widowed father-in-law. On a hot night one July in the dark of room 117, God had used cancer to usher my mother-in-law, his bride of half a century, into the throne room and glory ever after. We had sung that night, "What a day that will be when my Jesus I shall see." I had laid the cold cloth on the sweat beads stringing along her brow. I tear open his envelope, slide out the DaySpring card, read his slow Dutch scrawl. But it's the last words of his card that grab me:

"Thinking on the beginning of this year, who does He call to come Home? Is it me, Lord? May I be ready. Or us. Whoever."

Emotion wells, spills. How this letter, these words, and

now, after last night's dream wrestle? After my years of mornings?

Whoever. Ready for the end of here.

Whoever. Ready for the first meeting of Him there.

Whoever. *Soon.*

Will I have lived fully — or just empty?

How does one live ready, and always? Yes, ultimately, only Jesus. Yes, this premature dying to self, birthing into the cross-life, the grace cocoon before emerging into the life unending. Without this Jesus, no, no one can be ready.

But, someone, please give me — who is born again but still so much in need of being born anew — give me the details of *how* to live in the waiting cocoon before the forever begins?

In my reality-dream (dream-reality?), I gasp for more time, frantic for more time. But I have to wonder: more time for more what? The answer to that determines the road these so-short days take.

Hard questions drive me hard to distraction. I check e-mail. More words sent this way, this time from a mother. Her seventeen-year-old has been diagnosed with, yes, specter of that word too real, cancer. I try to breathe. Today, it's hard. What are the messages of God? Her mother types the words across my screen: "Any words?"

I stumble away.

Obviously, I have no words, no answers. I am groping for my own way. Desperately feeling along today for a way to live through this fleeting blink of a life.

How do we live fully so we are fully ready to die?

I stack the linen closets. I think of all the things I might never live to do.

I think of all the things I am going to miss.

My eyes will never know China's jade-green Li River. I'm never going to see those black-haired boys under straw-brimmed hats fish off their bamboo rafts with the ringed cormorants, the mist rising behind over the karst formations, surreal and dark. I am never going to be ascending the Loita Hills of Kenya to witness the dance of gazelles migrating up by the millions from the Serengeti. I am not going to be swimming the sapphire waters of some South Pacific grotto, or sitting up late listening to the wind whisper through the Sequoia woods, or spending my golden years scaling the summit of emerald Machu Picchu.

I run my hand across the thick of the terry towels. I'm a farmer's wife. I'm the homeschooling mother of six children. There are no fancy degrees, titles, diplomas hanging on these finger-smudged walls. Are there places that must be known, accomplishments that must be had, before one is really ready? I know the theological answers, but do my blood and my pulse?

I remember once sitting at the hairdresser's. The woman beside me reads, and I read her title in the reflection of the mirror: *1000 Places to See Before You Die.* Is that it? Are there physical places that simply must be seen before I stop breathing within time, before I inhale eternity?

Why? To say that I've had reason to bow low? To say that I've seen beauty? To say that I've been arrested by wonder?

Isn't it here? Can't I find it *here*?

These very real lungs will breathe in more than 11,000 liters of air today,[1] and tonight over our farm will rise the Great Hexagon of the blazing winter stars—Sirius, Rigel, ruby Aldebran, Capella, the fiery Gemini twins, and Procyon, and in the center, scarlet Betelgeuse, the red supergiant larger than twice the size of earth's orbit around the sun — and I will embrace the skin of a boy child that my body grew from a seed. The low heavens outside the paned windows fill with more snowflakes than stars, no two-stacked crystals the same; the trees in the wood draw in collective green breath to the still of January hibernation, and God in the world will birth ice from His womb, frost of heaven, bind the chains of the Pleiades, loose the cords of Orion, and number again the strands on my head (Job 38:31; Matthew 10:30).

Isn't it here? The wonder? Why do I spend so much of my living hours struggling to see it? Do we truly stumble so blind that we must be affronted with *blinding* magnificence for our blurry soul-sight to recognize grandeur? The very same surging magnificence that cascades over our every day here. Who has time or eyes to notice?

All my eyes can seem to fixate on are the splatters of disappointment across here and me.

I close the bathroom linen closet. Pick up a brush to swish toilets. I don't need more time to breathe so that I may experience more locales, possess more, accomplish more. Because wonder really could be here — for the seeing eyes.

So — more time for more *what*?

The face of Jesus flashes. Jesus, the God-Man with his own termination date. Jesus, the God-Man who came to save me from prisons of fear and guilt and depression and sadness. With an expiration of less than twelve hours, what does Jesus count as all most important?

"And he took bread, gave thanks and broke it, and gave it to them ..." (Luke 22:19 NIV).

This. I live in this place, make porridge, scrub toilets, do laundry, and for days, weeks, I am brave and I do get out of bed and I think on this. I study this, the full life, the being fully ready for the end. I start to think that maybe there is a way out of nightmares to dreams? Maybe?

I thumb, run my finger across the pages of the heavy and thick books bound. I read it slowly. In the original language, "he gave thanks" reads *"eucharisteo."*

I underline it on the page. Can it lay a sure foundation under a life? Offer the fullest life?

The root word of *eucharisteo* is *charis*, meaning "grace." Jesus took the bread and saw it as *grace* and gave thanks. He took the bread and knew it to be *gift* and gave thanks.

But there is more, and I read it. *Eucharisteo*, thanksgiving, envelopes the Greek word for grace, *charis*. But it also holds its derivative, the Greek word *chara*, meaning "joy." *Joy*. Ah ... yes. I might be needing me some of that. That might be what the quest for more is all about—that which Augustine claimed, "Without exception ... all try their hardest to reach the same goal, that is, joy."[2]

I breathe deep, like a sojourner finally coming home. That has always been the goal of the fullest life—joy. And my life knew exactly how elusive that slippery three-letter word, *joy*, can be. I think of it then again, that night of nightmares, the flailing, frantic, moon-eyed lunge for more. More *what*? And this was it; I could tell how my whole being responded to that one word. I longed for more life, for more *holy joy*.

That's what I was struggling out of nightmares to reach, to seize. Joy. But where can I seize this holy grail of joy? I look back down to the page. Was this the clue to the quest of all most important? Deep *chara* joy is found only at the table of the

euCHARisteo—the table of thanksgiving. I sit there long ...
wondering ... is it that simple?

Is the height of my *chara* joy dependent on the depths of my
eucharisteo thanks?

So then as long as thanks is possible ... I think this through.
As long as thanks is possible, then joy is always possible. *Joy is
always possible. Whenever,* meaning—now; *wherever,* meaning—
here. The holy grail of joy is not in some exotic location or
some emotional mountain peak experience. The joy wonder
could be here! Here, in the messy, piercing ache of now, joy
might be—unbelievably—possible! The only place we need
see before we die is this place of seeing God, here and now.

I whisper it out loud, let the tongue feel these sounds, the
ear hear their truth.

Charis. Grace.

Eucharisteo. Thanksgiving.

Chara. Joy.

A triplet of stars, a constellation in the black.

A threefold cord that might hold a life? Offer a way up into
the fullest life?

Grace, thanksgiving, joy. *Eucharisteo.*

A Greek word ... that might make meaning of everything?

When children sleep under the scraps stitched into quilts
and the clock ticks too loudly through the dark hours and the
spiral galaxies spin in space, I lie under the afghan by the fire
and read the words of an old sermon. It is weeks later now,
and the mind stores things, waiting for such a time when God
aligns the stars. I read, "The greatest thing is to give thanks
for everything. He who has learned this knows what it means

to live.... He has penetrated the whole mystery of life: giving thanks for everything."[3] Breath leaves the lung.

I whisper in the dark: *Eucharisteo!*

It really might be the mystery to the fullest life ...

I lie on relief. I might have found the holy grail ... and lost it, moved on. And yet really—hadn't God set the holy grail in the center of Christianity? *Eucharisteo,* it's the central symbol of Christianity. Thanksgiving. The table with its emblems is the essence of what it means to live the Christ-life. Sunday after Sunday in our nondenominational Bible church, we're formally invited to take the bread, the wine. Doesn't the continual repetition of beginning our week at the table of the Eucharist clearly place the whole of our lives into the context of thanksgiving?

And too ... it's the most common of foods, bread. The drink of the vine has been part of our meal taking across centuries and cultures. Jesus didn't institute the Eucharist around some unusual, rare, once-a-year event, but around this continual act of eating a slice of bread, drinking a cup of fruit from the vine. First Corinthians 11:26 reads, "whenever you eat this bread and drink this cup" (NIV)—*whenever.*

Like every day. Whenever we eat.

Eucharisteo—whenever: now. Joy—wherever: here.

Doesn't Christ, at His death meal, set the entirety of our everyday bread and drink lives into the framework of *eucharisteo*? The Big Dipper lurks low outside the window. Yet how does the framework of *eucharisteo* undergird a life? Penetrating the mystery is like discovering galaxies; there is always more.

I stand the next morning on planks of light lying down across the floor, and I bake bread, yeasty dough moist between

my fingers, and that one word works me, again and again—
eucharisteo. I won't let it go this time. I'll enter into the mystery.

I shape loaves and think how Jesus took the bread and gave
thanks ... and then the miracle of the multiplying of the loaves
and fishes.

How Jesus took the bread and gave thanks ... and then the
miracle of Jesus enduring the cross for the joy set before Him.

How Jesus stood outside Lazarus's tomb, the tears streaming
down His face, and He looked up and prayed, "Father, I thank
you that you have heard me ..." (John 11:41 NIV). And then
the miracle of a dead man rising! Thanksgiving raises the dead!
The empty, stiff cadaver surging, the veins full of blood, the
alveoli of the lungs filling with oxygen, the coronary arteries
full of the whoosh of thrumming life.

How there is thanks ... and then the mind-blowing
miracle! I lay loaves into pans and feel years of the angst lying
down too.

Eucharisteo—thanksgiving—*always precedes the miracle.*
The bread rises.

And I stand in the kitchen stirring a kettle of lunch's lentil
soup, the one that calls for the salsa and the carrots and the
hungry children, and I read while stirring and I have to sit
down to let the words find their places: "The only real fall
of man is his noneucharistic life in a noneucharistic world."[4]
That was the fall! Non-*eucharisteo*, ingratitude, was the fall—
humanity's discontent with all that God freely gives. That
is what has scraped me raw: ungratefulness. Then to find
Eden, the abundance of Paradise, I'd need to forsake my non-
eucharisteo, my bruised and bloodied ungrateful life, and grab
hold to *eucharisteo*, a lifestyle of thanksgiving. Might a life of

eucharisteo really work the miracle of the God-communion? I rise from the chair.

That's when I begin to track it whenever I open my Bible, the red pen in hand, hunt down the trail of *eucharisteo* through Scripture. Where it leads barbs, and I am surprised and I reel.

"*On the night when he was betrayed*, the Lord Jesus took some bread and *gave thanks to God for it*. Then he broke it in pieces ..." (1 Corinthians 11:23–24, emphasis added). Jesus, on the night before the driving hammer and iron piercing through ligament and sinew, receives what God offers as grace (*charis*), the germ of His thanksgiving (*eucharistia*)? Oh. Facing the abandonment of God Himself (does it get any worse than this?), Jesus offers *thanksgiving* for even that which will break Him and crush Him and wound Him and yield a bounty of joy (*chara*). The mystery always contains more mysteries.

Do I really want this way?

I listen to Matthew 11 for a whole week while exercising, panting hard, skin flushed with life, before I snare this truth— and it snares me:

> Then Jesus began to denounce the cities in which most of his miracles had been performed, because they did not repent. "Woe to you, Korazin! Woe to you, Bethsaida! ... If the miracles that were performed in you had been performed in Sodom, it would have remained to this day." (Matthew 11:20–21, 23 NIV)

And then what does Jesus directly do, in the face of apparent failure, when no one responded to His teaching and things didn't work out at all? He lives out *eucharisteo*. "At that time, [*precisely at that failing time*] Jesus answered and said, 'I thank thee, O Father, Lord of heaven and earth ...'" (Matthew

11:25 KJV). In the midst of what seems a mess, in the tripping up and stumbling down of all hopes, Jesus gives thanks?

What precedes the miracle is thanksgiving, *eucharisteo*, and it is a Greek word with a hard meaning that is harder yet to live. Do I really want to take up this word?

But I wonder it one Sunday as they pass the broken loaf on that plate of silver, from Paula Van de Kemp to Ron Collins to Tammi Lindsay reaching for it over her kids. Maybe I already take up *eucharisteo*'s hard meaning every time I take Communion? In a very tangible, physical act, aren't I enacting my thanksgiving for His pain? In a very real way, in a digestible, consuming-oneness way, I'm celebrating greater gain through great loss. "Is not the cup of thanksgiving for which we give thanks a participation in the blood of Christ? And is not the bread that we break a participation in the body of Christ?" (1 Corinthians 10:16 NIV). The Eucharist invites us to give thanks for dying. To participate in His death with our own daily dying and give thanks for it. Then Mrs. Klumpenhower passes me the silver plate, and I tear off my small chunk of bread, chunk of the dead-and-risen-again wheat. I feel the granules between the fingers. I lay the torn bread on the tongue and I remember and press it to the roof of my mouth and the bread melts and I give thanks for the dying.

I swallow it down.

This constellation in the dark—grace, thanksgiving, joy— it might be like that—reaching for stars. So hard. *So hard.*

Is there some easier way to the fulfilling life?

The day I peel back chapter 17 of Luke's gospel, I think I have my answer.

I sit at the prayer bench before my bedroom window. Outside, our boys roll millions of flakes into a snow fort. I read the passage, one I remember from the musty basement of the Knox Presbyterian Church Sunday school. I think I know this one. Jesus restores ten lepers to wholeness. And only one returns to offer any thanks. I remember the moral too, Mrs. Morrison and her glossy red lipstick: "How often do you remember to say thanks?" Yes, I think I know this one.

I skim.

"One of them, when he saw he was healed, came back, praising God in a loud voice. He threw himself at Jesus' feet and thanked him — and he was a Samaritan" (Luke 17:15 – 16 NIV). Yes, thankfulness, I know. Next verse.

> Jesus asked, "Were not all ten cleansed? Where are the other nine? Was no one found to return and give praise to God except this foreigner?" Then he said to him, "Rise and go; your faith has made you well." (Luke 17:17 – 19 NIV)

Wait. I trace back. Hadn't Jesus already completely healed him? Exactly like the other nine who were cured who hadn't bothered to return and thank Him. So what does Jesus mean, "Your faith has made you well"? Had I underinterpreted this passage, missed some hidden mystery? I slow down and dig. I read Jesus' words in Young's Literal Translation, "And [Jesus] said to him, 'Having risen, be going on, thy faith hath saved thee.'" Saved thee? I dig deeper. It's *sozo* in the Greek. Many translations render *sozo* as being made "well" or "whole," but its literal meaning, I read it — "to save." *Sozo* means salvation. It means true wellness, complete wholeness. To live *sozo* is to live the full life. Jesus came that we might live life to the full; He came to give us *sozo*. And when did the leper receive *sozo*—the saving to the full, whole life? When he returned and gave thanks. I lay down my pen.

Our very saving is associated with our gratitude.

Mrs. Morrison hadn't mentioned this. But ... of course. If our fall was the non-*eucharisteo*, the ingratitude, then salvation must be intimately related to *eucharisteo*, the giving of thanks.

I look back to the text. That is what it says: "Thy faith has saved thee." And the leper's faith was a faith that said thank you. Is that it? Jesus counts thanksgiving as integral in a faith that saves.

We only enter into the full life if our faith gives thanks.

Because how else do we accept His free gift of salvation if not with thanksgiving? Thanksgiving is the evidence of our acceptance of whatever He gives. Thanksgiving is the manifestation of our *Yes!* to His grace.

Thanksgiving is inherent to a true salvation experience; thanksgiving is necessary to live the well, whole, *fullest* life.

"If the church is in Christ, its initial act is always an act of thanksgiving, of returning the world to God," writes Orthodox theologian Alexander Schmemann.[5] If I am truly in Christ, mustn't my initial act, too, always be an act of thanksgiving, returning to Jesus with thanks on the lips?

I would read it much later in the pages of the Psalms, at the close of a Communion service as the bread and the wine were returned to the table, the Farmer handing his Bible over to me, his finger holding the verse for me to see because he had just read it there, what I had been saying, living, believing, and the chin would quiver before I'd brim at the way God shows His salvation: "He who sacrifices thank offerings honors me, and he prepares the way so that I may show him the salvation of God" (Psalm 50:23 NIV).

Thanksgiving—giving thanks in everything—prepares the way that God might show us His *fullest* salvation in Christ.

The act of sacrificing thank offerings to God—even for the bread and cup of cost, for cancer and crucifixion—*this* prepares the way for God to show us His *fullest* salvation from bitter, angry, resentful lives and from all sin that estranges us from Him. At the Eucharist, Christ breaks His heart to heal ours—Christ, the complete accomplishment of our salvation. And the miracle of *eucharisteo* never ends: thanksgiving is what precedes the miracle of that salvation being fully worked out in our lives. Thanksgiving—giving thanks in everything—is what prepares the way for salvation's whole restoration. Our salvation in Christ is real, yet the completeness of that salvation is not fully realized in a life until the life realizes the need to give thanks. In everything?

I would never experience the fullness of my salvation until I expressed the fullness of my thanks every day, and *eucharisteo* is elemental to living the saved life.

Mrs. Morrison hadn't told me this either.

And sitting there before the window, I'm struck, a comet blazing across the empty dark of my life. All those years thinking I was saved and had said my yes to God, but was really living the no. Was it because I had never fully experienced the whole of my salvation? Had never lived out the fullest expression of my salvation in Christ? Because I wasn't taking everything in my life and returning to Jesus, falling at His feet and thanking Him. I sit still, blinded. This is why I sat all those years in church but my soul holes had never fully healed.

Eucharisteo, the Greek word with the hard meaning and the

harder meaning to live—this is the only way from empty to full.

I watch our boys carve in the wall of their snow fort.

They dig and their cheeks flame with the heat of the work, their hair damp with the effort. I think of the mother of the daughter with cancer, my father-in-law asking if I'm ready to go Home. No. I still have no words. Our tallest son has a shovel and the youngest son, a garden spade, and they dig into their wall. I have just one word. A word to seize and haul up out of a terminal nightmare, a word for fearless dying, for saved, fully healed living, a word that works the miracle that heals the soul and raises the very dead to life.

The packed snow of the fort gives way and there it is. A door in the wall.

Eucharisteo.

The way through is hard. But do I really want to be saved?

CHAPTER 3

first flight

Gratitude bestows reverence, allowing us to encounter
everyday epiphanies, those transcendent moments of awe that
change forever how we experience life and the world.
Sarah Ban Breathnach

The window in the den is open wide, the carved loon and the
mallard sitting still on the sill, the heartwood of a tree hewn
into a longing wing.

In a friend's kitchen, I work too, cutting cucumbers.

It's drifting in on July, and I can hear it, up from the
riverside, peals of child laughter, this stream running smooth,
and the seedy cucumber disks fall to the china plate, their own
green platters full of summer. She has a vase by the sink.

Tall with the foxglove spires, their full pink lips flecked
with drops of scarlet, and I can just see how she would have cut
each stalk careful and carried it in here, beauty for the women
come to the tap for water. A medicinal bloom for heart failure,
I remember reading that of foxgloves, a heart strengthener. Did
she think of that when she cut them, thinking of me coming?

The men voices wander in the open window too, with the
smoke and the sizzling, their broad backs hanging over flame
and the grill all dripping. I'm hungry. My blade slices rings of

the green. She stands at the stove, stirring a sauce, us parents cooking for the broods we have borne, and I almost don't hear her when she says it.

"You've changed." She turns to me, and I turn to catch the words.

"I have?" She's caught me off guard. I'm thick-tongued and the cheeks flame and I reach for the pitcher, to pour the cups full and distract from her catching me trying to take wing.

"Yes ... you've changed." Shelly sets her pot on a trivet, her eyes on me, and I can feel them and I just set out the glasses.

I don't say it, but I am thinking she may be right and I had felt it for months, the maturing, the swelling, the something different that had begun to happen. But I had thought the re-creation was still embryonic, a bud of hope. I hadn't thought it had fully bloomed. I hadn't thought that anyone could see the light in the eyes.

"It's that list you've been writing, isn't it?" She clatters down bowls.

I concentrate on pouring the water steady into each empty cup.

A fly cuts the surface of one full glass. I can see it—the wounding of water.

"Yes ..." There. A moment. And yes. "It's The List."

The wound of the water smoothes ... fades ... heals.

I may have always known that change takes real intentionality, like a woman bent over her garden beds every day with a spade and the determined will to grow up something good to strengthen the heart.

I may even have known that change requires more than

merely thinking the warm and fuzzy thoughts about a door and a way through and that Greek word, *eucharisteo*, holding the mystery to the full life and ever after.

But none of that at all meant that I knew what to do.

How in the world, for the sake of my soul, do I learn to practically pick up *eucharisteo*, the word I had underlined as a firm foundation to lay down under all of my days?

How in the world, for the sake of my joy, do I learn to use *eucharisteo* to overcome my one ugly and self-destructive habit of ingratitude (that habit that causes both my cosmic and daily fall) with the saving habit of gratitude—that would lead me back to deep God-communion.

To live—at all—I needed to know.

I had read that too, written by a wise man of old, Jean Pierre de Caussade: "When one is thirsty one quenches one's thirst by drinking, not by reading books which treat of this condition."[1] If we are dying of thirst, passively reading books about water quenches little; the only way to quench the parched mouth is to close the book and dip the hand into water and bring it to the lips. If we thirst, we'll have to drink.

I would have to *do* something.

But I hadn't known at all the day I laid aside the books about *eucharisteo* and picked up a pen to begin that list that I was really taking down, swallowing, the first real drink and how I'd transform. Or that the transformation would be so visible.

It was a dare, like a love dare of sorts, and I take it one clear November morning, not at all unlike that long ago November morning that her blood soaked the ground and I can never forget. It is the beginning of list season. Lists of holiday menus, lists of handmade projects, lists of have-to-buys. They're scattered and stacked across the counter, around my desk, when a friend's dashed-off digital line blinks up on my screen. She dares me, and I don't even blink. Could I write a list of a thousand things I love? I read her line again. As in, begin *another* list? To name one thousand blessings — one thousand gifts — is that what she means? Sure, whatever.

It's not like I thought that this is the carving, the flying, the healing of my wounds. Sometimes you don't know when you're taking the first step through a door until you're already inside.

I grab a scrap paper out of the ash-woven basket at the end of the counter, one with a child's drawing of St. Patrick, I think, headed to Ireland because he's in a boat and those really do look like shamrocks on his sleeve — and I flip it over. Across the backside, on a whim, a dare, I scratch it down: Gift List. I begin the list. Not of gifts I want but of gifts I *already have*.

1. Morning shadows across the old floors

2. Jam piled high on the toast

3. Cry of blue jay from high in the spruce

That is the beginning and I smile. I can't believe how I smile. I mean, they are just the common things and maybe I don't even know they are gifts really until I write them down and that is really what they look like. Gifts He bestows. This writing it down — it is sort of like … unwrapping love.

It might fit like a glove.

16. Leafy life scent of the florist shop

17. The creak of her old knees

18. Wind flying cold wild in hair

And when the house sleeps all heavy and only the dog barks crazy out on the lawn up at the cold round moon, I look down at Day 1 of counting all the way up to one thousand gifts. I run my hands across the page. I see again frames of the day, a life album in miniature. Writing the list, it makes me feel ... happy. All day. I can hardly believe how it does that, that running stream of consciousness, river I drink from and I'm quenched in, a surging stream of grace and it's wild how it sweeps me away. And I add one more to the list. To feel it all again. I can't understand why it does that. And yet ... too ... the list, it feels foreign, strange. Long, I am woman who speaks but one language, the language of the fall—discontentment and self-condemnation, the critical eye and the never satisfied.

And this, wasn't this ... I finger the corner of the page neatly numbered.

Well, if all these were gifts that God gives—then wasn't my writing down the list like ... receiving. Like taking with thanks. *Wait.*

"And he took bread, gave thanks and broke it, and gave it to them ..." *Gave thanks.*

This crazy-dare gift list—it's language lessons in *eucharisteo!* For real?

But *eucharisteo*—it's the word Jesus whispered when death prowled close and His anguish trickled down bloody. He took the bread, *even the bread of death*, and gave thanks. I look down at my list. This thanks that I am doing—it seems so ... crude. Trivial. If this list is the learning of the language of *eucharisteo*—this feels like ... guttural groanings. But perhaps the "full of grace" vocabulary begins haltingly, simply, like a child, thankful for the childlike.

But doesn't the kingdom of heaven belong to such as these?

At first, it's the dare that keeps me going. That and how happy it makes me—giddy—this list writing of all that is good and pure and lovely and beautiful. But what keeps me going is what I read in that Bible lying open on my prayer bench looking out the window to the snow fort. The fort with a door in the wall. It's Paul writing the letter to the Philippians. I read the fourth chapter. I almost don't see it, but Paul repeats it twice in only two sentences, so I don't miss it:

> I have learned how to be content with whatever I have. I know how to live on almost nothing or with everything. I have learned the secret of living in every situation, whether it is with a full stomach or empty, with plenty or little."
> (Philippians 4:11–12)

I read it many times, groping for the latch.

There it is—the secret to living joy in every situation, the full life of *eucharisteo*. Twice Paul whispers it: "I have learned ..." Learned. I would have to learn *eucharisteo*. Learn *eucharisteo*—learn it to live fully. Learn it like I know my skin, my face, the words on the end of my tongue. Like I know my own name. Learn how to be thankful—whether empty or full. Could the list teach me even that hard language? Over time? Gratitude in the midst of death and divorce and debt— that's the language I've got to learn to speak—because that's the kind of life I'm living, the kind I have to solve. If living *eucharisteo* is the key to unlocking the mystery of life, this I want. I want the hunt, the long sleuth, the careful piecing together. To learn how to be grateful and happy, whether hands full or hands empty. That is a secret worth spending a life on learning. Even if it takes a Rosetta Stone of decades.

I wake the next morning and I grip my pen, ink to crack the code.

~

Mr. Klumpenhower slides the mail into the clunky mailbox at the end of the lane, the one I painted Martha Stewart's burnt maple syrup but it really is more a barn red. I stand at the window and I hold the pen. I write it down in my journal:

22. Mail in the mailbox

And when my grandma's bona fide wood-handled pressure cooker from the fifties, full with the potatoes, bobbles the steam all dancey over kitchen windows come noon, I hold the pen and I write it down clear:

23. Grandma's pressure pot still dancing

Thanks is what multiplies the joy and makes any life large, and I hunger for it.

And when I'm in the produce section of Zehrs Markets looking for a just-ripe clump of bananas and I look over and see an old man all white-whiskered and bent, looking for the just-right card in the Hallmark aisle, I grab the journal from my bag and I hold the pen and I write it down wobbly:

24. Old men looking for words just perfect

I know how this makes me feel. I think I'm beginning to know why. How *eucharisteo* always precedes the miracle, even joy in a supermarket.

So I can't say I'm surprised when I read the words of Martin Luther, author of those ninety-five theses nailed to the door of the Castle Church in Wittenberg, but he did say, "If you want to change the world, pick up your pen."[2] This does feel like my own reformation, all things wooden-hard giving way to the sky. Recording gifts to reform. I pick up a pen and write of the God-gifts—all these things I had blithely and blindly brushed past before—and the list is my thanks, and *eucharisteo* is, I swear an oath, opening up the heights.

He says it too, John Piper—the things I am discovering, me with a hunt pen in hand—that moving the ink across the page opens up the eyes, that he may not understand how it sheds light, focuses its lens, but he only knows "that there are eyes in pencils and in pens."[3]

Eyes in pencils and in pens. I hold the seeing pen, the one with eyes, eyes that, in due time, might just decode the whole of *eucharisteo*.

I am hard after it.

Because the picking up of a pen isn't painful and ink can be cheap medicine. And I just might live.

I hold the pen. The cataracts clear.

37. *Windmills droning in day's last breeze*
38. *Wool sweaters with turtleneck collars*
39. *Faint aroma of cattle and straw*

"A nail is driven out by another nail; habit is overcome by habit."[4] Erasmus said that, contemporary and admirer of Martin Luther. When I read this thought, I am surprised because I had never known and I am sad for all that would have changed if only I had.

I look down at the pen, this pen I keep wielding, one writing her way all the way to one thousand. This pen: this *is* nothing less than the driving of nails. Nails driving out my habits of discontent and driving in my habit of *eucharisteo*. I'm hammering in nails to pound out nails, ugly nails that Satan has pierced through the world, my heart. It starts to unfold, light in the dark, a door opening up, how all these years it's been utterly pointless to try to wrench out the spikes of discontent. Because that habit of discontentment can only be driven out by hammering in one iron sharper. The sleek pin of gratitude.

I hammer.

54. *Moonlight on pillows*
55. *Long, lisped prayers*
56. *Kisses in dark*

And in a house sleeping, my heart rings.

In the morning, my Farmer Husband comes in from the barn smelling of hogs.

"We lost another litter this morning." He washes at the sink, dries those rough mitt hands, dark and work-worn, on a gingham towel draped over the cupboard. "All of them stillborn."

I smother a sigh with a smile, weak and resigned. He takes it regardless. "Yeah ..." He too smiles soft, a hand letting go, and our eyes hold each other long.

At the table, I pour milk over porridge. The Farmer sinks down into his chair at the end, lowers his head in prayer. He thanks God for the sustenance. I pray for some of that too.

I watch him eat. His three-day stubble, it's brushed with flakes of cracked corn, remnants of what he fed to the sows this morning. The neck front of his T-shirt is stained with sweat. He works four hard hours in the barn feeding hundreds of sows, and the sun is just now meandering up to the table. The glass of orange juice set out for him sits untouched. I know what he would never tell me: more cold sores on the inner wall of his mouth. Stress.

It's just that this thing, this sickness getting to sows — getting to him — has no name. It's been months. He's sent feed samples to an international lab, run various water trials, called in the vet to run a multipronged battery of tests. Nothing. No diagnosis for this spike in late-term miscarriages, the loss of litter after still-shriveled litter.

"I told Greg that I think it's viral, not environmental." He reaches for a second piece of toast. The Farmer and the vet have known each other since grade school and the soccer fields and Good News Bible Club.

"He asked if we could reconfigure production data to analyze symptoms by parity." I hand him his two vitamin C tablets. "Some strange patterns. And the thing that makes no sense? Sows testing pregnant when they aren't. You can hear the swoosh, swoosh with the ultrasound, but she's not pregnant. Why?!"

I'm getting good at feeble half smiles.

I clear off the table and he reads Scripture. We do this at the close of every meal. This morning, the book of Amos, the prophet-herdsman with the name that means "burden bearer."

Late afternoon, the back door latches close and water runs at sink. That's always him, washing up first. I turn to the clock. He's in before dark? Before I get to the mudroom, he slips past me to the study. "I think I'm on to something."

He's already hunched over keyboard, tapping in some search. I stay in the kitchen, chop up onions, wear smells of my own. I can hear the click of the cursor, him tracking a lead.

Then sauté, then broth, then vegetables to the pot. The sun has turned off the lights, gone to bed. In the dark of the study, his face is lit by the blue web. Soup simmers low, flavors bubbling, and I slip in behind him in front of the screen. His shoulders are tight, man tense with the trail; I rub the muscles deliberate, deep. "Anything?"

"It looks like it ..." He mutters the words more to himself than to me. "If this isn't it, I don't know what is. Everything just ... lines up."

My thumbs work circles into the sinews. I scan cyberwords. The words make me wince. "You think so?"

His cursor lingers at the end of a paragraph ... then he spins his chair around, pulls me down to his lap. "I think that's it— that's the name." He murmurs the words near my ear.

"If that's ..." I point to the screen, to that name too long to pronounce. "If that's really what's going on out in the barn, are you OK?"

I can feel his relief, the way it drains into me.

"Yes ... and no. I don't like what it is, or that it looks like it's nearly impossible to eradicate, but you know what?"

I turn to find his eyes, the way he and I meet, touch. His hands around me tighten, us melded in hope.

"I'm strangely happy."

It's true. No furrow plows across his brow. His maritime eyes lay calm.

"God's good. Just naming it ... *Just naming it.* When you don't have the name for something, you're haunted by shadows. It ages you."

I press my lined forehead onto his.

"But when you can name something ..."

When you can name something.

My list of naming God-gifts lies open on the counter . . .

117. Washing the warm eggs

118. Crackle in fireplace

119. Still warm cookies

Naming is Edenic.

I name gifts and go back to the Garden and God in the beginning who first speaks a name and lets what is come into existence. This naming is how the first emptiness of space fills: the naming of light and land and sky. The first man's first task is to name. Adam completes creation with his Maker through the act of naming creatures, releasing the land from chaos, from the teeming, indefinable mass. I am seeing it too, in the journal, in the face of the Farmer: naming offers the gift of recognition. When I name moments—string out laundry and name-pray, *thank You, Lord, for bedsheets in billowing winds, for fluff of sparrow landing on line, sun winter warm, and one last leaf still hanging in the orchard*—I am Adam and I discover my meaning and God's, and to name is to learn the language of Paradise. This naming work never ends for all the children of Adam. Naming to find an identity, our identity, God's.

It's late, and in the lamplight when the bones finally rest, I read and turn a page and run unexpected into these words,

> Now, in the Bible a name . . . reveals the very essence of a thing, or rather its essence as God's gift. . . . To name a thing is to manifest the meaning and value God gave it, to know it as coming from God and to know its place and function within the cosmos created by God. To name a thing, in other words, is to bless God for it and in it.[5]

I read the words again. The heart palpitates hard. I don't

hear the clock or the slosh hum of the dishwasher. All I can see, think, is that my whim writing of one thousand gratitudes, the naming of the moments — this is truly a holy work.

This naming really *does* call now a gift, a gift of God. I read again: "To name a thing is to manifest the meaning and value God gave it." I look at a day, a thing, an event in front of me, and it may look manna-strange: "What is it?" But when I name it, the naming of it manifests its meaning: to know it comes from God. *This is gift!* Naming is to know a thing's function in the cosmos — to name is to *solve mystery.*

In naming that which is right before me, that which I'd otherwise miss, the invisible becomes visible.

The space that spans my inner emptiness fills in the naming. I name. And I know the face I face.

God's! God is in the details; God is in the moment. God is in all that blurs by in a life — even hurts in a life.

GOD!

How can I not name? Naming these moments may change the ugly names I call myself.

I put a pen to a journal, to name solve, and I shake it when it runs dry, trace circles, and I coax out ink.

~⌒

Some days I coax hard. I am tired. I don't know if it's the way the honey light runs down the walls and sticks to all the dust lying still on every surface, or if a fog films over the eyes, or if I am plain deceived. But that morning the washing machine hums early and the kids, all six, already studying long, I try taking up *eucharisteo* because I have known it before, that joy-miracle that might happen even now and here.

243. Clean sheets smelling like wind
244. Hot oatmeal tasting like home
245. Bare toes in early light

I do feel that. Happy when I name. But the porridge pot
soaks in the sink and I don't know. How much is my tongue,
tail of the heart, learning the real language of *eucharisteo*?
(I didn't know then what was to come.) I forget Eden and
naming and nails, and it all seems just a bit ... juvenile.
Contrived. This is the whole of the secret learning? I confess,
even after all that I've seen and tasted and touched, I do scoff.
I yearn for the stuff of saints, the hard language, the fluency of
thanksgiving in all, even the ugliest and most heartbreaking.
I want the very fullest life. I wonder, even just an inkling—is
this but a ridiculous experiment? Some days, ones with laundry
and kids and dishes in sink, it is hard to think that the insulting
ordinariness of this truly teaches the full mystery of the all
most important, *eucharisteo*. It's so frustratingly common—it's
offensive.

Driving nails into a life always is.

I pick up the journal. Paul had twice said it, and I mustn't
forget it. He said he had to *learn*. And learning requires
practice—sometimes even mind-numbing practice. C. S.
Lewis said it too, to a man looking for fullest life: "If you think
of this world as a place intended simply for our happiness,
you find it quite intolerable: think of it as a place of training
and correction and it's not so bad."[6] It might even be good.
So I, too, can be like our children and the everyday training,
memorizing of the Latin paradigms with the practicing chants:
amo, amas, amat. The washing machine dings and I light. This
is why I had never really learned the language of "thanks in

all things"! Though pastors preached it, I still came home
and griped on. I had never *practiced*. Practiced until it became
the second nature, the first skin. Practice is the hardest part
of learning, and training is the essence of transformation.
Practice, practice, practice. Hammer. Hammer. Hammer.

This training might prove to be the hardest of my life. It
just might save my life.

Some days I pick up a camera and it's a hammer.

The lens is my ink, for cameras have sensor eyes, and pixels
record. I slide it into a pocket, a thin point-and-shoot, and
find another way to chronicle, to force the lids open; another
way to receive the moment with thanks reverential. When
he comes in from the barn, the Farmer finds me with my
hammer in hand, leaning over a plate of cheese grated and
sitting in sunlight. It is true. I do feel foolish. I mean, it's curls
of mozzarella and cheddar piled high in a pond of golden
day. And I'm changing the settings for macro, pulling in for
a close-up frame. He's fed 650 sows with one strong arm this
morning, flicked on a welder and melded steel. It is quite
possible that the God-glory of a ring of shredded cheese may
be lost on him.

It isn't.

"I like finding you just like this." He wraps one arm around
my bowed middle, draws me close and up into him strong.

"Crazy like this?" I blush silliness, and he brushes close with
the four-day stubble. He laughs.

"*Perfect* like this." He nods toward the cheese plate. "You
being happy in all these little things that God gives. It makes
me very happy."

Happy in all these little things that God gives. Ridiculously happy over slips of cheese. That I am, and it's wild, and, oh, I am the one who laughs. *Me! Changed! Surprised by joy!*

Joy is the realest reality, the fullest life, and joy is always *given*, never grasped. God *gives* gifts and I *give* thanks and I unwrap the gift given: *joy*.

It is true, I never stop wanting to learn the hard *eucharisteo* for the deathbeds and dark skies and the prodigal sons. But I accept this is the way to begin, and all hard things come in due time and with practice. Yet now wisps of cheese tell me gentle that this is the first secret step into *eucharisteo*'s miracle. Gratitude for the seemingly insignificant—a seed—this plants the giant miracle. The miracle of *eucharisteo*, like the Last Supper, is in the eating of crumbs, the swallowing down one mouthful. Do not disdain the small. The whole of the life— even the hard—is made up of the minute parts, and if I miss the infinitesimals, I miss the whole. These are new language lessons, and I live them out. There is a way to live the big of giving thanks in all things. It is this: to give thanks in this one small thing. The moments will add up.

I, too, had read it often, the oft-quoted verse: "And give thanks for everything to God the Father in the name of our Lord Jesus Christ" (Ephesians 5:20). And I, too, would nod and say straight-faced, "I'm thankful for everything." But in this counting gifts, to one thousand, more, I discover that slapping a sloppy brush of thanksgiving over everything in my life leaves me deeply thankful for very few things in my life. A lifetime of sermons on "thanks in all things" and the shelves sagging with books on these things and I testify: life-changing gratitude does not fasten to a life unless nailed through with one very specific nail at a time.

Little nails and a steady hammer can rebuild a life—
eucharisteo precedes the miracle.

I snap a picture of cheese.

⁓

I roll out the dough, sprinkle the ring cheese on round
pizza thin. I feel how the sun lies down warm across hands and
how thanks soaks through the pores. I think how God-glory in
a cheese ring might seem trifling. Even offensive, to focus the
lens of a heart on the minute, in a world mangled and maimed
and desperately empty.

I know there is poor and hideous suffering, and I've seen
the hungry and the guns that go to war. I have lived pain, and
my life can tell: I only deepen the wound of the world when
I neglect to give thanks for early light dappled through leaves
and the heavy perfume of wild roses in early July and the song
of crickets on humid nights and the rivers that run and the stars
that rise and the rain that falls and all the good things that a
good God gives. Why would the world need more anger, more
outrage? How does it save the world to reject unabashed joy
when it is joy that saves us? Rejecting joy to stand in solidarity
with the suffering doesn't rescue the suffering. The converse
does. The brave who focus on all things good and all things
beautiful and all things true, even in the small, who give
thanks for it and discover joy even in the here and now, they
are the change agents who bring fullest Light to all the world.
When we lay the soil of our hard lives open to the rain of grace
and let joy penetrate our cracked and dry places, let joy soak
into our broken skin and deep crevices, *life* grows. How can
this not be the best thing for the world? For us? The clouds
open when we mouth thanks.

This thanks for the minute, this is to say the prayer of the most blessed of women about to participate in one of the most transformative events the world has ever known. Mary, with embryonic God Himself filling her womb, exalts in quiet ways: "My soul doth magnify the Lord" (Luke 1:46 KJV).

So might I; yes, and even here.

Something always comes to fill the empty places. And when I give thanks for the seemingly microscopic, I make a place for God to grow within me. This, *this*, makes me full, and I "magnify him with thanksgiving" (Psalm 69:30 KJV), and God enters the world. What will a life magnify? The world's stress cracks, the grubbiness of a day, all that is wholly wrong and terribly busted? Or God? Never is God's omnipotence and omniscience diminutive. God is not in need of magnifying by us so small, but the reverse. It's our lives that are little and we have falsely inflated self, and in thanks we decrease and the world returns right. I say thanks and I swell with Him, and I swell the world and He stirs me, joy all afoot.

This, I think, this is the other side of prayer.

This act of naming grace moments, this list of God's gifts, moves beyond the shopping list variety of prayer and into the other side. The other side of prayer, the interior of His throne room, the inner walls of His powerful, love-beating heart. The list is *God's* list, the pulse of His love — the love that thrums on the other side of our prayers. And I see it now for what this really is, this dare to write down one thousand things I love. It really is a dare to name all the ways that *God* loves me. The true Love Dare. To move into His presence and listen to His love unending and know the grace uncontainable. This is the vault of the miracles. The only thing that can change us, the world, is this — all His love. I must never be deceived by the simplicity of *eucharisteo* and penning His love list. Cheese. Sun. Journal. Naming. Love. Here. It all feels startlingly hallowed, and I breathe shallow. I should take the shoes off.

I am bell and He is sure wind, and He moves and I am rung and I know it for what it is: this is the other side where Daniel, man of prayer, lived. Change agent, mover and shaker Daniel, second-to-the-king Daniel, sleeping-on-perfect-peace-in-the-den-of-the-lions Daniel. Daniel is a man of power prayer, not because he bends the stiff knees and makes petitions of the High Throne three times daily. Rather, his prayers move kings and lion jaws because Daniel "prayed three times a day, just as he had always done, *giving thanks* to his God." (Daniel 6:10, emphasis added). Three times a day, Daniel prayed *thanksgiving* for the everyday common, for the God-love spilling forth from the God-heart at the center of all. The only real prayers are the ones mouthed with thankful lips. Because gratitude ushers into the other side of prayer, into the heart of the God-love, and all power to change the world, me, resides here in His love. Prayer, *to be prayer*, to have any power to change anything, must first speak thanks: "in everything, by prayer and petition, *with thanksgiving*, present your requests to God" (Philippians 4:6 NIV, emphasis added). "*First*, I tell you to pray for all people, asking God for what they need and *being thankful to him*" (1 Timothy 2:1 NCV, emphasis added). Prayer without ceasing is only possible in a life of continual thanks. How did I ever think there was another way to enter into His courts but with thanksgiving?

It's that one wondrous mound of grated cheese, rung in the sunlight and captured in frame, that makes me think it. What that ancient wise woman Julian of Norwich stated:

The highest form of prayer is to the goodness of God.... God only desires that our soul cling to him with all of its strength, in particular, that it clings to his goodness. For of all the things our minds can think about God, it is thinking upon his goodness that pleases him most and brings the most profit to our soul.[7]

The gift list *is* thinking upon His goodness—and this, *this* pleases Him most! *And* most profits my own soul and I am beginning, only beginning, to know it. If clinging to His goodness is the highest form of prayer, then this seeing His goodness with a pen, with a shutter, with a word of thanks, these really are the most sacred acts conceivable. The ones anyone can conceive, anywhere, in the midst of anything. *Eucharisteo* takes us into His love. I am struck and I long chime: Daniel is only a man of prayer because he is a man of thanks, and the only way to be a woman of prayer is to *be a woman of thanks*. And not sporadic, general thanks, but three times a day *eucharisteo*. Was it the power of *everyday thanksgiving* prayer that shut the gaping mouths of the lions ravenous? Lions would count as hard *eucharisteo*.

I slide a pizza out of oven and cheese has melted over all and through all and someday I would tell Shelly that life change comes when we receive life with thanks and ask for nothing to change.

I cut the pizza round into slices. And the porcelain dove, etched with the word *peace*, the one that hangs in hope by my corner kitchen window—she looks to soar into hard winds.

CHAPTER 4

a sanctuary of time

All we have to decide is what to do
with the time that is given us.
J. R. R. Tolkien

April sun pools into a dishwater sink, liquid daylight on hands.

The water is hot. I wash dishes. On my arms, just below
the hiked sleeves, suds leave delicate water marks. Suds glisten.
And over the soaking pots, the soap bubbles stack. This fragile
tension arched in spheres of slick elastic sheets.

Light impinges on slippery film.

And I only notice because I'm looking for this and it's the
rays falling, reflecting off the outer surface of a bubble ... off
the rim of bubble's inner skin ... and where they meet, this
interference of light, iridescence on the bubble's arch, violet,
magenta, blue-green, yellow-gold. Like the glimmer on raven
wing, the angles, the hues, the brilliant fluid, light on the
waves.

I touch wonder and fragility quivers ... and bulges. Merges.
Melds. Ripens full round, time shimmering clear.

And bursts.

Science may explain mechanics, but how do the eyes of the
soul see? I seize the pen on the sill, and I can record another

one. With my hand still dribbling dishes, with the breath all caught, I etch it down in that journal always lying out flat.

362. *Suds . . . all color in sun*

I lay down the pen. Dry my hands on the dish towel, dab at water spots transfusing into ink.

The house is a mess.

The pots pile, husks of the lunch labor. Bits of potato harden to counter. Books and pages and paper and pencils and crayons stagger senseless across the study table, ideas lost and left. Domino tiles hail across the floor. The children have all tumbled out, out to the air and the spaces wide open. I wash up undone on an island of quiet. The loud and blur of the morning ache across my shoulders. The washing machine works, and the porcelain dove, the one with "peace" scrolled deep into wing, hangs by one clear thread. From the sink, I can see her spin, spin, this way, then that, around and around and dizzy around.

After that night of the nightmares, I had said it, that I didn't need more time to do or see or experience anything more. But look at the remains of a morning and it's obvious I'm craving it deep: more time to manage just the life I already have. The work, the kids, the meals, the laundry, the ministry, a life so full it can seem empty. And then, on top of all that, who has time to take on yet one more thing and keep a gratitude journal, count gifts? Who has time to tally up one thousand of them? Can our time-crammed lives handle yet one more *thing*?

I drain the sink, suds exhausted to oily scum.

~

I refill. The tap runs fresh water. I watch the stream from

the faucet foam up fresh soap. I only see it because I'm
looking ...

362. Suds ... all color in sun

I fill the sink with the circle of bowl, and batter floats up
in suds. I wash. I see my reflection in the stainless of the tap.
I know you, those seeking eyes. You're the one in dire need
of time, that thing we can't buy, what we sell of ourselves
to get more of what we think we want, what we sacrifice to
seemingly gain. They say time is money, but that's not true.
Time is life. And if I want the fullest life, I need to find fullest
time. I wipe a water spot off the tap; there is a reflection of
me. Oh yes, I know you, the *busyness* of your life leaving little
room for the *source* of your life. I'm the face grieving.

God gives us time. And who has time for God?

Which makes no sense.

In Christ, don't we have *everlasting* existence? Don't Christians
have all the time in eternity, life everlasting? If Christians run out
of time — wouldn't we lose our very own existence? If anyone
should have time, isn't it the Christ-followers?

I hold the bowl in hand, take that knit cloth, and work
it around the bowl's lip. I think back, remembering that
stark morning in May when I sat with the dead as I do every
Tuesday — but that Tuesday, I won't forget.

While children play keys at the piano teacher's, I wait down
the street among the tombstones, looking for keys of my own.

I sit at cemetery's edge, reading, and two white-crowned
women stand alone by a hole in the ground at the other end
of the graveyard. What are they waiting for in shy spring
light, jackets pulled round tight? A white pickup truck with
its dangling hoist backs up to earth's gaping mouth. A man in

green work pants gets out of the pickup, hooks on to concrete box, lowers it into black void, a cradle for the casket.

Then a black hearse creeps slowly into the cemetery, slow across grass. Here comes the casket—the remains of the living. I lay aside my book.

Is there no preacher coming? Just two elderly ladies—and a funeral director with his grave digger? And one black crow presiding high from the pile of dirt dug up, a shadow ready for the flight.

Who awaits in the hearse with only two gathered for the burial? And did he, the deceased, push to get through each day so he'd be first lunging over the finish line, life done? Did the dashing to grab fistfuls of life fill his emptiness . . . fill the emptiness of a coffin?

"We are merely moving shadows, and all our busy rushing ends in nothing" (Psalm 39:6).

The women, shoulder to shoulder, brush away flies. And when the funeral director and grave digger open up the back of the hearse and slide the coffin out, in that stark moment of earth-finality, a question once asked of a pastor haunts through the rows of headstones and I hear it sure again.

What was the pastor's most profound regret in life?

They carry the wooden box across the graveyard. It's the weight of regrets that weighs a coffin down. And I hear the answer of the pastor ring.

Being in a hurry. Getting to the next thing without fully entering the thing in front of me. I cannot think of a single advantage I've ever gained from being in a hurry. But a thousand broken and missed things, tens of thousands, lie in the wake of all the rushing. . . . Through all that haste

I thought I was *making up time*. It turns out I was *throwing it away*.[1]

In our rushing, bulls in china shops, we break our own lives.

Haste makes waste.

And I had paused before driving out of the cemetery and looked back to the grave digger and funeral director walking through headstones and I hear this too, words of another woman seeking: "On every level of life, from housework to heights of prayer, in all judgment and efforts to get things done, hurry and impatience are sure marks of the amateur."[2]

I scrub the bowl hard, try to scrape away the regrets of my life lived amateur.

Because that is the way I have lived. From the time the alarm first rings and I stir on our pillows touching, stretch over his bare back and check those relentless hands keeping time on that clock. The time, always the time, I'm an amateur trying to beat time. The six kids rouse. We race. The barn ... and hurry. The breakfast ... *and hurry*. The books, the binders ... and hurry! In a world addicted to speed, I blur the moments into one unholy smear. I have done it. I do it still. Hands of the clock whip hard. So I push hard and I bark hard and I fall hard and when their wide eyes brim sadness and their chins tremble weak, I am weary and I am the thin clear skin, reflecting their fatigue, about to burst, my eyes glistening their same sheer pain.

The hurry makes us hurt.

And maybe it is the hurt that drives us on? For all our

frenzied running seemingly toward something, could it be that we are in fact fleeing—desperate to escape pain that pursues?

Whatever the pace, time will keep it and there's no outrunning it, only speeding it up and pounding the feet harder; the minutes pound faster too. Race for more and you'll snag on time and leak empty. The longer I keep running, the longer the gash, and I drain, bleed away.

Hurry always empties a soul.

And it's those six souls there I love, those six under spruce trees, there out my window. Twelve arms gathering fallen cones. Twelve legs bent. The Boy-Man's arms rake a pile of dead grass, winter's refuse. The Tall-Girl tucks Little-One's blowing wisps of blonde under spring hat. Two little boys bent, tossing cones into pail, their heads touching in joke and I see their faces laughter light, their shoulders shaking in fun. And oh, I know that sound and I smile.

The crusted pan that baked the chocolate-melt bars slides off the tower of bowls, crashes to the floor. I pick it up and watch it sink into sink.

I speak it to God: I don't really want *more* time; I just want *enough* time. Time to breathe deep and time to see real and time to laugh long, time to give You glory and rest deep and sing joy and just enough time in a day not to feel hounded, pressed, driven, or *wild* to get it all done—yesterday. In a world with cows to buy and fields to see and work to do, in the beep and blink of the twenty-first century, with its "live in the moment" buzz phrase that none of the whirl-weary seem to know how to do, who actually knows how to take time and live with soul and body and God all in sync? To have the time to grab the jacket off the hook and time to go out to all air and sky and green and time to wonder at all of them in all this light, this time refracting in prism.

I just want time to do my one life well.

A soap bubble bursts next to my skin.

~

A soap bubble, skin of light and water and space suspended in sphere. Who has time for that?

Hadn't I? Only because I was looking. Because that list of one thousand gifts has me always on the hunt for one more … and one more — to behold one more moment pregnant with wonder.

The wonder right in the middle of the sink. Looking for it like this. I lay the palm under water and I raise my hand with the membrane of a life span of moments. In the light, the sheerness of bubble shimmers. Bands of garnet, cobalt, flowing luminous.

I see through to the pattern. I see. The way my life, vapor, is shaping. I hadn't noticed.

It's 362.

362. *Suds… all color in sun*

That's my answer to time.

Time is a relentless river. It rages on, a respecter of no one. And this, this is the only way to slow time: When I fully enter time's swift current, enter into the current moment with the weight of all my attention, I slow the torrent with the weight of me all here. *I can slow the torrent by being all here.* I only live the full life when I live fully in the moment. And when I'm always looking for the next glimpse of glory, I slow and enter. And time slows. Weigh down this moment in time with attention full, and the whole of time's river slows, slows, slows.

The bubble in my hand quavers, a rainbow at fringes.

And blind eyes see: It's this sleuthing for the glory that slows a life gloriously. It's plain, bubble straight through: Giving thanks for one thousand things is ultimately an invitation to slow time down with weight of full attention. In this space of time and sphere, I am attentive, aware, accepting the whole of the moment, weighing it down with me all here.

I tilt my hand more to the light and the wave frequencies reinforce on bubble's dome and color bands deepen, fire-blue swirling flame into lurid scarlet. A kaleidoscope planet. Full attention fills the empty ache.

This. Is this *eucharisteo* the way to that elusive fullest life, the one that lives in the moment? What my sister urges when I get angsty and knotted about tomorrow, when I sorrow for what is gone, her words always tugging me to stay right here — "Wherever you are, be all there."[3] I have lived the runner, panting ahead in worry, pounding back in regrets, terrified to live in the present, because here-time asks me to do the hardest of all: just open wide and receive.

Light on soap film, its energy traveling, reflection, refraction on a wall a few millionths of an inch thick. Light waves permeate and collide, crest to crest and crest to trough. Yellow marbleizes into indigo dark. I do see this. I hold it.

This is where God is.

In the present. I AM—His very name. I want to take shoes off. I AM, so full of the weight of the present, that time's river slows to a still ... and God Himself is timeless. The bubble trembles slight. Or is it my hand? It's not the gifts that fulfill, but the holiness of the space. The God in it. Far curvature of the bubble eddies, violet sliding down. This is supreme gift, time, God Himself framed in moment. I hardly breathe ... and time is only of the essence, because time is the essence of God, I AM. This I need to consecrate: time.

I may never wear shoes again.

The bubble arches into the dome of a cathedral. There. What I am to do? Make every moment a cathedral giving glory ... I am Jacob and the Lord is in this place and I was not aware of it (Genesis 28:16). And it is *eucharisteo* curving the moment into a cupola of grace, an architecture of holiness[4]— a place for God. Thanks makes now a sanctuary. And I take my vows: I will not desecrate this moment with ignorant hurry or sordid ingratitude. I will be Jacob, and I will name this moment the "house of God" (Genesis 28:19). Crystalline orb gleams in the light of the window.

The clock ticks slow. I hear it for what it is: good and holy. Time, what God first deemed holy above all else (Genesis 2:3). Thank God for the time, and very God enters that time, presence hallowing it. True, this, full attention slows time and I live the full of the moment, right to outer edges. But there's more. I awake to I AM here. When I'm present, I meet I AM, the very presence of a present God. In His embrace, time loses all sense of speed and stress and space and stands so still and ... holy.

Here is the only place I can love Him.

The bubble glints luster, pearl pried from the oyster.

I hold it as long as it has life. Then I wipe slow the wet hands, grab my journal and put pen to paper, plunging pole into terra firma, new territory claimed, and the banner flaps wild in wind. Here is the only place I can love Him. I have time for God ...

363. *Rays reflecting hues off translucent globes*

364. Sound of spruce cones thumping buckets with spring

365. Cackle of crows high in the limbs, iridescence on wings

I am a hunter of beauty and I move slow and I keep the eyes wide, every fiber of every muscle sensing all wonder and this is the thrill of the hunt and I could be an expert on the life full, the beauty meat that lurks in every moment.

I hunger to taste life.

God.

~

I cut squares of chocolate-melt bars in half and the knife slides clean straight through. A ladybug walks the windowsill, spring stroll all in parade of red and black dots. Her back parts into wing, then shies. I jot her down, 366. I slow time! It's ridiculous how much joy a moment can hold.

Dishes soak. The clock ticks, and I hear it like a song in easy time. I lick the chocolate off fingertips and swallow sweet down and I try to open it up all the way wide.

Why is *eucharisteo* the answer to the time starved and soul famished?

I haul out a stack of white china dishes. One dessert square for each china plate. Count again, slow—is there enough?

Like the God-Man counting His too-few loaves and not-enough fishes. The one I remember from felt boards and figures pressed out smooth, where "Jesus then took the loaves, *gave thanks*, and distributed to those who were seated as much as they wanted" (John 6:11 NIV, emphasis added).

Gave thanks. He'd done it there too? Again? I'd missed it and all of my life?

I'd never considered those two words, the bridge words

there in the middle, the crossing over that took the not enough and made it enough.

Gave thanks.

Eucharisteo.

Jesus embraces His not enough ... *He gives thanks* ... And there is more than enough. *More than enough!*

Eucharisteo always, always precedes the miracle.

And who doesn't need a miracle like that every day? *Thanksgiving makes time.*

Really? Give thanks and get time? Give thanks ... slow time down with all your attention — and your basket of not-enough-time multiplies into more than enough time.

I have extra squares. I bank them along the rim of the plate and realize for the first time what has never been the problem of my life.

The real problem of life is never a lack of time.

The real problem of life — *in my life* — is lack of thanksgiving.

Thanksgiving creates abundance; and the miracle of multiplying happens when I give thanks — take the just one loaf, say it is enough, and give thanks — and He miraculously makes it more than enough. I have beheld suds in sun, and I have known miracles like that.

I am a mother-tired, but when my soul doth magnify, my time doth magnify. I look out to the six I carried on the hip and in the heart and need all the hours for. And #362 and all the *eucharisteo* that came before tell me this: I redeem time from neglect and apathy and inattentiveness when I swell with thanks and weigh the moment down and it's giving thanks to God for this moment that multiplies the moments, time made enough.

I am thank-full. I am time-full.

Leaning, light out the door, iron dinner bell in hand, I ring and it's gratitude that invites me to the here grandeur, to the embrace of I AM, to come multiply my little time into enough time and the glory of now I ring for children to come, come.

The table is set. There is enough and more than.

Though I'd be tried and sore tested.

They tramp in loud and fling themselves out of their coats like cicada splitting skins, leave boots a trail of droppings.

The Tall-Girl lets the door swing loose and it slams the fingertips of Little-One and she yelps a pain dance of salty tears.

In the tussle out of a stubborn sleeve, a big brother swipes hard the head of a little brother and Small-Son wails the mad fists and there are coats and boots and still all the dominoes and dishes and books and who has time for *all this more?* More work? More stuff? More stress? I can feel my pulse quicken fierce. Entering fully into the moment can overwhelm, a river running wild. I will forget, and again, and again, but today I do remember. I breathe and I reel and I hold my ground and my tongue in this torrent coming down. I've staked my claim to the miracle. I know the way to the Promised Land.

I do what I always need to do. I preach it. I preach it to the person I need to preach to the most. I preach to me. The skin's tugged hard by the rush of time and I say it aloud in current pounding past, words I need like water: *Calm. Haste makes waste. Life is not an emergency. Life is brief and it is fleeting but it is not an emergency.* I pick up a coat and thank God for the arms that can do it. *Emergencies are sudden, unexpected events — but is anything under the sun unexpected to God?* I call a son back and hand him a hanger and thank God that he can do this too. *Stay calm, enter the moment, give thanks.* I thank God for boots and we line them straight and the little hands help. *And I can always give thanks because an all-powerful God always has all these things—* all things—*always under control.* I breathe deep and He preaches to me, soothing the time-frenzied soul with the grace river in whisper.

Life is not an emergency. Life is eucharisteo.

Eucharisteo.

I, too, soothe the cheek of the mad-fisted child. I give thanks for that one curl that always lies on his forehead, beckoning invitation, and him held close in the arms, I know it. That life is so urgent it necessitates living slow.

It's only the amateurs—and that I have been and it's been ugly—who think slow and urgent are contradictory, opposite poles.

He lays his head on my shoulder. I stroke his hair, wind my finger round that curl. I can feel the heat of his cheeks. I can feel time's current in my blood ease ... meander. Is this what the life experts know?

That in Christ, urgent *means* slow.

That in Christ, the most urgent necessitates a slow and steady reverence.

For a moment, longer, I hold son—and life—and I hold it mindfully ... attentively ... thankfully. Life at its fullest is this sensitive, detonating sphere, and it can be carried only in the hands of the unhurried and reverential—a bubble held in awe.

I carry the small son boy to the table.

When those hungry eyes and empty tummies circle round the table, smiles big just like their daddy's when he's eyeing something good heaping high on a platter, they are all story and loud talk and hardly able to restrain the waiting for the nod and I grin it too, "You may …"

They dive.

I watch them feast. They quiet. Taste buds savor it long. It's that same recipe my mama baked up when I was a kid, cowlicks sliding up the front of my hair, just like theirs.

The Boy-Man mumbles, his mouth sticky full. "I am not eating mine fast." His tongue licks chocolate off lip. "Wanna taste it all."

"Oh, when I was your age I used to just scarf my food down." I pull back one of the paint-flecked spindled chairs, one of the worn ones that used to sit around the walls of the community center during old-time Saturday night dances. It only wobbles a bit. "My Grandma Ruth would shake her head, disgusted at me. Like this."

And I show them and I wag my finger too, just the way she did, and they grin chocolate.

"She'd say, 'My lands, child! That is *no* way to eat. It took time to make this meal. And you'd better take some time to taste it. Slow down, like so.' Then she'd chew slow and deliberate like. And tell me again, so I'd remember, 'Food is meant to be savored.'"

The Tall-Girl's jaw slows. I wink. She smiles, brushes her lip with her finger.

"Pork chops, potatoes, peas, it was all just food to me." I hand down the plate with extras for the boys looking eager. They kneel up on chairs to eye out that one square that's just a smidge bigger. "But Grandma's apple pie? Her butterscotch squares? She didn't have to tell me to slow down then!" A boy takes a big bite, too big, smiles knowingly. I look around at their faces, their taste buds all alive, eyes shining delight in the sweet.

When did I stop thinking life was dessert?

I push back from the table. Push away from regrets. They need something to drink. I clatter out the stainless steel glasses. Pour out the cold milk and think of the strangers walking briskly, blithely along to Emmaus, oblivious to the God-skin before their eyes. Only in the slowing, the sitting down at the table, when His hands held the bread and the thanks fell from His tongue, do the open-eyed, the wide-eyed, see the Face they face (Luke 24:13 – 35). The fast have spiritually slow hearts.

I carry the cups back to the table.

My drained, empty body has stopped and my soul has caught up and if I give thanks here, Whom might I recognize? I pass two cups down to the end of the table. It takes a full twenty minutes after your stomach is full for your brain to register satiation. How long does it take your soul to realize that your life is full? The slower the living, the greater the sense of fullness and satisfaction. The body and soul can synchronize. This moment I enter. Racing time tempers. And the neurons brand into memory—the Tall-Girl collecting crumbs on the end of a fingertip, the light reflecting off the curve of her skin, the near man-sized hands grabbing glass, swigging down milk, hands that once clenched my finger in first life, Small-Son lisping out a joke and all their happy banter, this taste of chocolate and children, and I don't reach forward and I don't reach back and I weigh the moment down with full attention here.

Life is dessert—too brief to hurry. You don't wolf it down. The Little-One's tongue searches about for smudge of chocolate she can feel on her cheek.

"More milk?"

She nods, eyes large, laughing yes.

I pour more. And I have an appetite to *celebrate—yes, let us eat cake!*—and nibble on bare toes, to pick armfuls of poppies, to hold a heart up against me, stronger, surer, to sit long with my mama in the last of afternoon light. "Wherever you are, be all there" is only possible in the posture of *eucharisteo. I want to slow down and taste life, give thanks, and see God.*

There are four appointments scratched on the calendar this week and two evening meetings slotted and all six kids have swimming lessons and there are piano recitals and exams looming at week's end and ... and ... and days flood torrential—but full attention slows the current. Don't I always have the choice to be fully attentive? Simplicity is ultimately a matter of focus. *Eucharisteo, eucharisteo.* That keeps the focus simple—sacred.

I watch the hands move grace on the clock face. I'm growing older. These children growing up. But time is not running out. This day is not a sieve, losing time. With each passing minute, each passing year, there's this deepening awareness that I am filling, *gaining* time. We stand on the brink of eternity.

The Small-Son pauses between bites, wiggles his tooth with tip of his tongue. I watch him and I smile. He sees me watching and he grins. He takes that last bite of chocolate-melt and with mouth still full of gooey good, he serenades soft, "I love you, Mom ... and all this."

And all this.

This cathedral moment, this God, this time before it bursts. *All this.*

I am Jacob and this moment is the house of God and I reach for the plate.

I want to savor long whatever time holds.

what in the world, in all this world, is grace?

One act of thanksgiving,
when things go wrong with us,
is worth a thousand thanks when things
are agreeable to our inclinations.
Saint John of Avila

The front porch flag Mama bought for me from Burvey's General Store flaps in a lazy gust of back road July.

It's early morning, first light, and I'm watering flowers. Before the heat of high noon coming. The scarlet profusion, the petunias, the begonias from the market, the wintered-over geraniums. The water soaks into earth and I watch it go. Water in, flowers out, miracle there on the porch. The watering can empty, I lean a bit at the rail. Watch the bees drone honeyed heaviness over purple of coneflowers, work for a queen. Then, sudden, thrum out of nothing, a ruby-jeweled hummingbird. I hold the breath. Make the self invisible. It darts, blossom lip to blossom lip.

Her long bill swills back July sun transfigured into nectar. I watch her, become her, drink the sweet right out of now.

I'm still transfixed when the ricochet of words rip up the back.

"Levi's hand went through a fan at the barn!"

The knees go weak. Our oldest son pants hard against the door frame, feed chop from his chores still mussed down his shirt.

I drop the watering can and I run.

I hold the edges of the skirt tight and, bare feet across gravel yard, I fly scared. It's the naked heel pressing the sharp of the stones that push the memories through and I am four again, child running after mother, the mother running to the child crushed away red. Now I am the mother, the eyes shot white through, and I run for my child, child maimed and bleeding away. I do remember to breathe, to hold each breath long, so I won't give way when I find Levi. He will be howling. He will be … I can hardly imagine how those fan blades, each two feet long, each a whacking two pounds, each whirring at blurring speeds, circulating air for hundreds of sows, might hack up a little boy's hand.

Or hack it off.

I know it, even in running down the lane to the barn, the diaphragm rising, bracing; this may be it. The hard *eucharisteo.* Now I know that I don't want to know it yet … Ever.

How to lay the hand open for this moment's bread—when it will hurt.

Three hours later, the gravel in the lane crackles, Levi and I home from ER. Bent over his bandages, Levi whimpers, rocks the swaddling back and forth, back and forth. She's waiting for us in the lane. My mama who has wept and rocked and who

has had the child taken from the hand—she meets me there in
the gravel lane, the angst carved hard across her forehead.

I speak to Mama, me who still has my child.

"He has a hand."

I open the door to help seven-year-old Levi out of the
passenger seat. I steady Mama too with details. "And . . . he has
all ten of his fingers." She drops her head in relief, holds her
hand to her chest, exhales.

"He's cut up bad. But only the index is broken. They're
booking us for a surgeon." The surgeon would tell us that the
weight and speed of that fan blade slamming into the finger
snapped the bone in half and rotated it full round. Without
surgery, the scalpel blade careful to limit nerve damage, to
open up the finger and spin the bone, Levi's right index finger
would warp, useless crook.

Levi, eyes hollowed with shock, holds up his bandaged
hand to show my pale-faced mama.

"But hey—he has a hand!" I rub hope into the small of his
back, into Mama's fear.

Her tension lines loosen, and she leans into me, laying her
hand firm on my shoulder and she whispers it sure. "*God's
grace*," she whispers. "*God's grace*." She pats my shoulder and
I feel her relief . . . and something dark . . . angry . . . ugly.

I guide Levi into the house, one arm around, one shielding
his wrappings. And a slippery question serpentines up me,
nearly shakes my tongue with its words but I refuse it. Refuse
the opening of lips to the wondering. But the words still come
quiet, hard and black, squeezing me tight.

And if his hand had been right sheared off?

What of God's grace then?

Can I ask that question?

I get a pillow for Levi, all weary from crying. I lift his head, slip some comfort under him heavy with hurt and just stroke his hair. His eyelashes still, his chest breathes the slumber and I think of what I had heard on the radio on the way home from ER, the announcer static crackly. The obituaries after the noon farm news. A thirteen-year-old Mennonite boy, just down the road from the red-roofed dairy farm my husband grew up on. A farm boy, an accident. Date of death. Siblings. Funeral details. No mention of the state of his mama's heart, delta fractures splitting her through.

Why in the world, everywhere I turn, every page, always death? I'd like some happy, blithe, Pollyanna words, please. For a happy, blithe, Pollyanna life. My gratitude journal lies open on the counter. I retrieve it, flip back through pages, and run my hand over penned numbers, memories of the Pollyanna moments. And I can see it in the looking back, how this daily practice of the discipline of gratitude is the way to daily practice the delight of God and what in the spring had been #362 *suds in the sink*, grew over weeks and months and I read

457. *Brown eggs fresh from the henhouse*
485. *Hair bows holding back curls*
513. *Boys jiggling blue Jell-O*
526. *New toothbrushes*

and I remember realizing when I was already over half and fixed on counting, couldn't stop, always looking for just one more in this unfolding of a chronicle of grace, our life story in freeze frames of thanks

613. *Paper bag puppet shows*

647. Pinky skin of newborn pigs

663. Opening jars of preserves

664. Nylons without runs

and not only was the numbering leaving traces of our days; this counting blessings was the unlocking of the mystery of joy, joy, "the gigantic secret of the Christian,"[1] joy hiding in gratitude and who but the Jesus people are the most thankful? And then it had seemed like it might be over all too soon …

748. Mama delivering chicken soup to the back door

783. Forgiveness of a sister

882. Toothless smiles

891. Earthy aroma of the woods

Come early winter, I jotted haltingly, not wanting it to end:

904. First frost's crunch

924. Scooping out squash, all steaming

943. Stepping over a dog when coming in through the dark

971. Kettle whistling for tea on a cold afternoon

And when I wrote the one thousandth gift, I had written careful:

1000. Resurrection bloom, an amaryllis, a gift a year in the coming

My mother-in-law had given us that amaryllis bulb the year before. I had set it in the kitchen windowsill, under the porcelain dove. I had waited. A full rotation of the earth through the galaxy, I had waited. Cancer had left Mom Voskamp's remains buried deep. And then. Her bulb had trumpeted a call: *Fully live! Live fully!*

My one thousandth gift. I had swallowed hard. God had used the dare to give me this; led me all the way to give me this as the thousandth gift, exactly like this, to unfurl just this:

Live fully! Mom Voskamp spoke to me from the grave. Here are gifts worth waiting 365 days for, gifts worth counting to one thousand for, gifts that will unbelievably emerge out of the deathly dark. Joy is always worth the wait, and fully living worth the believing. The pursuit! The bloom had trumpeted for weeks.

Was it all over now?

I had turned the page. And into another year, another spring, another year of beans and corn and wheat under sun, I had kept writing it down, a free-for-all, a journal in my purse, one by my bed, another on the counter by the sink, a file on my computer, because the dare to write *one thousand* gifts becomes the dare to celebrate innumerable, *endless* gifts! That initial discipline, the daily game to count, keeping counting to one thousand, it was God's necessary tool to reshape me, remake me, rename me, and now how could I stop being Ann full of grace?

Or was this now only the beginning of really becoming?

Daily discipline is the door to full freedom, and the discipline to count to one thousand gave way to the freedom of wonder and I can't imagine not staying awake to God in the moment, the joy in the now.

But awakening to joy awakens to pain.

Joy and pain, they are but two arteries of the one heart that pumps through all those who don't numb themselves to really living. Pages of the gratitude journal fill endlessly. Yet I know it in the vein and the visceral: *life is loss.* Every day, the gnawing ...

What will I lose? Health? Comfort? Hope? Eventually, I am guaranteed to lose *every* earthly thing I have ever possessed.

When will I lose? Today? In a few weeks? How much time have I got before the next loss?

Who will I lose? And that's definite: I will lose *every* single person I have ever loved. Either abruptly or eventually. All human relationships end in loss. Am I prepared for that?

Every step I take forward in my life is a loss of something in my life and I live the waiting: How and of what will I be emptied today?

I return to Levi and pull the blanket up over our boy curled round his wound. I watch him sleep.

Does anyone whisper in the dead boy's house, "*God's grace . . . God's grace*"?

What in the world, in a world of certain loss, is grace?

And the more of the blessings I name, this theological problem deepens, the kind that manifests itself between the breakfast table and last light out. If I am numbering gift moments to one thousand and now beyond—what moments in my life count as blessings? If I name this moment as gift, grace, what *is* the next moment? Curse? How do you know how to sift through a day, a life, and rightly read the graces, rightly ascertain the curses?

What is good? What counts as grace? *What is the heart of God?*

Do I believe in a God who rouses Himself just now and then to spill a bit of benevolence on hemorrhaging humanity? A God who breaks through the carapace of this orb only now and then, surprises us with a spared hand, a reprieve from sickness, a good job and a nice house in the burbs—and then finds Himself again too impotent to deal with all I see as suffering and evil? A God of sporadic, random, splattering goodness—that now and then splatters across a gratitude journal? Somebody tell me:

What are all the other moments?

~~~

Levi moans. I brush his cheek soft. Is there Tylenol in the kitchen? My Bible lies open by the gratitude journal. I look for a bottle of pills to ease the pain, and I remember the summer I was twelve.

We beat it down a gravel road in a cloud of dust, and I looked over at the billboard that the van Veens had planted back in their woods. I asked Dad why anyone would bother putting a sign up in their woods if no one could make out the words. He looked at me squinting, and my mama made me an optometrist's appointment. Next time we drove by van Veens' words in the woods, I wore glasses, horn-rimmed frames. And I saw the words as clear as a bell and I read them plain: "Believe on the Lord Jesus Christ, and thou shalt be saved" (Acts 16:31 KJV).

The woods spell out words. I need a lens to read them.

Every dark woods has words. And every moment is a message from The Word-God who can't stop writing His heart.

But who can read His messages?

I feel around the back of the medicine cupboard for the bottle. I squint hard, but I can't read the cryptic, indecipherable text of injured farm boys, anemic marriages, terminal mamas ... war, famine, disease. What do all the words written in the world really spell out? I had read it in Job, what makes reading God's message in every moment a form of art, fullest life: God speaks to us not in one language but two: "For God does

speak—now one way, now another" (33:14 NIV). One way,
His finger writing words in stars (Psalm 19:1–3), His eternal
power written naked in all creation (Romans 1:20); and now
another way, the sharp Holy Writ on the page that makes a
careful incision into a life, blade words that kindly cut the
tissue back to where soul and spirit join, tenderly laying bare
the intents of the heart (Hebrews 4:12).

I hold the medicine bottle, but have I found pills for the
pain?

To read His message in moments, I'll need to read His
passion on the page; wear the lens of the Word, to read His
writing in the world. Only the Word is the answer to rightly
reading the world, because The Word has nail-scarred hands
that cup our face close, wipe away the tears running down,
has eyes to look deep into our brimming ache, and whisper,
"I know. I *know*." The passion on the page is a *Person*, and the
lens I wear of the Word is not abstract idea but the eyes of the
God-Man who came and *knows* the pain.

How does the *Word* read the world?

I lay out two Tylenol for Levi in the palm. Levi moans,
swallows it down. I hold the glass of water and I tell him the
pain will ease in a bit and I don't think about the surgery, that
hand throbbing sore.

He closes his eyes, tired. I pull up the blanket again, let
him find comfort in the dark. And I go looking for medicine
of my own. Slipped in books, in purse, taped to the fridge,
mirror over the sink, these cue cards are yellowed old. Tattered
remnants of those days after I drove away from the locked
ward of the psychiatric hospital, my belly swollen heavy with

our first child, and I left Mama behind, her heart swollen too heavy with the emptiness of the child she watched bleed away before her eyes. At the door of the ward, before the steel had slammed hollow shut, she'd slipped me her wedding band so it wouldn't get stolen. I wore it home on the finger next to my own band. I had cried blind all the roads back, and I spent that night writing out these lenses through which to read a world.

Ten years, longer, I've carried these cards.

I stand in our bedroom by the window and hold a card to the light. I can hardly now make out the water-splat words of Isaiah 14:24, "Surely, just as I have intended so it has happened, and just as I have planned so it will stand" (NASB). As God plans ... *so it stands.*

I read the faded ink below, and I remember what I felt the day I copied those words, "Does disaster come to a city unless the LORD has planned it?" (Amos 3:6). And I feel it again today and I breathe: A good God plans everything. *Everything.* So a good God can only ... make plans for good? He only gives good gifts? A thing of evil cannot be created by a good God?

From the bedroom window, I watch a shadow move across the lawn, move out long across our wheat fields. That is what a shadow is, an empty space, a hole in the light. Evil is that—a hole in the goodness of God. Evil is all that lacks the goodness of God, a willful choice to turn away from the full goodness of God to that empty of His goodness.[2] I watch the grey shadows slink away over the hill, the sun driving them east.

All God makes *is* good. Can it be that, that which seems to oppose the will of God actually is used of Him to accomplish the will of God? That which seems evil only seems so because of *perspective*, the way the eyes see the shadows. Above the clouds, light never stops shining.

But *what* perspective sees good in dead farm boys, good in a little girl crushed under tires of a truck right in front of her mother's eyes, good in a brother-in-law who buries his first two sons in the space of nineteen months—and all the heinous crimes and all the weeping agony and all the scalding burn of this world? The sun rolls across wheat warm. I lean against the windowsill and watch it. I hear the echo, truth words whispering down time's cavern, words that Julian of Norwich heard:

> See that I am God. See that I am in everything. See that I do everything. See that I have never stopped ordering my works, nor ever shall, eternally. See that I lead everything on to the conclusion I ordained for it before time began, by the same power, wisdom and love with which I made it. How can anything be amiss?[3]

Perspective—how we see.

And how should anything be amiss? I can see her name on that stone, five letters of my little sister named "loved one," and I won't shield God from my anguish by claiming He's not involved in the ache of this world and Satan prowls but he's a lion on a leash and the God who governs all can be shouted at when I bruise, and I can cry and I can howl and He embraces the David-hearts who pound hard on His heart with their grief and I can moan deep that He did this—*and He did.*

I feel Him hold me—a flailing child tired in Father's arms.

And I can hear Him soothe soft, "Are your ways My ways, child? Can you eat My manna, sustain on My mystery? Can you believe that I tenderly, tirelessly work all for the best good of the whole world—because My flame of love for you can never, *ever* be quenched?"

I only close my eyes ... Enter the dark too. Sometimes we need time to answer the hard *eucharisteo*.

How do we converse with a God who may not seem to honor our honor?

In the quiet, Levi sleeping, I wonder, cue card in hand— if I had the perspective of the whole, perhaps I'd see it? That which seems evil, is it a cloud to bring rain, to bring a greater good to the *whole* of the world? Who would ever know the greater graces of comfort and perseverance, mercy and forgiveness, patience and courage, if no shadows fell over a life? I dare flip the cue card over and I make out words on the back side, "See now that I, I am He, and there is no god besides Me; It is I who put to death and give life. I have wounded and it is I who heal" (Deuteronomy 32:39 NASB). I nod. I know. *I know.* And these truth words reconfigure the battlefield under my feet.

I grip the card and I know all our days are struggle and warfare (Job 14:14) and that the spirit-to-spirit combat I endlessly wage with Satan is this ferocious thrash for joy. He sneers at all the things that seem to have gone hideously mad in this sin-drunk world, and I gasp to say God is good. The liar defiantly scrawls his graffiti across God's glory, and I heave to enjoy God ... and Satan strangles, and I whiten knuckles to grasp real Truth and fix that beast to the floor.

It's just that the eyes are bad—my perspective. "Your eye is a lamp that provides light for your body," Jesus said. "When your eye is good, your whole body is filled with light. But when your eye is bad, your whole body is filled with darkness. And if the light you think you have is actually darkness, how deep that darkness is!" (Matthew 6:22–23). If Satan can keep my eyes from the Word, my eyesight is too poor to read light—to fill with light. Bad eyes fill with darkness so heavy the soul aches because empty is never truly empty; empty is only a full, deepening darkness. So this is what it is to be. Eve in the Garden, Satan's hiss tickling the ear, "Did God actually say . . . ?" (Genesis 3:1 ESV).

No Scripture glasses to read what God is trying to write through a prodigal child? Scrawl my own quick editing on the half-finished story: *failure.* Satan's tongue darts.

Not wearing a biblical lens to decipher the meaning of a doctor's ominous diagnosis? Just read Satan's slippery interpretation: *cheated.*

Not using anything to bend the light of this world so I can read my own messy days? Spray on another layer of graffiti: *worthless.*

So I have been ambushed.

Without God's Word as a lens, the world warps.

I slip the cue card into my back pocket, glasses slipped on. I catch a glimpse of myself in the bureau's antique mirror, the glass wavy and flecked with age. I only slightly distort.

The phone rings. Levi still dozes. I lunge across the bed, try to grab the receiver before the next ring. It's John, my brother-in-law. He has the details of the Mennonite family's funeral arrangements for their young son.

"I can't fathom that kind of grief." I'm thinking of shadows and holes. It hurts to talk. Levi breathes heavy on the couch, whole and here.

"I talked to the uncle." John's voice is steady. "They have peace. They look at how the accident happened, this series of unlikely events. Change even one, and none of this would have happened."

Levi groans. I sit by him, tuck the blanket over his shoulders, John speaking quietly on the other end of the line. "The family accepts. God meant it this way."

I shake my head, shake off disbelief, shake off this weight pressing hard on the chest.

They can whisper it in the dead boy's house too?

God's grace, God's grace.

The unwavering faith of fissured hearts that stand in funeral parlors looks in the eyes of those offering condolences and speaks it with sure voices, "The LORD gave, and the LORD has taken away; blessed be the name of the LORD" (Job 1:21 NKJV). Twice I'd stood in the same pew as John had at the funerals of both of his sons, and I had turned and I had seen for myself, how John stood with the congregation and sang it clear, "Blessed be the name of the Lord." Twice John sang his lifelong favorite Scripture before the coffins of his sons. I can still see him brave through each line sung, the tears of faith streaming down his cheeks into his smile. My throat had swelled raw in this sad awe, and I had turned away, drowning in grief waters all my own. The kind of faith I had witnessed in John, that spoke in the dead boy's home, that kind of faith puts real vertebrae into a verse like Ephesians 5:20: "*always* giving thanks *for all* things in the name of our Lord Jesus Christ . . ." (NASB, emphasis added). That lets the Word take on their flesh, their lips speaking hardest *eucharisteo.*

I hang up the phone and I stand for a long while, just watching Levi breathe. Watching Levi live. He had an extra serving of ice cream on his plate last night and licked the mint right off the plate. He might not have. He slept in a bed last

night, on clean sheets, and beside his brother. *What if he hadn't?*
He woke and walked out across the dew grass this morning,
the blades all sewed up in dangled gossamer of spiders. *Why
him?* He worked alongside his dad in the barn, swept the
broom hard; and when his dad said he was growing quite the
muscles, he had laughed. *He might not have.*

Who deserves *any* grace?

A line of cumulous white races across July, dragging grey
shadows across our fields. Levi whimpers, slips his bandaged
hand higher on the pillow. And I remember words of evening
graces and morning miracles:

> *Here dies another day*
> *During which I have had eyes, ears, hands*
> *And the great world round me;*
> *And with tomorrow begins another.*
> *Why am I allowed two?*[4]

Why doesn't anyone ask *that* why question?

Why are we allowed two? Why lavished with three? A
whole string of grace days?

Isn't even one grace enough? Me with child alive, thinking
of faces of mothers in cemeteries—my own mama—I want to
yell, "NO!" *No, it is not!* I want to take both fists and splinter
that door with an ungrateful demanding for more. Why can't
we be allowed days indefinitely? How can God ever expect us
to say good-bye to the eyes, ears, hands of those we cherish
more than our own?

Is it because His heart awaits us at Home? Because if we
don't say good-bye here, when will we meet Him there?
Because these are the lens words for a life: Precious in His eyes
is the homecoming of the saints (Psalm 116:15). Blood seeps

through the edge of Levi's bandage. I put the bottle of Tylenol back in the cabinet. I pull the pen out of the gratitude journal's coiled spine, the one lying open on the counter always naming, endlessly naming, to one thousand and ad infinitum and I write it slow:

Levi's index finger
Bandages and pain relief

That we are allowed two—a grace miracle I hardly ever notice.

When I realize that it is not God who is in my debt but I who am in His great debt, then doesn't *all* become gift?

For He might not have.

When the night sky frays to day, smudged light coming up over fields, I wake Levi. Today's our date with the city hospital, an operating table, a surgeon. He's sleepy. He drags to the back door, holding his splint and bandaged hand to his chest, and I tie his shoelaces. The Farmer leans against the open door and takes my hand and I take Levi's other one. We will pray for the going, the cutting, the healing. Then it comes, this murmur, and from my lips ...

"Lord ..." All the feelings since the blade and the breaking, all my questioning and asking, they swell, hot lava to the surface, and I choke it back, the thick farming hand squeezing mine.

" ... that I'd day after day after day greedily take what looks like it's good from Your hand—a child gloating over sweet candy ..." My voice catches hard. I've been a thief, trying to hoard away all the good.

" ... but that I'd thrash wild to escape when what You give from Your hand *feels* bad—like gravel in the mouth. Oh, Father, *forgive* ... Should I accept good from you, and not trouble?" (Job 2:10).

I pray Job's words and heat flows down liquid.

What if that which feels like trouble, gravel in the mouth, is only that—*feeling*? What if faith says *all is* ... I think it. But do I really mean it?

I gather up Levi and hand and the man at the door kisses us both good-bye and we wind through the dawn dark. The radio snaps out sound bites of presidents, celebrities. Lights flicker in milking parlors, farmers at chores. I click off the radio and flip over to Scripture on CD. The gospel of Matthew. In the slumber of towns, the odd kitchen light flashes by. *Jesus said ... And then Jesus replied ... And a voice from heaven said ...* My fingers wrap hard around the steering wheel. At a graying intersection of two empty country roads, I idle long, stunned. It's coming out of the same stereo speakers, like the voices of presidents, dignitaries. *These are the words of God.*

Headlights make holes in the slate morning. I nudge Levi gentle, awed, "We're listening to *God*." And out of the speakers, I hear Him clear:

But Jesus told him, "No! The Scriptures say,

> 'People do not live by bread alone,
>   but by every word that comes from the mouth of God.' "
> (Matthew 4:4)

I listen and I live fully on what comes straight from His mouth. That Serpent, he's slithered with the lie that God doesn't give good but gives rocks in the mouth, leaves us to starve empty in wilderness and we'll just have to take lessons from Satan on how to take the stones of the careless God and make them into bread to feed our own hungry souls. And I hear it straight out of the speakers on a July morning breaking, the Son of God saying there is only *one* way to live full and it is "by every word that comes from the mouth of God."

It is all that Jesus used to survive in the desert, in His wrangle with silver-tongued Lucifer, only this: "It is written." And it's *the Word of God* that turns the rocks in the mouth to loaves on the tongue. That fills our emptiness with the true and real good, *that makes the eyes see,* the body full of light.

I glance at the clock ... Levi is to roll into the operating theatre in three hours. The Word of God whispers through the speakers. Levi drifts back to sleep. The countryside splits open, the earth unpeeled into sun. The wheat wears gold.

I drive out of dark and into morning glory.

I awaken to the strange truth that all new life comes out of the dark places, and hasn't it always been? Out of darkness, God spoke forth the teeming life. That wheat round and ripe across all these fields, they swelled as hope embryos in womb of the black earth. Out of the dark, tender life unfurled. Out of my own inner pitch, six human beings emerged, new life, wet and fresh.

All new life labors out of the very bowels of darkness.

That fullest life itself dawns from nothing but Calvary darkness and tomb-cave black into the radiance of Easter morning.

Out of the darkness of the cross, the world transfigures into new life. *And there is no other way.*

Then ... *yes:* It is dark suffering's umbilical cord that alone can untether new life.

It is *suffering* that has the realest possibility to bear down and deliver *grace*.

And grace that chooses to bear the cross of suffering *overcomes* that suffering.

I need to breathe.

I roll down the window. I inhale the pungency of a passing hayfield in bloom of clover, ditches with those all together wild black-eyed Susans swaying in early air. I try to think straight, truest straight. My pain, my dark—all the world's pain, all the world's dark—*it* might actually taste sweet to the tongue, be the genesis of new life?

Yes. And emptiness itself can birth the fullness of grace because in the emptiness we have the opportunity to turn to God, the only begetter of grace, and there find all the fullness of joy.

So God transfigures all the world?

Darkness transfigures into light, bad transfigures into good, grief transfigures into grace, empty transfigures into full. God wastes nothing—"makes everything work out according to his plan" (Ephesians 1:11).

We pull into the hospital parking lot, and I park across from the entrance sign that reads Oncology. A mother pushes a wheelchair down the sidewalk, bald-headed son gripping a stuffed tiger. I open the door for Levi.

I wear my lenses, and I pray to see. Who knows when you might climb a mount of transfiguration?

∽

Levi and I sit on hard chairs, waiting. The turquoise paint in the waiting room is chipped. They're in the midst of renovations, plastic draping off one corner of the room—

everywhere, transfiguring. We sit in a room with bodies
broken and casted, bent over the walkers ... burned, the skin
dressed in gauze, the skin exposed, grafted, mottled, scarred.
No one speaks. We try not to stare at each other but I can't
keep myself from saying it to God, this raw sob echoing St.
Teresa of Avila's: "If this is how You treat Your friends, no
wonder You have so few!"[5] Can I be that honest?

I am David lamenting, "O Lord, why ...?" (Psalm 10:1).
Why this broken world punched through with losses? "O
Lord, how long?" (Psalm 13:1). How long until every baby
thrives and all children sleep down the hall from a mom and
dad wrapped up in love, and each womb swells with vigorous
life, and every single cancer clinic sits empty and we all grow
old together? How long? I know a neighboring Mennonite
woman folding away the clothes of her dead son and I sit in a
room full of the battered and busted and I lament: *please.* And
He takes the empty hands and draws me close to the thrum of
Love. *You may suffer loss but in Me is anything ever lost, really? Isn't
everything that belongs to Christ also yours? Loved ones lost still belong
to Him—then aren't they still yours? Do I not own the cattle on a
thousand hills; everything? Aren't then all provisions, in Christ also
yours? If you haven't lost Christ, child, nothing is ever lost. Remember,
"through many tribulations we must enter the kingdom of God" [Acts
14:22 NASB], and in "sharing in [my Son's] sufferings, becoming
like him in his death" you come "to know Christ and the power of his
resurrection" [Philippians 3:10 NIV].*

And I nod it soft. *Yes, Father, You long to transfigure all, no
matter how long it takes. You long to transfigure all.*

The wrinkled man in the wheelchair with the legs
wrapped, the girl with her face punctured deep with the teeth
marks of a dog, the mess of this world, and I *see*—this, all this,

is what the French call *d'un beau affreux*, what the Germans call *hübsch-hässlich* — the *ugly-beautiful*. That which is perceived as ugly transfigures into beautiful. What the postimpressionist painter Paul Gauguin expressed as *"Le laid peut être beau"* — The ugly can be beautiful. The dark can give birth to life; suffering can deliver grace.

In infant psychology at university, I learned that newborns, shown side-by-side images of two faces, spend more than 80 percent of their time looking at the attractive face. So to see through the ugliness to beauty, won't I need to wear a lens? I'll need my own transfiguration to enter a kingdom where the Prince is born into a manure-smeared feed trough, where Holy God touches leper sores, breaks bread with cheats, where God wounds Himself through with nails on a cross and we wear the symbol as beauty.

Is the Son of God nauseated by the stench of twelve years of soaked menstrual cloths when He speaks tenderly to the bleeding woman? Is He repelled by the crazed eyes, the foul talk, or bad breath of the demon-possessed man. Staggeringly, doesn't even Beauty Himself become the ugly-beautiful? "There was nothing beautiful ... about his appearance" (Isaiah 53:2). He became ugly that we might become beauty. The God of the Mount of Transfiguration cannot cease His work of transfiguring moments — making all that is dark, evil, empty into that which is all light, grace, *full*.

I take to heart the words of Thomas Aquinas, who defined beauty as *id quod visum placet* — beauty as that which being seen, pleases.[6] And if all the work of transfiguring the ugly into the beautiful pleases God, *it is a work of beauty*. Is there *anything* in this world that is truly ugly? That is curse?

Levi looks up at the clock, counting minutes down. Levi,

with freckles sprinkled across the bridge of his nose, cowlick swiping his brush cut, with a hand, who breathes, boy who has been allowed the grace of two. He leans against my shoulder, lays his bandaged hand in my lap. I look down at his ugly-beautiful. And I see what I am. I'm amputated. I have hacked my life up into grace moments and curse moments. The chopping that has cut myself off from the embracing love of a God who "does not enjoy hurting people or causing them sorrow" (Lamentations 3:33), but labors to birth grief into greater grace. Isn't this the crux of the gospel? The good news that all those living in the land of shadow of death have been birthed into new life, that the transfiguration of a suffering world has already begun. That suffering nourishes grace, and pain and joy are arteries of the same heart—and mourning and dancing are but movements in His unfinished symphony of beauty. Can I believe the gospel, that God is patiently transfiguring all the notes of my life into the song of His Son?

What in the world, in all this world, is grace?

I can say it certain now: *All is grace.*

I see through the woods of the world: God is always good and I am always loved.

God is always good and I am always loved.

Everything is eucharisteo.

Because *eucharisteo* is how Jesus, at the Last Supper, showed us to transfigure all things—take the pain that is given, give thanks for it, and transform it into a joy that fulfills all emptiness. I have glimpsed it: *This, the hard* eucharisteo. The *hard* discipline to lean into the ugly and whisper thanks to transfigure it into beauty. The *hard* discipline to give thanks for all things at all times because He is all good. The *hard* discipline to number the griefs as grace because as the surgeon would cut open my son's finger to heal him, so God chooses to cut into my ungrateful heart to make me whole.

All is grace only *because all can transfigure.*

Levi reads his book, good hand holding it in lap, and I read the sacred script of pain bound in plaster, the illuminated manuscript of twisted bones, the text gilded of crutches hobbling. I wear the lens of the Word and all the world transfigures into the Beauty of Christ and *everything is eucharisteo.* And when I find Levi groan-writhing in post-op, blood leaching through gauze, his tongue all thick hot, I stroke his hair. I lean over stainless rail of the bed and I press my cheek to his flushed red and I ask soft if he'd like water and he nods. I put the straw to his lips.

In early light so new, heads hovering close over a glass of water in a hospital room, we drink the sweet right out of the world.

what do you want? the place of seeing God

Every time you feel in God's creatures something pleasing
and attractive, do not let your attention be arrested by them alone,
but, passing them by, transfer your thought to God and say:
"O my God, if Thy creations are so full of beauty,
delight and joy, how infinitely more full of beauty, delight
and joy art Thou Thyself, Creator of all!
Nicodemus of the Holy Mountain

"You will want to see this."

He takes my shoulders in his hands, large and field worn,
and draws me close. I fight the urge to writhe.

It's not him. Not his hands holding me, the whisper of
his voice, his eyes inviting me now. It's just that I'm feeling
time's strangling grip, struggling to make a cathedral of the
moment, to hallow it with the holy all here. It's late and I've
got an even later dinner to dish onto eight empty plates. A half
dozen children noisily, happily, ring the table with their hardly
washed hands and silly jokes replete with snorts and grunts and
dirty feet still needing bathing. And I haven't served the dinner
yet, haven't sliced up the loaf of bread yet, haven't put away

the basil, oregano, parsley, the peelings of carrots, the skins of onions, the jars of tomatoes. Still have to grate the cheese into circles in the soup bowls. Still have to wash the dishes, sweep the floors, wash up kids, turn down beds, kneel for the prayers weary and long and needy. My gratitude journal is buried under a mess of papers over the sink's sill with yesterday's snippets of the list that never ends:

Book pages turning
Child sobs ebbing
Boys humming hymns
Click of a seat belt
Fender rattling with stones of gravel roads
Wind rushing through open truck window
Horse hooves clopping down a side road
Laundry flapping
Buggy clattering
Squeak of old swing swaying
Laughter

—but nothing counted today. And I know my camera is lying facedown in a cupboard and my windows are finger smudged and my head is right spun and when I carry the water pitcher to the table it leaves drops of clear on the counter, round rim of a circle, one large in the center, and it looks like an eye.

For a moment, I notice.

I stare back.

Then wipe it away.

The aping racket rises and I feel it mount and I almost yield to its vise, almost acquiesce, almost desecrate the space with words that snap. "Can't I just see whatever it is later?"

But he's holding on to me gentle. He's smiling broadly. He's leaning his face into all my knotted angst, and his hands slide down my arms, bold, blind love, and his thick fingers twine mine. "Come."

"Right now?" Can't he see the kids, hear the kids, *feel* the crush of all these kids?

He's grinning silly, man-boy with a secret he can hardly contain.

He leads me the impossible distance of a whole two steps to the windowsill. I'm transfixed. Wonder gapes the mouth open and spirits the words away.

His whisper brushes the curl of my ear, "When I saw it, I knew you'd want it too."

Want it? Who can breathe? I am moon-eyed and moonstruck. I turn to find his eyes to find words. "Serve dinner? So I can ..." So I can what? What is it exactly that I want to do?

" ... So I can run out there?"

He's laughing at me all wide-eyed, but I don't care and he's used to it, he who made vows to a woman seeker and hunter and chaser. No—he didn't actually make vows to that woman. But this is the woman I am becoming. That *eucharisteo* is making me—fulfilling thanks vows to God. I am starved and the feast makes me wild. Because really, who gets to touch the moon? Tonight, she's close. I might.

He grins, nods go, and I breathe relief and I remember to grab the camera off the shelf but forget to close the cupboard and I am gone, out the back door, across the back lawn, apron still on.

I take flight. I feel foolish, like a woman taking photographs of cheese, but I feel four again, the spring after we buried Aimee, and my younger-by-only-twelve-months-and-thirteen-days brother John, he and I ran whole lengths of fields at twilight to touch the sun, an ember burning up the horizon. I remember how the swallows had swooped, the flame light thick with bugs for their bills. My mama had sat at field's edge rocking my only five-month-old sister and watched us chase and she smiled, understanding the hoping. We ran and ran. My dad drove a tractor down the field, tilling up the earth.

I am old now. Why am I after the moon tonight? I have known all these years since that you can never run all the way to the end and lay your hand up against awe. I have grieved this. Are the staid Mennonite neighbors peering out their kitchen windows to see the farmer's wife flapping across the wheat stubble? I do have shoes on. Are my own children nose-pressed to the window watching my race?

The moon rounds immense, incandescent globe grazing ours. Her gravity pulls, pearl filling deepening sky, stringing me unto the universe.

If I race to field's edge, earth's rim, can I stroke her lustrous curve, drink her lily-white skin?

I laugh. I *am* still a child.

She is a harvest moon aching, swaying over the golden fields, womb swelling round with glory, and she's rising away. I gather my apron close, run faster through the wheat stubble. Who am I to see glory with unveiled face? Is that what the child seeks?

Is that why I escape motherhood at the dinner hour, because I can't see the glory there, here, right in the moment? *Still?* And me slowing for the hunt, looking for even one thousand more gifts, sanctuaries in moments, seeking the fullest life that births out of the darkest emptiness, all the miracle of *eucharisteo.* Yes—maybe *that* woman-child. The one who lives her life in circles, discovering, entering into, forgetting and losing, finding her way round again, living her life in layers—deeper, round, further in. I know *eucharisteo* and the miracle. But I am not a woman who ever lives the full knowing. I am a wandering Israelite who sees the flame in the sky above, the pillar, the smoke from the mountain, the earth open up and give way, and still I forget. I am beset by chronic soul amnesia. I empty of truth and need the refilling. I need come again every day—bend, clutch, and remember—for who can gather the manna but once, hoarding, and store away sustenance in the mind for all of the living?

An arrow of geese catch the moon before I do, black silhouettes shooting her through. I run harder. The flock lifts her higher into night coming down, lonely cries heralding the coming autumn. They pierce me through. There at our fence line where our wheat field gives way to foreign land, I gasp to inhale, crumple to earth. The moon on the geese wings climbs.

I am of terra; they are of heavens. I've only come to witness. *Is this why I've come?*

The weight of all this stark beauty crushes lungs. Mine burn.

I had written it down after I had read it, that I might hope to remember it: the Hebrew word used throughout Scripture to describe God's glory, *kabod*, is derived from the root word meaning "heaviness."

Dusk and all the arching dome and the field and the great-bellied moon, it all heaves, heavy with the glory. I heave to breathe: The whole earth is full of His glory. Sky, land, and sea, heavy and saturated with God—why do I always forget? Yeah, I'm no different than Jacob, Jacob waking from sleep before full moon rising. "Then Jacob awoke from his sleep and said, 'Surely the Lord is in this place, and I wasn't even aware of it!' But he was also afraid and said, 'What an awesome place this is! It is none other than the house of God, the very gateway to heaven!'" (Genesis 28:16–17). This moment, this place, is none other than a gate into heaven. God's glory rains down, weighs down earth's tented heights, and grace tears through, ripping sky canvas and me clear open. Everywhere windows and gates, and I did not know it. No. I *have* known it and I have forgotten it and I remember it again.

The weight of God's glory, not illusory or ephemeral, but daily and everywhere, punctures earth's lid and heaven falls through the holes. I kneel in wheat, moonstruck.

Bowed at the edge of the world, Jesus asks me spun in circles, me coming to, only to lapse and to forget again, He asks soft of me who is yet again lost what He asked of the man born blind: "What do you want me to do for you?" (Luke 18:41).

Why have I run?

A mama with children, a wife with full house, a Father's child living *eucharisteo* and even the hard—His eye is on me under the moon, penetrating my own shroud. His breath falls warm. He *knows* what I want, need. Has He called me because He wants me to do my own plumbing of the soul? *What do you want?*

Isn't that the sole question we all need to circle back to, over and again? And who knows the answer?

I feel in it my chest first, before any answer or layer of answer finds shape in image, words. (For all real answers, don't they come in strata, gradations of understanding?) My body knows it, the way tension drains from shoulders and a heart unknots. I loosen, breathe long. I slow. Moonlight cascades and

a smile spreads in its wake. *What do you want?* Why have I run?
A summer of traveling to the city with Levi for follow-up visits
with the surgeon. A summer of physiotherapist appointments
and daily bending exercises, trying to work his gnarled joint,
stretch through the scar tissue stiff. Yes, the whole of life, these
exercises to break down the knotting scar tissue from the fall.
A summer of pain. Always the running. A summer of grace.
Always the revelation. Pain is everywhere, and wherever
the pain there can be everywhere grace, and yes, Jesus, I am
struggling and I get turned around but I think I know, at least
in part, what I want. If I had never run, if I had never fallen,
and here, I am not sure I would have known with blazing
clarity. I may not know all that it means, but this *is* what I
want.

This kingdom laden with glory, this, the pearl of great
price, the field I'd sell everything to possess. This is the pearl
that crams me with a happiness that throbs, serrated edge, pit
open wide for more of His glory.

The only place we have to come before we die is the place
of seeing God.

This is what I'm famished for: more of the God-glory.

I whisper with the blind beggar, "Lord, I want to see"
(Luke 18:41).

That's my moaning pulse: "*See. See.*"

~

The camera.

I slip the camera out of the pocket of my apron. How can
this sensor, point-and-shoot in the palm of my hand, capture
what the eye sees, the soul memorizes? I kneel low on wheat
stalks at the edge and I frame up the moon. I want to see

beauty. In the ugly, in the sink, in the suffering, in the daily, in all the days before I die, the moments before I sleep. Isn't beauty what we yearn to burn with before we die? What else so ignites, hot flame? Beauty is all that is glory and God is Beauty embodied, glory manifested. This is what I crave: I hunger for Beauty. Is that why I must keep up the hunt? When I cease the beauty hunt, is that why I begin to starve, waste away?

I laugh—because haven't I run? Pursued? I must be *Sehnsucht* for beauty, that word C. S. Lewis used from the German—to long for (*sehnen*) like a mania (*sucht*). I have run because I long for beauty like a mania, a woman leaving dinner, running in apron for the cast of the moon. When I can't find it—is that why my soul goes a bit wild, morose, crazed? Strange—I hadn't even noticed that I'd been hungry for Beauty until I ran for the moon. Today frayed, unraveled at the edges a bit with dishes and dirt and paraphernalia dumped by kids. But only yesterday I had been numbering moments, counting graces. I thought I had felt soul-nourished. Is that it? Like an addiction, a compulsion that can't stop its seeking, do I always want to see *more* beauty—*more* of the glory of God? Because that is what I am made for—to give Him more glory. More *eucharisteo*, more. And not only yesterday. But today— *manna today or I starve.*

The moon has all my gaze, God-glory heavy and mounting. I kneel here, needing to know how a hung rock radiates— ethereal? This beauty is not natural, not of nature. This beauty is not merely form and color but God's "shining garment's hem."[1] Beauty is the voice endlessly calling and so we see, so we reach. Doubt the philosophies, doubt the prophecies, doubt the Pharisees (especially the ones seen in mirrors), but who can doubt this, Beauty? Beauty requires no justification, no explanation; it simply is and transcends. See beauty and we know it in the marrow, even if we have no words for it: Someone is behind it, in it. Beauty Himself completes.

I am alive!

Focus and click, focus and click.

A hunter trying to capture. And none of the shots are close enough, wide enough, radiant enough for the hunter. What is this that I feel sitting here, coursing through me relentless, hot, ardent? I *have* to seek God beauty. Because isn't my internal circuitry wired to seek out something worthy of worship? Every moment I live, I live bowed to something. And if I don't see God, I'll bow down before something else.

Is worship why I've run for the moon? Not for lunar worship, but for True Beauty worship, worship of Creator Beauty Himself. God is present in all the moments, but I do not deify the wind in the pines, the snow falling on hemlocks, the moon over harvested wheat. Pantheism, seeing the natural world as divine, is a very different thing than seeing divine God present in all things. I know it here kneeling, the twilight so still: nature is not God but God revealing the weight of Himself, all His glory, through the looking glass of nature. I had told it once to a questioning son that *theology* is but that born of *theos* and *logy*—God and study—and theology is to study God. I had always thought of the hefty concordances on the high shelf in the study, but isn't this, too, the deep study of the Spirit God? The revelation of God over the farm?

How I want to see the weight of glory break my thick scales, the weight of glory smash the chains of desperate materialism, split the numbing shell of deadening entertainment, bust up the ice of catatonic hearts. I want to see God, who pulls on the coat of my skin and doesn't leave me alone in this withering body of mortality; I want to see God, who gives gifts in hospitals and gravesides and homeless shelters and refugee camps and in rain falling on sunflowers and stars falling over hayfields and silver scales glinting upriver and sewage flowing downriver. *Eucharisteo* is everywhere and I want to see *eucharisteo* everywhere and I want to remember how badly I really want to see.

Here. How could I have forgotten how badly I wanted this? To bow down and rightly worship.

It is still, stalk still.

One lone stem of wheat bows its head before me. Behind it, the perfect backdrop of pure moon full, pregnant with the grandeur.

I reach out my hand, run my finger up its silk slender shank. This is how. I learn how to say *thank you* from a laid-low head of wheat. From the wind rustling glory through the dried blades of grass raised, from the leaves in the silver maple hushed awed still. I pay tribute to God by paying attention. I raise one hand high. And another hand high. I bow the head down. I lay the body down. "The life of true holiness is rooted in the soil of awed adoration. It does not grow elsewhere," writes J. I. Packer.[2] I am bowed like wheat, raised like grass blades, grounded and rooted to now, and from Him and through Him and to Him are all things and all is His and everything that has breath praises Him and I whisper it again, again, again, remembering, remembering, remembering.

Eucharisteo, eucharisteo, eucharisteo.

Isn't He the face of all faces? He is infinite and without end, without jaw or sockets, everywhere eye. The face of the moon, the face of the doe, the face of derelict, the face of pain, His the countenance that seeps up through the world, face without limitation, face that "plays in ten thousand places."[3]

All beauty is only reflection.

And whether I am conscious of it or not, any created thing of which I am amazed, it is the glimpse of His face to which I bow down. Do I have eyes to see it's Him and not the thing? Satan came in the scales that gleamed, a thing of beauty, and he lured the first woman and she was deceived. Beauty, the disguise, can slide dangerous. True, authentic Beauty requires of us, lays claim to us, and it is this, the knees bent, the body offered in *obedience*. A pantheist's god is a passive god, but omnipresent God is Beauty who demands worship, passion, and the sacrifice of a life, for He owns it. Do I have eyes to see His face in all things so I'm not merely dazzled by the trinket, glitzy bauble dangling for the ogling, till it flakes and breaks and I strain for more to lie prostrate before?

I rise slowly, roll face to sky darkening navy, strung with that one large pearl; I lie quiet. I lie long. August lies out. A sparrow flits low, a surprise. That moon is so white. I could lie here forever, murmuring the only language of the God-glory: gratitude. It's all so ... unlikely. I have never before run. I have never before stretched out prostrate. Why am I out in this evening field, lying under moon? Is *eucharisteo* opening the eyes wider, the heart deeper? Is this paradox—that giving thanks for what is, creates an appetite for more—not for more things, but for seeking more of God to give more glory?

Looking is the love. Looking is evidence of the believing. The moon swings higher. I remember reading it only weeks before, sitting in the surgeon's waiting room with Levi, the

hospital renovation progressing slowly, the patients healing
only slightly faster. (Transfiguration can be the long miracle.)
Levi had daydreamed out the waiting room window, listened
to the stories of car accidents and work injuries from the
bandaged, and I had held my book. I'd read how the Israelites
looked about and saw much to bemoan, much to complain
about: "and they began to speak against God and Moses.
'Why have you brought us out of Egypt to die here in the
wilderness?' they complained. 'There is nothing to eat here
and nothing to drink. And we hate this horrible manna!'"
(Numbers 21:5). I had looked around at the wounded all
waiting. I had turned back to the page. And what does God
send the ingrates? What came to the ingrates in the Eden
beginning? A slithering blanket of snakes that coil around the
complaints of the Israelites, open wide and pierce the flesh
with the fang. Always, ingratitude makes the poison course.
The cure against thanklessness's bite?

The remedy is in the retina.

> Then the LORD told him, "Make a replica of a poisonous
> snake and attach it to a pole. All who are bitten will live if
> they simply *look at it*!" So Moses made a snake out of bronze
> and attached it to a pole. Then anyone who was bitten by a
> snake could *look* at the bronze snake and be healed! (Numbers
> 21:8–9, emphasis added)

How we behold determines if we hold joy. Behold glory
and be held by God.

How we look determines how we live ... *if* we live.

A patient's name was called and a father helped a son to his
feet and the boy leaned hard.

And I had read how Jesus says, "In the same way that Moses

lifted the Serpent in the desert so people could have something
to see and then believe, it is necessary for the Son of Man to
be lifted up — and everyone who looks up to him, trusting
and expectant, will gain a real life, eternal life" (John 3:14 – 15
MSG). I had looked up from my book and into the face of a
boy with his ear bandaged and I didn't want to imagine what
had happened. I had tried to take it in: Isn't Jesus Himself
saying that people need to see and then believe — that looking
and believing are the same thing? That in the right inner
looking, we can gain the right outer life ... the *saved full* life?
I had read it and had forgotten (always!) but I remember it now,
mooning under the moon, "Faith is the gaze of a soul upon a
saving God."[4]

Faith is in the gaze of a soul. Faith is the seeing soul's eyes
upon a saving God, the saving God of twisted bodies, the
saving God of harvest moons. Is that summer's last cricket
strumming lonely? The diameter of the night orb fills all the
atmosphere over our farm. Faith is the seeing eyes that find the
gauze to heaven torn through; that slow to witness the silent
weight, feel the gold glory bar heavy in palm, no matter the
outer appearance. Seeing is the spiritual life. " ... they might
see with their eyes, hear with their ears, understand with their
hearts, and return and be healed" (Isaiah 6:9 – 10 NASB).
"Looking comes first," wrote Lewis in *The Great Divorce*.[5]
First, the eyes. Always first, the inner eyes.

Two crickets sing now in echo. That leper who had
returned with thanks — his faith that *gave thanks* was counted
by Jesus as *saving faith*. And now this — that faith is not a once-
in-the-past action, but faith is always a way of *seeing*, a seeking
for God in everything. And if the eyes gaze long enough to
see God lifted in a thing, how can the lips not offer *eucharisteo*?

The truly saved have eyes of faith and lips of thanks. *Faith is in the gaze of a soul.*

Has His love lured me out here to really save me?

I sit up in the wheat stubble, drawn. That He would care to save. Moon face glows. We are head to head. I am bare; He is bare. All Eye sees me. An ample hoop rung with brilliance, the moon is like a wheel of chrysolite riding up the sky, full of the radiance of the glory of the Lord. I want to be cherub, all eye, looking back. To be like the cherubim, with "eyes all over their bodies, including their hands, their backs, and their wings" (Ezekiel 10:12). To be Moses, who "kept right on going because he kept his eyes on the one who is invisible" (Hebrews 11:27). *That is what makes us persevere through a life: to see Him who is invisible!* It is my prayer with the last crickets of summer: O Lord, open the eyes of my heart, the eyes of my hands, the eyes of my mouth, the eyes of my feet. I long to live all eye.

A gust of wind rattles hollow through dried leaves of a patch of soybeans. The leaves in the silver maple murmur of fall coming, fall coming. I feel too bared. Can I live all eye and gaze on God and live?

I must, to believe, and so said Jesus, but I too remember, "'But you may not look directly at my face, for no one may see me and live '" (Exodus 33:20). And yet there are days where I know it in the shadows: "Truly you are a God who hides himself" (Isaiah 45:15 NIV). (Or is it me who hides?) Other times, Jacob times, I know it is the only way to be delivered from the blackness: "So Jacob called the name of the place Peniel, saying, 'For I have seen God face to face, and yet my life has been delivered'" (Genesis 32:30 ESV). And yet at all times, I wonder: Can anyone with the oily stains of a pride-splotched heart see God?

I look down at the stained skirt of my apron, washed in moonlight. And I think I can stand here? I think I can brave this Beauty? Not an empty, tinny beauty but a Fierce Beauty, Flaming Fire who burns through the thick masks and leaves the soul disrobed. I am naked and I am right ashamed. I know how monstrously inhumane I can be. Raging at children for minor wrongdoings while I'm the one defiling the moment with sinful anger. Hoarding possessions while others die of starvation. Entertaining the mind with trivial pretties when I haven't bowed the head and heart in a prayer longer than five minutes in a week. My tongue has had a razor edge and my eyes have rolled haughty and my neck has been stiff and graceless and I have lived the filth ugly, an idolater, a glutton, and a grace thief who hasn't had time for the thanks.

I wrap the hem of my splattered apron around a finger. I cannot raise the eye. We've read it around the table at the close of the meal, us all with Bibles open, and we've read the verse with one voice: "God blesses those whose hearts are pure, for they will see God" (Matthew 5:8). What am I doing out here? I am filthy rags. Is sight possible? I've only got one pure thing to wear and it's got Made by Jesus on the tag and the purity of Jesus lies over a heart and His transparency burns the cataracts off the soul. The only way to see God manifested in the world around is with the eyes of Jesus within. God within is the One seeing God without. God is both the object of my seeing and the subject who does the act of all real seeing, the Word lens the inner eye wears. To sit in the theater of God and see His glory crack the dark, to open the eyes of my heart to see the fountain of His grace—thousands of gifts—I have to split heart open to more and more of Jesus. Who can split open the eyelids but Jesus? He tears the veil to the Holy of Holies, gives

me the only seeing I have. I have been lost and now I am found
and I sing it softly, before the flying of the flocks south: "Be
thou my vision, O Lord of my heart . . ."

The lunar pearl overwhelms and I am all eye to the world.
It is strange, how joy pains. In the burn of the ache, there is
this unexpected sensation of immense moon slowly shrinking
and God expanding, widening and deepening my inner spaces.
Is that why joy hurts — God stretching us open to receive more
of Himself?

I ache-gaze on bits and blades of creation and all things
created fade, diminish, and only the features of the Creator
shimmer, magnified. My eye sees through to the heights and
Him and things beneath are seen for what they are: but finite
talismans pointing up. That full moon rising higher holds me
rapt. This is where I see it.

God always sits here.

~

Joy that fills me under full moon is the joy that always
fills God. What I've run to brush up against, to press all my
throbbing emptiness into, these heavy glory waters endlessly
flood from Him and He spills. Skirts of stars swirl through
black space and waterfalls canter over stones, manes of runaway
horses, and lone mushroom tilts in the shadows of soundless
forest and God sees it all. This is His endless experience
because this is who He is, beauty overflowing. My moon
wonder is but a glimpse, foretaste, of what God always sees,
experiences. He is not tyrant or despot. I smile under the
moon.

For God is happiest of all.
Joy is God's life.

Don't I yearn for it to be mine?

Is this why I've run? Answering the invitation to live in Him who is happiest of all? I am a child again and tonight I have run to the end of the horizon and this time I have touched Him and I twirl in full apron skirt, spinning hem brushing the grass heads bowed and I laugh *joy*. It's dawning, my full moon rising: I was lost but know I am found again, Jesus, and I know what I want: to see deeply, to thank deeply, to feel joy deeply. How my eyes see, perspective, is my key to enter into His gates. I can only do so with thanksgiving. If my inner eye has God seeping up through all things, then can't I give thanks for anything? And if I can give thanks for the good things, the hard things, the absolute everything, I can enter the gates to glory. Living in His presence is fullness of joy — and seeing shows the way in.

The art of deep seeing makes gratitude possible. And it is the art of gratitude that makes joy possible. Isn't joy the art of God?

It's true! What that ancient man Irenaeus, very disciple of the apostle John, wrote: "The glory of God is the human being *fully* alive and *the life of the human consists in beholding God*" (emphasis added).[6] For all the reasons He called me to come across field, He surely called me for this. Don't I give God most glory when I am fully alive? And I am most fully alive beholding God!

I spin happy, and in the radiant expanse, engulfed, I glimpse the endlessness of God. My desires, don't they stretch out endless, like God? Desire has no end, no bounds, but fuels all living, all lungs, and I spin. Our endless desires are fulfilled in endless God.

I stop the whirl. The grass heads still. I can see the house lights glowing in the back bank of windows up on our knoll.

I should go to dishes and children needing baths and stories
and prayers. But I just don't want this moon to end. The desires
submerge into God. I want to see God endlessly. I long to
merge with Beauty, breathe it into lungs, feel it heavy on skin.
To beat on the door of the universe, pound the chest of God
with the psalmist: "One thing I ask of the Lord, this is what
I seek ... all the days of my life, to gaze upon the beauty of
the LORD, and to seek him in his temple" (Psalm 27:4 NIV).
Faith is the gaze of the soul and I want to *see in*. So I can *enter
in. Enter into God.* I would read it long after my moon chase,
words of C. S. Lewis, and I would startle at my unknowing
echo of his cry:

> What more, you may ask, do we want? Ah, but we want so
> much more—something the books on aesthetics take little
> notice of. But the poets and the mythologies know all about
> it. We do not want merely to *see* beauty, though, God knows,
> even that is bounty enough. We want something else which
> can hardly be put into words—to be united with the beauty
> we see, to pass into it, to receive it into ourselves, to bathe in
> it, to become part of it.[7]

Yes.

Is the longing for the Beauty the happiest place of all?
Longing to gaze upon the Beauty of the Lord and to seek
Him, the place where all the joy spills from. No matter
how manifested, beauty is what sparks the romance and we
are the Bride pursued, the Lover pursuing, and known or
unbeknownst, He woos us in the romance of all time, beyond
time. I ache for the oneness. Would *eucharisteo* take me even
into that? I would pursue and He would pursue and how could
I have known where all this journey would lead?

The moon climbs, a radiating disk gliding, shimmering space rock that slides on invisible gossamer, and behind me, somewhere in thickening dusk, children call, running across fields. "Mama? Mama!" And they find me and laugh that I've chased the moon and I laugh that I have too. How I laugh and it feels so right.

"Did you catch it?" Hope-Girl asks, breathless and grinning.

"No, I didn't catch the curve of the moon." I look up, wishing. "But I did find what I wanted" ... what He longed for me to know.

All eye, all eye.

The hills darken black. We walk up the last knoll, our shadows outlined in the sun smoldering down in the west. The children talk, laugh, holler. I am happy. I smile, slip a hand into a pocket, cool night air drifting in. I'm no pilgrim at Tinker Creek, no recluse at Walden Pond. I can't live in moon moments. (Could I?) I live with the broken bodies. Wasn't He awakening me to Beauty everywhere, because beauty is the way of the inner eye? The wheat stubble scratches my legs as I walk the fields. One hand fingers the hem of my splotchy apron. I am going back. I look up, try to find her again. I'm reluctant to untether from the moon. The world I live in is loud and blurring and toilets plug and I get speeding tickets and the dog gets sick all over the back step and I forget everything and these six kids lean hard into me all day to teach and raise and lead and I fail hard and there are real souls that are at stake and how long do I really have to figure out how to live full of grace, full of joy—before these six beautiful children fly the coop and my mothering days fold up quiet? How do you open the eyes to see how to take the daily, domestic, workday vortex and invert it into the dome of an everyday cathedral? Could I go back to my life and pray with eyes wide open?

Praying with eyes wide open is the only way to pray without ceasing.

If I unwrap *eucharisteo* down to its next layer, will I find more of the answer? His love had invited me into this part of the answer—wouldn't He lead on into the rest? I half spin apron skirt, half smile—Him happiest of all. Wouldn't He show me? The children run on ahead, their voices carrying long through the night coming on.

I come slow up the field, watching their black silhouettes fly, and the mind numbers gifts:

Laughter at twilight
Glow of the front porch light
The last cry of geese

I could live blind, either in black or in blaze. I'll be all eye, all blinded by glory.

The windows of home burn bright.

seeing through the glass

Nothing here below is profane
for those who know how to see.
Pierre Teilhard de Chardin

The last of the sunflowers stands tall in the kitchen garden
right off the porch. It's early, too early, really. The picket fence
gate at the side of the garden lies open. I have scissors in hand
and hopes for just a ring or two of fresh petals. In the house,
empty vases line the counter. Emptiness opened wide for
beauty filling. So I have gone looking, always looking.

The finches, yellow on wing, flit among the high leaves.
The ground is damp from the night dreams. I stretch high on
the toes to reach a crowning sunflower, perfect. A few lower
ones, bowed, still new. I walk the rows of giants and I gather.
My arms are wet with dew, full of summer.

In the house, I trim stems, shear off lower leaves, fill the
open vase mouths, and I arrange. I set the vases of the golden
heads out. One on the side table by the window, another at
the end of the hand hewn-mantel, beam from a barn that the
school bus drove past all my childhood. I bring beauty in. I
take the last to the table, set its bouquet in the middle of the
quilted runner of pinwheel stars that Mama stitched for my

birthday, thrifted cotton ginghams, old men's shirts, faded summer work. For a moment, I bend, fingering petals.

I peer into a wide circle of sunflower, a mother searching a child's face.

My boys come in from the barn.

I lay out bread. They banter, hard, the brother-scrape. I stir orange juice, keep breathing, ask them to be kind. I brought the beauty in: why now smash the vases? One of the boys tosses in slices of bread for toast, careless. I set out plates in sun. The Tall-Son lathers butter on toast, but only his. I notice.

"Son, your brother? Could you butter his toast?" He reaches for peanut butter, fires me a white-hot glare. Morning flashes.

How'd I stumble into shadow and cross fire?

"*Please.* Might you pass a piece of toast down to your brother?"

"Sure." His sarcasm slaps. I steady myself on the table's edge.

Nothing could have braced the gut for what he did next, shrapnel ripping intestines.

He whips a piece of toast into his brother's face.

Why throw toast in your brother's face?

His brother rages red and I'm sucker punched and it's toast, yeah, but isn't it his heart and I shake the head stunned, losing words, and the child I ripened with, bore down and birthed from the heart, he turns on a Tuesday, tears out a few more of the pulsing chunks and *where did I go so wrong*?

Who cares about bringing the beauty in when all the inner rooms reek? It's toast and it's not toast and I can't shrug it off because it's the profanity of it, the desecrating of one made in the Image. I slam hands down on the table when I'd like to grab hold of his throat. Can I exchange the clay eyes shot red for the sacred seeing?

"Why?" My mother-anger could crack vases.

He's smirking.

"*Why* would you throw that at him?" I'm too shrill, too gaped, too blind-white angry.

Straw comes in all shapes and the back of a camel can be weak and *it's toast* and surely there's something behind it that I should seek out but I don't even care. It's my own face that obscures the face of God. How can I help this son of mine see when I can't see? The parent must always self-parent first, self-preach before child-teach, because who can bring peace unless they've held their own peace? Christ incarnated in the parent is the only hope of incarnating Christ in the child—yet how do I admit that people made in the Image can make me blind to God, my own soul contorting, skewing all the faces? Why gouge out your own eyes when crusading for Beauty? Pain drives us to the mad acts.

I am mad. I'd like to will myself out of it but the blood is pounding loud in my ears and the sons slash at each other with the dagger eyes. *Why?* Can I just go back to the moon and the brazen glory? Wind and trees and sky wake me and I'm Peter on the mountaintop, stirring to see The Glory in all its God-radiance, stammering out that it's good to be here; let's build shelters and never depart (Luke 9:28–36). But there's always the descent from the mount. The meeting of the crowd, the complaining, the cursing. Obvious and immediate transfigurations exhilarate the faith, but the faithful can forget transfigurations, faces that once changed appearances. We betray Who we know. Didn't Peter?

How to be a contemplative here, seeing the fullness of God with the six children 24/7, the one farm, the six hundred sows, eight hundred piglets, only a whole lot of craziness? I hang my head. A boy pounds a plate with a clenched fist. The other blithely butters toast. *How do I fix this? Them? Me?* In the messy, Jesus whispers, "What do you want?" and in the ugly, I cry, "I want to *see*—see You in these faces." He speaks soft, "Seek My face." I want to answer with David, "My heart says to you, 'Your face, LORD, do I seek'" (Psalm 27:8 ESV) but I'm desperate to grab someone, anyone, and shake hard, "*How do I have the holy vision in this mess?* How do I see grace, give thanks, find joy in this sin-stinking place?"

The moon and the geese fly high, unsullied and wide-eyed, and I'm too twisted.

A boy drives a plate hard back down the table at his brother. And God tries to gently drive the words of Caussade from the knowing of my head to the bleeding of the heart:

> You would be very ashamed if you knew what the experiences you call setbacks, upheavals, pointless disturbances, and tedious annoyances really are. You would realize that your complaints about them are nothing more nor less than blasphemies—though that never occurs to you. Nothing happens to you except by the will of God, and yet [God's] beloved children curse it because they do not know it for what it is.[1]

A blasphemer.

I pull out a chair from the table, sink down. The sunflower heads have turned low. The Tall-Son is chewing his toast too loud at the other end of the table. What compels me to name these moments upheavals and annoyances instead of grace and gift? Why deprive myself of joy's oxygen? The swiftness and starkness of the answer startle. *Because you believe in the power of the pit.*

Really? I lay my head on the table. Do I really smother my own joy because I believe that anger achieves more than love? That Satan's way is more powerful, more practical, *more fulfilling* in my daily life than Jesus' way? Why else get angry? Isn't it because I think complaining, exasperation, resentment will pound me up into the full life I really want? When I choose—and it *is* a choice—to crush joy with bitterness, am I not purposefully choosing to take the way of the Prince of Darkness? Choosing the angry way of Lucifer because I think it is more effective—*more expedient*—than giving thanks?

Blasphemer.

Blasphemer.

I rake my fingers through my hair. Who's the real sinner at breakfast on Tuesday, the one with the stinking pig in the temple?

Senses are impaired if they don't sense the Spirit and somebody, *tell me*, how do I tear open tear-swollen eyelids to see through this for what it really is?

If there are wolves in the woods—expect to see wolves; and if there is God in this place—*expect to see God.*

Can I be so audacious? To expect to see God in these faces when I am the blasphemer who complains, who doesn't acknowledge this moment for Who it is?

"Do you even care what he did to me first?" Future-man is standing now, hands stuffed hard into pockets, glowering. His stack of toast is growing cold.

I should want to care, and I try to will myself, but I'm hard, so tired. I turn away. *See, somehow I've got to see, got to feel.*

How did Jesus do it again? He turned His eyes. "And

looking up to heaven, he gave thanks and broke the loaves.
Then he gave ..." (Matthew 14:19 NIV). He looked up to
heaven, to see where this moment comes from. Always first
the eyes, the focus. I can't leave crowds for mountaintop, daily
blur for Walden Pond—but there's always the possibility of the
singular vision. I remember: Contemplative simplicity isn't a
matter of circumstances; it's a matter of *focus*.

One boy is turned, shaking his head, angry, at the window,
the world; the other is eating another slice of toast, defiant.
I take a deep breath, say nothing to them, but I look up to
heaven and I speak it to Him here because there are wolves in
the woods and there is God in this place and I haven't done this
before and it feels strange but I give thanks aloud, in a whisper:
"Father, thank You for these two sons. Thank You for here
and now. Thank You that You don't leave us in our mess." My
heart rate slows. Something hard inside softens, opens, and this
thanks aloud feels mechanical. But I can feel the heart gears
working. "Thank You for toast. Thank You for cross-grace
for this anger, for the hope of forgiveness and brothers and
new mercies." I look for the *ugly beautiful,* count it as grace,
transfigure the mess into joy with thanks and *eucharisteo* leaves
the paper, finds way to the eyes, the lips. This, this is what
Annie Dillard meant:

> Seeing is of course very much a matter of verbalization. Unless
> I call my attention to what passes before my eyes, I simply
> won't see it. It is, as Ruskin says, 'not merely unnoticed, but in
> the full, clear sense of the word, unseen.' ... I have to say the
> words, describe what I'm seeing.... But if I want to notice the
> lesser cataclysms of valley life, I have to maintain in my head a
> running description of the present.[2]

I speak the unseen into seeing and I can feel it, this steady breathing in the rhythm of grace—*give thanks (in), give thanks (out).* The eyes focus, apertures capturing Beauty in ugliness. There's a doxology of praise that splits the domestic dark.

The sun spreads out across the table, a cloth, and sunflowers ring light. I see it. All the world is window. No material is opaque. If we are willing to see—people, circumstances, situations, relationships—all is transparent.

All of this globe is but glass to God.

And *eucharisteo* washes the glass. *Eucharisteo*, wholesale worship, its redemptive work wiping away the soot of days cindered.

I look over at my son tearing away at toast. Why am I a habitual reductionist? Why do I reduce God in this moment to mere annoying frustration? Why do I reduce The Greatest to the lesser instead of seeing the lesser, this mess, as reflecting The Greatest? I have to learn how to see, to look through to the Largeness behind all the smallness. *Isn't He here?*

The humiliated son can stand it no more, pushes away from the table, pushes past his fuming brother, slams the door behind him. I exhale. Remember: Gratitude redeems, making us the realists. Mouth thanks to the heights and see the real reality. Give thanks to keep the gaze on heaven.

Glass to God.

Eucharisteo *always precedes the miracle.*

Why do I have spiritual Alzheimer's, *always forgetting*?

I can feel it, the grip on my shoulders, and it's St. John who whispers it clear too, how to find God in the mess:

> *We [actually] saw His glory.... For out of His fullness (abundance) we have all received* [all had a share and we were all

supplied with] one grace after another and spiritual blessing upon spiritual blessing and even favor upon favor and *gift [heaped] upon gift.* (John 1:14, 16 AMP, emphasis added)

That's the mystery map to the deep seeing! We saw His glory ... *because* ... we have all received one grace after another. We *have* all received one grace after another, but we only recognize the glory of God in this moment *when we wake to the one grace after another.* "If you want to be really alert to seeing Jesus' divine beauty, his glory ... *then make sure you tune your senses to see his grace,*" urges theologian John Piper (emphasis added). "That's what his glory is full of."[3] Grace— *that* is what the full life is full of, what the God-glory is full of. To see the glory, name the graces. Retune the impaired senses to sense the Spirit, to see the grace. Couldn't I do that anywhere? *Why is it so hard?* Practice, practice.

I run my hand across the table, gathering crumbs, and look carefully into the face of my son. His arms are stiff, his jaw set, his eyes near mine and drenched black-blue, like the day I first held him. This day too has bruising of its own. I glimpse Who this moment really is and I'm tender. The swine flees.

I lay a hand on his shoulder, but he bristles, skin grown from this skin and sick of this skin. "Can you tell me more? I'm ready. I really do want to understand." I climb his eyes down into who he is. He's echo-black.

He jerks his shoulder to flip away my hand, steps back from my stench. We eye each other and mine beg and his ice. The lips I once traced after the lullabies, they turn surly and hard.

"You never see what he does!" He leans into my face. "But you sure do always see what I do!" He wants to stare me down, shoot me down. This is old pus, infected wounds. This is not about toast. Is it ever all about now? His howl fills the face, his and mine. Heart that once beat under mine, how did we get here? *How did I fail you?* How did I see things all wrong? I am Hagar lost with boy and the boy bangs the table with his fist and I want to step back, flee. Who can witness the dying, but how can I leave him?

"Then God opened her eyes and she saw a well of water" (Genesis 21:19 NIV).

Hagar and her boy were dying of thirst with a well less than bowshot away.

What insanity compels me to shrivel up when there joy's water to be had here?

In this wilderness, I keep circling back to this: I'm blind to joy's well every time I really don't want it. *The well is always there.* And I *choose* not to see it. Don't I really want joy? Don't I *really* want the fullest life? For all my yearning for joy, longing for joy, begging for joy—is the bald truth that I prefer the empty dark? Prefer drama? Why do I lunge for control instead of joy? Is it somehow more perversely satisfying to flex control's muscle? Ah—*power*—like Satan. Do I think Jesus-grace too impotent to give me the full life? Isn't that the only reason I don't always swill the joy? If the startling truth is that I don't really want joy, there's a far worse truth. If I am rejecting the joy that is hidden somewhere deep in this moment—am I not ultimately rejecting God? Whenever I am blind to joy's well, isn't it because I don't believe in God's care? That God cares enough about me to always offer me joy's water, wherever I am, regardless of circumstance. But if I don't believe God cares, if I don't want or seek the joy He definitely offers somewhere in this moment—I don't want God.

Blasphemer.

In His presence is fullness of joy. *He is in this moment.*

The well is always here. God is always here—precisely because He does *care.*

God faithfully provides water for His people everywhere.

But how do you make yourself want joy? I look across at my son glaring me down.

When you know you're Hagar and you finally come to the end of yourself and all the water in your own canteen is gone and you *know* that you and your son are going to *die* if you don't get some joy to the lips and down the parched throat— and now; when you can no longer stand to see those you love *die* all around you from your emptiness; when the emptiness is so dark you are driven to struggle again for joy, to *cry* for joy to the Joy God there and you beg, sob—remember: *You have to want to see the well before you can drink from it.* You have to want to see joy, God in the moment.

I cradle the son's glare with the beholding eyes.

Thank You, Lord, for that one strand that always curls near his ear, that scar he ripped across his cheek when he was three, those eyes sky like his father's.

I am praying with the eyes wide open and prayer becomes revelation. My eyes change and he changes in them and I remember, as G. K. Chesterton observes, how "our perennial spiritual and psychological task is to look at things familiar until they become unfamiliar again."[4] The unfamiliar becomes the real and the real is only seen by the lovers and I count him as grace, I embrace now as love, and I know how lovers alone see the true.

Love is not blind; love is the holy vision.

For a glancing moment, I am Hagar healed, Hagar who had spoken once before in a desert exile:

Thereafter, Hagar used another name to refer to the LORD, who had spoken to her. She said, "You are the God who sees me." She also said, "Have I truly seen the One who sees me?" So that well was named Beer-lahai-roi (which means "well of the Living One who sees me"). (Genesis 16:13 – 14)

Hagar had known God sees for she had met Him before, needy in the sands, yet when sent away the second time, Hagar had forgotten. She had laid her son down to die and couldn't see any well. In the domestic cloud of dust and family, I too can forget the One who sees me, but in *eucharisteo*, I remember. I cup hands and all the world is water.

The well, it is still there.

There is always a well — All is well.

I choke out my son's name. His skin is transparent ... glass. And he stares long, brims ... quavers ... falls. And I cradle him, the Boy-Man, flood over shoulders.

"You wear anger to hide all this sadness?" I lay a hand on his back, whisper words. He pulls away, bites lip quivering, dams it up.

"Where do you find happiness anymore?" I ache for the once-laughing child now struggling into his teens and the man-skin. He stares out the window, away, murmurs it to no one and anyone. "I think I am happy ... when I am alone."

I ache toward him sitting by the window and I am mother searching child's face and I crack ... I brim ... I fall ... and the tears scald. Oh, son ... *So thirsty.*

There is always a well.

I remember a moon and the face of Him who is happiest of all who wants us to be happiest in Him and oh, son, I know, I know, *this peopled life.* Jacob wrestled with God and called the place Peniel, meaning "God's face." This daily joy struggle, above all, it is a Jacob-wrestle to see God in the faces we face. How do I help my son, so thirsty?

Tell him what *eucharisteo* is doing. How I'm wrestling to name graces to see glory in the moment, graces to see glory in the faces. I could tell him stories of people like us, living the strain of everyday family life, who tried *eucharisteo* too. How we tried a ten-day *eucharisteo* experiment. Ten days of *eucharisteo* as a stress intervention, *eucharisteo* as a practical miracle, not on the mount, but in the faces and the crowd. Whenever we felt stress in relationships, we audibly gave thanks. I could tell him how one woman wrote, "I can feel the gratitude starting to soak into my soul. I'm becoming someone else, *a new person,* one that I like better than the old."

How another voiced, "I'm learning to express gratitude before stress gets a chance to creep up in a lot of situations.... I'm so thankful for what God has allowed our humble attempt at gratitude to work in our home! *I just can't help but share how life changing this gratitude experiment has been!*"

That another's words make me cry joy because it is my life story?

"Learning slowly to not be so reactionary while *inserting verbal gratitude into stressful situations is almost like being healed of mental blindness. I have begun to 'see' again.*"

My human experience is the sum of what the soul sees and I see precisely what I attend to and what the eyes focus on is what the life is. See the well, son, *the well.*

He's sitting now, turned toward the window and fields and gnawing his lip, trying to stem the hollow burn running down his cheeks, and I finger for words.

"I get it, you know." He doesn't turn. Brushes his cheek with the back of his hand. What day when I wasn't looking did his hand become like his father's? Like a man's. He's weeping. My son is crying and he's letting me in, sharing what it's like to be behind his eyes. *Eucharisteo* gave me this ... It *was* just toast. Ugly toast. And He showed me how to give thanks for it. And then the miracle—a soft heart. To let me hold his heart.

"I get how hard it is to live with the people and find the joy." I lower into the chair across from him. The babe has become me. His hair is darkening, only a few lighter strands now in his cowlick, like my cowlick—one I inherited from my father.

"You see it every day here. How I wrestle for joy, for seeing God in the faces ... you see how I fail." I reach across the table for him. Stretch my hand out to touch his. His knuckle's cut. From welding steel? From the miter saw? Always creating, designing ... dreaming.

He turns slightly—toward me. He lets me touch him. *Oh son.* He is not alone; I am not alone. I want to hold him in my arms, make my skin, his skin, right again. Return to Eden. I can't change our skin. Maybe our eyes? I catch his. He doesn't look away. He lets the eyes hold him.

"Can I help you find the laughter again? I'm looking too."

My eyes beg. His thaw. He shifts, sighs. I almost miss his murmur.

"I've already tried giving thanks."

Oh.

"You knew? I mean, you knew that giving thanks is the way into joy? Because thanksgiving is the way we enter into God?"

"I hear you doing it all the time." He slumps into the chair, lays his head on the table.

The thrash for joy can be gory, loud.

Did he see it on the counter too, the constant counting of gifts in the journal under the words "Ugly Beautiful" scratched across the page?

Toppling closets (books!)
Toys all over the floors (boy joy!)
Two-month-old paint tape around trim (someday soon!)
Mismatched socks
Lost library book
Apple cores, apple cores, apple cores
Dusty shelves
Splattered mirrors . . .

Does he see me doing the hard *eucharisteo*, counting the ugly as grace, transfiguring the ugly into beauty with thanks? Does he see?

"And?" I pull my chair closer, gently squeeze his hand.

"It's just so ... hard." He mutters, closes his eyes.

He knows my skin; I know his.

"Hard. Yes. *So hard.*" He lies with his eyes closed. I feel it too, boy of mine. Days, just close my eyes to it all. "It's hard, *eucharisteo.* I am trying, really trying: Practice. *The discipline of thanks only comes with practice.*" I know, son. *So many days, so hard.* I want to give up too. But give up the joy-wrestle ... and I die.

"The practice of giving thanks ... *eucharisteo* ... this is the way we practice the presence of God, stay present to His presence, and it is always a practice of the eyes. We don't have to change what we see. Only the *way* we see." I whisper it to the son with the eyes closed. His chin trembles. Eyes leak tears. *Oh, son. So hard.* To see all this material world as transparent, glass to God. To practice migrating one thousand gifts on paper to one thousand all eyes to one thousand smiles on lips. To transfigure the principle to the skin.

But if we don't intentionally commit to the hard practice of seeing, don't we die in barren wilderness? Anger, frustration, emptiness?

I lay my hand on my son's cheek, his tear-wet cheek. We are of a piece.

"Son? You can't positive-think your way out of negative feelings. About your brother, about me, about people. Feelings work faster than thoughts; blood runs faster than synapses." His eyelashes quiver. "The only way to fight a feeling is with a feeling."[5]

I stroke his cheek slow.

I move closer, hoping my words might revive. "Feel thanks and it's *absolutely impossible* to feel angry. We can only experience *one emotion* at a time. And we get to choose — which emotion do we *want* to feel?"

He lies still. Sometimes acknowledging what we really want is hardest of all.

I wrap an arm around him, his back warm in sunlight, and lay my head on his one broad shoulder. Under my face, his shoulder rises and falls, labored breaths. Death sadness. *I must still try to give my son water.*

"Can I tell you a story?" I can feel his muscles relax. Since the day I first held him, I've told stories to this curl of ear. He and I, stories, this is our space.

"There was once a wrestler like us. His name was Jacob. And on a night when he was all alone, staring up at the stars in the dark, unable to sleep because he was scared to go meet his brother the next day, this brother that he had run away from because the brother had wanted to actually take his bare hands and kill him. Talk about taut family ties."

"Esau." *Ah.* He's listening. His voice, hope in the sands. I smile into his shoulder, squeeze him tight.

"Yes. Esau. Jacob was terrified to meet his brother Esau. And all night long, he wrestles hard with a man, flailing and thrashing and struggling and he grips his fingers deep into the leg, the torso of the man, and he utterly refuses to let go, right till the sun embers kindle up the horizon. It's hard. He's exhausted. He's confused." I sit up. Rub my son's back in slow, wide circles. The midmorning sun's rays through the window are strengthening.

"And when the man can't overpower or throw off Jacob, he touches the socket of Jacob's hip on the sinew of the thigh. The man breaks Jacob. Then day breaks. And he commands Jacob to let him go." I run my fingers up through his hair, that cowlick of mine.

"But Jacob, he refuses to let the man go. He doesn't even really know who the man is, can't clearly see his face, but he begs, "I will not let you go until you bless me." And the man turns to Jacob and gives him a new name. Names him Israel, the God-wrestler. Says to him, "You've wrestled with God and you've come through." All that while Jacob hadn't known who he was wrestling. Just a man in the dark, a man he couldn't see. And in the black, all that night, it was the face of *God* over him that he was struggling against. *God is behind the faces, son. Can we see?*" My hand rests on his head and my chest hurts.

"And you know what Jacob named the place? Peniel— means 'God's face.' He said, 'I saw God face-to-face and lived to tell the story!'"

I smile. "But there's more to the story ... There's always

more to every story." His lips twitch a sad smile and I see
it. I half grin. "A long time ago, a preacher named James H.
McConkey asked a friend of his, a doctor, 'What is the exact
significance of God's touching Jacob upon the sinew of his
thigh?'"

"And the doctor told him, 'The sinew of the thigh is the
strongest in the human body. A horse couldn't even tear it
apart.'"

These are the words I have never forgotten, what preacher
McConkey said: "Ah, I see. The Lord has to break us down at
the strongest part of our self-life before He can have His own
way of blessing with us."[6]

Like this morning, breaking us down at the tough parts ...
Then we see. *See the blessing.*

I lean in close to my boy's ear.

"And when Jacob went out the next morning to meet that
brother he dreaded? After the dark of the wrestle, and being
torn right apart in his strongest part, by a man he didn't even
know was God — do you know what he said? He looked into
the face of his brother, that brother who had wanted to kill
him, and he said, 'To see your face is like seeing the face of
God' [Genesis 33:10 NIV]." I rest my hand on his arm, arm so
still.

"Wrestle with God, *beg to see the blessings* ... and all faces
become the face of God. *See, son?*"

Water? Do you see the water?

Under my hand resting on his arm, I can feel the drain of
his wrestle, mine. I look into his face. His eyelids rest easy.
His cheeks have dried. We've shaken and the blood has rushed
and we have felt the heat of the rage, the fire of the enemy, the
flame of True God's holiness, and we have done war. We've

dug in our nails and we haven't let go until the blessings; we have practiced, we have extended, we have clung and we've been rung out. We have panted it and we've cupped palm to the heavens, "Bless me, Bless me. I won't let go."

Like Jacob, we ask, breathless and heaving, where He is, who He is, for His name here, the only real blessing. "Please tell me your name." We have named the graces and there found His name, Glory, and in the face of man we have seen the face of God. Then Him, the blessing, God, joy-water in the desert.

But wells don't come without first begging to see the wells; wells don't come without first splitting open hard earth, cracking back the lids. There's no seeing God face-to-face without first the ripping.

Tear the thigh to open the eye.

Wrench the socket of the hip, the tough grizzle of the heart, and heal the socket of the eye. It takes practice, wrenching practice, to break open the lids. But the secret to joy is to keep seeking God where we doubt He is.

"Son?"

He lifts his head. He opens his eyes and he looks into me and this heart revives. *My son . . .* He blurs. *There is always a well. All is well.*

"You want to—want to practice *eucharisteo* with me?"

The round of our eyes hold us liquid round and within him I warm, and the love really sees.

"Yeah, Mom." He smiles slow. "Yeah . . . we could practice thanks together."

  . . . *Grace eyes*
  . . . *My hand near his*
  . . . *The calm after the storm*

The moon will rise and those who limp know how to see. Who can live with hand wide open?

Son turns his hand open toward mine. I lay mine down gentle.

The morning light makes halos of the bouquet of sunflowers, their faces all upturned.

how will he not also?

All I have seen teaches me
to trust the Creator for all I have not seen.
Ralph Waldo Emerson

God and I, we've long had trust issues.

Outside the laundry room window, snow falls, the down of angels.

The swing under the maple hangs still. The empty sandbox fills with white, and the lane down by the barn, up by the sheds, sleeps. Bread bakes in the oven. I can smell them, five earthy loaves in early winter. They'll be rising like old mountains, rounded, brown, smooth. My bread rising up on the top rack in Marjorie Knight's bread pans, same pans that baked the loaves she sliced up for me as a girl, my brother and I having biked the mile of gravel to her farm, up her long lane through the dark of the tall spruce trees. How many years has she been gone now too? I can still hear her laugh, the way all her words ran together like a stream of laughter, her mountain-humped back shuddering mild with each chuckling word. I stand in the laundry room. Smelling bread, remembering, folding towels. Watching snow fall. In the corner windowpane, I can just catch the hem of winter's quilt sloping down the barn . . . The barn.

That barn housing our livestock, our very livelihood, seems more like a house of death to me, the death of dreams, and in an instant, the bottom of the stomach gives way and I'm all pit and the towel stack teeters, falls to the floor. It's the market that really keeps falling, tumbling, the market prices for our pigs, and I'd felt weak when I read it in the farm paper last week, the dire prediction of family hog farming in Canada on the brink of extinction. It's true for us: Our once-thriving lives on this farm teeter on the edge of collapse and only a glimpse of that barn strikes rank fear into me and what we've already lost directly out of pocket piles far higher than those snowdrifts blowing in around the barn. Every day we get up and every day we work hard and every day we produce food that gouges deep out of us. How long until we are gone?

I turn my back to the window. I am bent in the refolding of the towels, refolding of the interior world, when the Farmer comes into the laundry room on his way out of the house back to the barn and the work we keep doing that's draining us dry. I can feel him watching me. A whisper of wind moans.

"Ann .... it's OK." Dare I brave his eyes?

But he's not looking at my face. He's looking at my feet.

"You." He shakes his head. "You! Look at your toes." I glance down. "They're all curled tight."

I hadn't noticed.

He lays his foot gentle on my curled ones, kneads my shoulders to stroke out all my worry. "We're going to be OK. Out there, the barn, the pigs, the sows. We're going to make it through this." He wraps his arm around my shoulder, pulls me up into that strength.

"Relax ... just trust. Just *trust.*"

Just trust? When the farm economy is imploding and all around us farming families are losing their land or being buried in loans and debts, us all just hanging on by the skin of the teeth? I take a deep breath, exhale. I lay a weak smile into his shoulder and all that faith.

Anxiety has been my natural posture, my default stiffness. The way I curl my toes up, tight retreat. How I angle my jaw, braced, chisel the brow with the lines of distrust. How I don't fold my hands in prayer ... weld them into tight fists of control. *Always control—pseudopower from the pit.* How I refuse to relinquish worry, babe a mother won't forsake, an identity. Do I hold worry close as this ruse of control, this pretense that I'm the one who will determine the course of events as I stir and churn and ruminate? Worry is the facade of taking action when prayer really is. And *stressed*, this pitched word that punctuates every conversation, is it really my attempt to prove how indispensable I am? Or is it more? Maybe disguising my deep fears as stress seems braver somehow.

I curl my big toes, crush them hard into floorboards. I've breathed the air of angst, bent the bones with anxiety.

I am five and lie in bed and dark night, eyes drilling ceiling with the fierce determination. My sister's little hands, ones I held as she tottered down the back walk, they're rotting in the dirt under a gravestone and I don't have to close my eyes to see the forces of the composting. If I don't close eyes, I won't die. In our house, we don't talk of heaven; the dead bury the dead.

Mama comes, shadow through the doorframe, and she sits and she sings and she rubs my feet. She strokes my hair. She coaxes sleep.

"I don't want to be dead in the dirt like Aimee."

Mama holds me and we rock and rock.

I am seven and the nurse clatters in with a tray of pea soup and I gag. Pea soup. But pea soup isn't acidic, doesn't scald the lining of the stomach wall. Dr. Munn stands in the hallway, tells Mama he thinks my fetal-curled agony is an ulcer. I am seven. I am seven and in second grade and I have an ulcer.

"Is she a particularly anxious child?"

I can't hear Mama's murmurs, only the fevered toddler with pneumonia whimpering in the crib by the big window looking out on the steepled church across the street.

When I return to school after that weeklong hospital stay, I sit in the desk behind Matthew Rowbotham and I tap him on the shoulder and I tell him straight out, "You can't tell me jokes anymore. Laughing makes my gut hurt too bad." In our house, we don't do much of that either, laugh.

I am seventeen and my hand lets it go, an empty jam jar, glass over concrete, and the shards rain across the garage floor. In the shattering, the tightness inside cracks. The pain drains. I finger for the sharpest edge, long and smooth, and lay it against the bare skin of the inner arm and I cut long and watch it all run, salty red tear. I don't want to die. I just want to bleed out of me.

The long years after my salvation and baptism at sixteen, I break and cut away the self-hatred, the anxiety, right at the wrist, right up the arm. Slicing the flesh burns, burns away pain, and the blood drops, the angst it ebbs, flowing far out and away. I try to pray.

I am twenty and waiting for the elevators in Varey Hall on a bitter cold day in February, when that first panic attack snaps me at jugular and I twist bits of the neck skin between fingers, tear for air. I'm wild for the door, the door. Claw through student swarm, the backpacks and books, to the lit exit sign.

Winter blasts my face and lungs gasp for air. Back in dorm, I sit in a rocking chair by fourth-floor window, open my Bible. I rock and rock.

My mind is all scrambled and my heart won't stop slamming the chest wall the day the psychologist hands me a slip of her scribbled ink, a prescription on a square of white, lays her hand on my shoulder. "It will help with the anxiety attacks, the agoraphobia."

Agoraphobia, "anxiety about being in places or situations from which escape might be difficult." It's my skin that is difficult to escape. I snap an elastic band around my wrist. For months, I swallow down the calm with the pills. I try to pray.

Fear is like this piano wire cutting round the wrists, life shackled, cutting deep, and the hands spasm, fists of control. Fear keeps a life small. The music dies and the joy drains. I've lived the strangle.

What if I opened the clenched hands wide to receive all that is? A life that receives all of God in this moment? How do you do that when the terror tears up your throat and you wear the burn scars of a razed past?

"You're really worried, aren't you?" His voice is soft. I catch that glance of his out the window, out to snow falling deep on barn, that roof over our livestock ... our dying livelihood.

"Yeah ... I guess I am." I exhale. Farming families gathered this week in our community facing bankruptcy, asking for prayer. Record low prices breaking generations of earth tillers, herdsmen.

"Is there going to be enough?" He tucks a lost strand behind my ear, and I whisper more of the honest. My voice races only a bit ahead of the wave of panic. Do I look in his eyes and let him see how scared I am? "Maybe I'm just stressed ..." That word again. *Stressed.*

Deep breath.

Stress isn't only a joy stealer. The way we respond to it can be sin. I stand in the laundry room looking out at the barn, knowing that stress stands in direct opposition to what He directly, tenderly commands: "Do not let your hearts be troubled. *Trust* in God; *trust also* in *me*" (John 14:1 NIV, emphasis added). I know an untroubled heart relaxes, trusts, leans assured into His ever-dependable arms. Trust, it's the antithesis of stress. "Oh, the joys of those who trust the LORD" (Psalm 40:4). But how to learn trust like that? Can trust be conjured up simply by sheer will, on command? I've got to get this thing, what it means to trust, to gut-believe in the good touch of God toward me, because it's true: I can't fill with joy until I learn how to trust: "May the God of hope fill you with all *joy* and peace as you *trust* in him, so that you may overflow" (Romans 15:13 NIV, emphasis added). The full life, the one spilling joy and peace, happens only as I come to trust the caress of the Lover, Lover who never burdens His children with shame or self-condemnation but keeps stroking the fears with gentle grace.

How can I trust when a troubled, joy-shriveled heart has pumped fear through the stiff veins of all my years?

I exhale. I'm still all knotted.

If I believe, then I must let go and trust. *Why do I stress?* Belief in God has to be more than mental assent, more than a clichéd exercise in cognition. Even the demons believe (James 2:19). What is saving belief if it isn't the radical dare to wholly trust? I read it in one of the thick commentaries, that two hundred twenty times that word *pisteuo* is used in the New

Testament, most often translated as "belief." But it changes everything when I read that *pisteuo* ultimately means "to put one's faith in; to trust."[1] *Belief is a verb, something that you do.*

Then the truth is that authentic, saving belief must be also? The very real, everyday *action* of trusting.

Then a true saving faith is a faith that gives thanks, a faith that sees God, a faith that deeply trusts? How would *eucharisteo* help me trust?

I read the verse several times in the Amplified Bible on an afternoon while young hands work scales up and down the piano keys, "Jesus replied, 'This is the work (service) that God asks of you: that you believe in the One Whom He has sent [that you cleave to, trust, rely on, and have faith in His Messenger]'" (John 6:29 AMP). That's my daily work, the work God asks of me? To trust. The work I shirk. To trust in the Son, to trust in the wisdom of this moment, to trust in now. And trust is that: work. The work of trusting love. Intentional and focused. Sometimes, too often, I don't want to muster the energy. Stress and anxiety seem easier. Easier to let a mind run wild with the worry than to exercise discipline, to reign her in, slip the blinders on and train her to walk steady in certain assurance, not spooked by the specters looming ahead. Are stress and worry evidences of a soul too lazy, too undisciplined, to keep gaze fixed on God? To stay in love? I don't like to ask these questions, sweep out these corners where eyes glare from shadows. But this I must ask and I do, out loud, to the C-scale being played with certainty: Isn't joy worth the effort of trust?

Because I kid no one: stress brings no joy.

In fact, stress may be far worse than that: "He who believes [who adheres to and trusts in and relies on the Gospel and

Him Whom it sets forth] ... will be saved ...; but he who does not believe [who does not adhere to and trust in and rely on the Gospel and Him Whom it sets forth] will be condemned" (Mark 16:16 AMP).

Without trust in the good news of Jesus, without trust in the good news of God's saving work even in this moment, without an active, moment-by-moment trust in the good news of an all-sovereign, all-good God, how can we claim to fully believe? This is the trust I lack: to know that if disaster strikes, He carries me even there. Trust in the wholeness of the gospel—including this moment, good news too—and be saved. Choose stress, worry, anxiety, reject what God has given now, which is good news too—refuse to trust—and be condemned.

I've just begun to feel around the outside edges of it, here in crumbling economics, the fretfulness of parenting, the dizziness of the twenty-first-century spin. Just begun to realize it, and it catches in the throat:

If authentic, saving belief is the act of trusting, then to choose stress is an act of disbelief ... atheism.

Anything less than gratitude and trust is practical atheism.

I wince. Perhaps the opposite of faith is not doubt. Perhaps the opposite of faith is fear. To lack faith perhaps isn't as much an intellectual disbelief in the existence of God as fear and distrust that there is a *good* God. If I don't emotionally believe, practically believe, in the goodness of God, *am* I a believer? Don't the believers have to believe? Don't the saved have to trust the Savior? For yes, salvation from sins, but this too: the salvation from fear.

True, certainly, there are organic, biological causes to anxiety, and there may certainly be underlying chemical issues that warrant medication. I have filled prescriptions. This has been right. All anxiety is not spiritual. And yet I know and haltingly confess: Much of the worry in my own life has been a failure to believe ... a wariness to thank and trust the love hand of God.

I make soup and I bake bread and I know my supreme need is joy in God and I know I can't experience deep joy in God until I deep trust in God. I shine sinks and polish through to the realization that trusting God is my most urgent need. If I deep trusted God in all the facets of my life, wouldn't that deep heal my anxiety, my self-condemnation, my soul holes?

The fear is suffocating, terrorizing, and I want the remedy, and it is trust. Trust is everything.

If fear keeps our lives small, does a life that receives all of God in this moment grow large too?

I light candles and slice bread for dinner.

Early Sunday morning, the Farmer still works in the barn with his crew of diligent kids, but I am slotted to serve in the nursery for first service at the chapel. He and the six kids will rush in from the barn later, make it in time for the second service. I drive on ahead to the chapel, through a countryside of snow glimmering around barn islands, bastions of hope, and I count gifts, do *eucharisteo*. Something always comes to fill the empty spaces and this is what I've come to do with white space. I invite thanks. For this is His will, thanks the one thing He asks to be done in everything and always and only because He knows what precedes the miracle.

I speak the graces aloud that I might see them, feel them: Thank you, Lord, for ...

Sculptures of drifts
Salvation of sinners, me, chief
Hoarfrost flaking off tree limbs, like the cold slipping off its necklace
All the clear sky descending into one black crow
Steam rising off barn...
Barns.

The edges of everything in sight darken. All that stands is a barn. I gaze at a barn up a lane and the eyes don't dart away. Time slows with me all here.

It's the absence of the thing that startles: I feel no fear.

I'm looking at barns, counting gifts, and I'm jarred: There is no choking angst. I am not anxious and I breathe easy and that worry child I've clung to, she deserts. I feel no fear and it makes no sense. The market still teeters, the future of our livelihood still hangs precarious, and there are still no guarantees, no assurances, no change. Nothing has materially changed since yesterday's fears, last week's anxiety. But *I* have. I'm changing. I am changing, deep changing, and I am giving thanks, doing *eucharisteo* and *eucharisteo* is *eureka* and I know why there's no fear and why had I never seen it before? I can mark the spot on Road 178, right at the bridge, where the epiphany blinds like snow:

Thanks is what builds trust.

I cross over a bridge.

The Maitland River curls glassy, barns along both banks. I cross the bridge, and the river's a ribbon of silver slipping under the bridge like a thread passing through eye of a needle. And in that moment, another strand of *eucharisteo* slips through the eye of my soul.

Who trusts the Bridge Builder?

Who trusts the Bridge Builder when you've seen your sister's crushed body bleed lifeless on gravel? When you wake to find the kitchen eerily empty again, her bed vacant again, Mama long gone again, checked into a locked psychiatric ward again? Who trusts the Bridge Builder when you wake to snow on your blankets and winter blasting through cracked walls and dinner for four is a fifty cent box of Kraft Dinner rationed in half and your dad tells you every single day that he just doesn't know how there is ever going to be enough?

How do you count on life when the hopes don't add up?

A morning in late November, joy shimmers.

The hopes don't have to add up. The blessings do.

I want to slam on the brakes right then and there on a side road in Howick Township, the light blinding.

Count blessings and discover Who can be counted on.

Isn't that what had been happening, quite unexpectedly? This living a lifestyle of intentional gratitude became an unintentional test in the trustworthiness of God—and in counting blessings I stumbled upon the way out of fear.

Can God be counted on? Count blessings and find out how many of His bridges have already held.

Had I not trusted all these years because I had not counted?

I glance back in the mirror to the concrete bridge, the one I've boldly driven straight across without second thought, and I see truth reflecting back at me: Every time fear freezes and worry writhes, every time I surrender to stress, aren't I advertising the unreliability of God? That I really don't believe? But if I'm grateful to the Bridge Builder for the crossing of a million strong bridges, thankful for a million faithful moments, my life speaks my beliefs and I trust Him again.

I fearlessly cross the next bridge.

I shake my head at the blinding wonder of it: Trust is the bridge from yesterday to tomorrow, built with planks of thanks. Remembering frames up gratitude. Gratitude lays out the planks of trust. I can walk the planks—from known to unknown—and know: He holds.

I could walk unafraid.

Is that why the Israelites kept recounting their past— to trust God for their future? Remembering is an act of thanksgiving, a way of thanksgiving, this turn of the heart over time's shoulder to see all the long way His arms have carried. "Gratitude is the memory of the heart,"[2] writes Jean Baptiste Massieu, but gratitude is not only the memories of our heart; gratitude is a memory of God's heart and to thank is to remember God.

I had read it this morning as I prayed the Psalms, the psalmist giving thanks for the memories:

> *Give thanks to the Lord of lords.*
> > *His faithful love endures forever.*
> *Give thanks to him who alone does mighty miracles.*
> > *His faithful love endures forever.*
> *Give thanks to him who made the heavens so skillfully.*
> > *His faithful love endures forever.*
> *Give thanks to him who placed the earth among the waters.*
> > *His faithful love endures forever.*
> *Give thanks to him who made the heavenly lights—*
> > *His faithful love endures forever. (Psalm 136:3–7)*

In memory, the shape of God's yesterday-heart emerges and assures of God's now-heart and reassures of His sure beat tomorrow. And for the first time I see why the Israelites are covenanted with God to be a people who remember with thanks. It is thanksgiving that shapes a theology of trust and the Israelites bear witness and I see.

Isn't this what ultimately Christ asks of us in the Last Supper? One of the very last directives He offers to His disciples, the one of supreme import but I too often neglect: to remember. *Do this in remembrance of Me.* Remember and give thanks.

This is the crux of Christianity: to remember and give thanks, *eucharisteo.*

Why? Why is remembering and giving thanks the core of the Christ-faith? *Because remembering with thanks is what causes us to trust — to really believe.*

I once read the words, "The foremost quality of a trusting disciple is gratefulness."[3] And for months of naming blessings, these words had spurred me on, that gratitude was the preeminent attitude of the Christ-follower (*think of it!*), that *eucharisteo returned me to God* as non-*eucharisteo* had caused the fall from God. And of course — *eucharisteo* is at the heart of Christianity. But I had never seen, until a crossing of a bridge, that gratitude truly is the foremost quality of a believing disciple precisely because *gratitude is what births trust . . . the true belief.*

It's only when you live the prayer of thanksgiving that you live the power of trusting God. I had never known what the door of *eucharisteo* might lead me into — and all the fears it might lead me out of. Light glints bright in my mirrors.

And in an empty pickup truck I hear voices scarred — the voices of people I have long loved and their voices cry pain and I honor them with the listening:

When your memories have an old man groping for your crotch, hot, foul breath on your face, and your skin crawls? Give thanks?

And an ultrasound screen stretches still and you're sent

home to wait for the uterine muscles to contract out the dead dreams?

Or the woman you lay down with, shared the naked and unashamed, she beds another man, hands you back the wedding albums, and says she never knew love for you, what then?

Remember and give thanks? For what? What if remembering doesn't kindle gratitude? What if remembering just leaves third-degree burns?

The words sear. I know their voices and I remember their faces and the sun spills from window glass, slants gold across steering wheel. Eyes on the road, yellow line dashing like a line on hold, I wait, just wait. In the wait, memories blister. And in the still, Spirit comes and He whispers a name.

Christ.

And I see a world through His lens: "He who did not spare his own Son, but gave him up for us all—how will he not also, along with him, graciously give us all things?" (Romans 8:32 NIV).

He gave us Jesus. *Jesus! Gave Him up for us all.* If we have only one memory, isn't this one enough? Why is this the memory I most often take for granted? He cut open the flesh of the God-Man and let the blood. He washed our grime with the bloody grace. He drove the iron ore through His own vein. Doesn't that memory alone suffice? Need there be anything more? If God didn't withhold from us His very own Son, will God withhold *anything* we need?

If trust must be earned, hasn't God unequivocally earned our trust with the bark on the raw wounds, the thorns pressed into the brow, your name on the cracked lips? How will He not also graciously give us all things He deems best and right? He's already given the incomprehensible.

Christ our Crossbeam.

The counting of all blessings is ultimately summed up in One.

All gratitude is ultimately gratitude for Christ, all remembering a remembrance of Him. For in Him all things were created, are sustained, have their being. Thus Christ is all there is to give thanks for; Christ is all there is to remember. To know how we can count on God, we count graces, but ultimately there is really only One.

And the radical wonder of it stuns me happy, hushes me still: *it's all Christ.* Every moment, every event, every happening. *It's all in Christ and in Christ we are always safe and "how will he not also . . .?"*

When bridges seem to give way, we fall into Christ's safe arms, true bridge, and not into hopelessness. It is safe to trust!

We can be too weak to go on because His strength is made perfect in utter brokenness and nail-pierced hands help up. It is safe to trust!

We can give thanks in everything because there's a good God leading, working all things into good. It is safe to trust!

The million bridges behind us may seem flattened to the earthly eye, but all bridges ultimately hold, fastened by nails.

It is safe to trust.

Each bridge I need cross, from one moment to moment the next, is wholly safe, each leading me deeper into Him and closer to Home.

And I hear that hurting voice again, her and me and all those aching voices I have known and they still cry: There are moments that as sure as I bruise don't *feel* like good things have been given. What of all the memories where Christ seems absent? When the bridge shakes and heaves, when "how will he not also?" reads more like "*he will not.*"

Trauma's storm can mask the Christ and feelings can lie.

I draw all the hurting voices close and I touch their scars with a whisper: sometimes we don't fully see that in Christ, because of Christ, through Christ, He does give us all things good—until we have the perspective of years.

In time, years, dust settles.

In memory, ages, God emerges.

Then when we look back, we see God's back.

Wasn't that too His way with Moses? "When my glory passes by, I will put you in a cleft in the rock and cover you with my hand until I have passed by. Then I will remove my hand and you will see my back" (Exodus 33:22–23 NIV).

Is that it? When it gets dark, it's only because God has tucked me in a cleft of the rock and covered me, protected, with His hand? In the pitch, I feel like I'm falling, sense the bridge giving way, God long absent. In the dark, the bridge and my world shakes, cracking dreams. But maybe this is true reality: It is in the dark that God is passing by. The bridge and our lives shake not because God has abandoned, but the exact opposite: God is passing by. God is in the tremors. Dark is the holiest ground, the glory passing by. In the blackest, God is closest, at work, forging His perfect and right will. Though it is black and we can't see and our world seems to be free-falling and we feel utterly alone, Christ is most present to us, I-beam supporting in earthquake. Then He will remove His hand. Then we will look.

Then we look back and see His back.

I look in my rearview mirror. The bridge I cross on the

way to the chapel has fallen behind hills. I can still see, in memory, the river's winding light, mirror on moving water.

God reveals Himself in rearview mirrors.

And I've an inkling that there are times when we need to drive a long, long distance, before we can look back and see God's back in the rearview mirror.

Maybe sometimes about as far as heaven — that kind of distance.

Then to turn, and see His face.

At the corner of Road 178 and Gorrie Line, turning north, winter sun now slips behind, shadows of the bare maples drawn long over fields, ditches. The Tinholt farm deep under snow to the south, pigs sleeping under those roofs. I remember it right then passing pig farms. And that God would bring that story to memory now.

How bread became a comfort when bombs fell in World War II, shattering earth and all that is within and children wept for parents, cried for food. Refugee camps offered beds to huddling, dirty frames but could not furnish rest. Blast of days haunted pitch of nights. Nothing comforted shell-shocked, gaunt children. Fear rimmed the eyes and the hearts pounded, too loud, and the sleep fled. I know how nights blinked with the saucer eyes, the vigilant, terrified eyes. But somewhere in the dark, up between each narrow row of beds, a hand came to pull up the thin sheets, a hand to touch each bony shoulder and offer the fear-chased something to seize.

A piece of bread.

Dazed child hands took the bread, tucked in with bread. They gave thanks and rested on pillows of trust. The bread hushed the fears with assurance: "The sun sets and He has provided and you've ate. Tomorrow the sun will rise and again

He will provide. You will eat bread again."[4] Hands clutch bread. And finally it comes: the terrified sleep deep.

I shake the head; sleeping with bread, a strange mental image. And yet really ... isn't that what that gratitude journal on the counter is? Opening the hand to receive the moments. Trusting what is received to be grace. Taking it as bread. Recount how we laughed today. How we cried today and it too was grace. How He fed us. We ate. We filled. We swept up the crumbs. So He lays us down to sleep. Trust tucks in. He has blessed today. Will He not bless again tomorrow? Sleeping with bread may seem strange, but Jesus knew the wilder.

He knew I'd only trust, rest, when I lived with bread in hand. When I eat manna.

Eucharisteo, remembering with thanks, *this is the bread.*

We take the moments as bread and give thanks and *the thanks itself becomes bread.* The thanks itself nourishes. *Thanks feeds our trust.*

And it swells up in me and I can't stop it, this surging sense of emancipation. Over a steering wheel in a white pickup, I can't help this glorious laugh, the laugh of the unafraid and the bold, the giddy hope of the bread carriers, the manna eaters.

Until Home and Promised Land and complete clarity, I'm a wanderer crossing bridges, wanderer eating manna, eating mystery. For really, as long as I live, travel, is there ever anything else to eat? I either take the "what is it?" manna with thanks, eat the mystery of the moment with trust, and am nourished another day — or refuse it ... and die. Jesus calls me to surrender and there's nothing like releasing fears and falling into peace. It terrifies, true. But it exhilarates. This, this is what I've always wanted and never knew: this utter trust, this enlivening fall of surrender into the safe hands.

There is no joy without trust!

I can feel all the sinews releasing, the opening of the heart chambers, the unfurling of a life into one reverberating, exultant *yes!* "For no matter how many promises God has made, they are 'Yes' in Christ" (2 Corinthians 1:20 NIV).

Yes in Christ!

To the Enfleshed Yes who said yes to this moment and yes to last year's illness and yes to the cracks of my childhood and yes to the nail and yes to my name in the Book of Life, hear me say YES! Not "I'm worried." Not "I'm stressed out." Not "I'm anxious." Not "I'm too afraid." Hear me say *thank you.* Hear me say YES! Watch me *live a life* of yes. To all that was and is and is to come. The power of sin and death and fear-sent-from-the-Enemy are forever ended because we can trust in the bridge even if it's caving, in God even when it's black, in manna-nourishment even when we don't know what it is. The God whom we thank for fulfilling the promises of the past will fulfill His promises again. In Christ, the answer to the questions of every moment is always Yes.

The answer is always YES!

You'd think I'd want to devour the bread. Epiphany's flicker, light here and gone. Come Monday morning, I forget. A child loses a book, has an exam, is late for practice. I stress over the trite, a phone call, what's for dinner, a deadline. And there are far longer, higher bridges: Where is a child's heart headed? Am I living God's best for this life or am I bankrupting any legacy of faith? What misery lurks in the next twenty-four hours and the next? Stress can be an addiction and worry can be our lunge for control and we forget the answer to this moment is always yes because of Christ.

My baby is five. She falls asleep in my arms after the close of dinner prayers, us still seated at table, and I hold her long after the Farmer has put the rest of the tribe to bed, her curls damp and etching into my skin and I don't move. Her face is turned toward mine, broad and open, eyelashes whisper of gold. I trace her lips, gentle curve of all things beautiful. The way her eyes danced today, soul light, the arch of her eyebrows and that lyrical laugh, heaven's echo that entirely undoes me. Her breath is warm on my face, all that is alive and warm and breathing inside of her now, falling upon me, and I can't capture it, hold it, this, her life now, me in this moment. She is leaving me, she's growing up and moving away from me, and she stirs and I sweep back the crop of the golden ringlets. *Stay, Little One, stay.* Love's a deep wound and what *is* a mother without a child and why can't I hold on to now forever and her here and me here and why does time snatch away a heart I don't think mine can beat without? Why do we all have to grow old? Why do we have to keep saying good-bye?

Again I refuse to walk the bridge into tomorrow's unknowns, and I shame the Bridge Builder with my worries, my demand to just let me stay here, or go back, but no, not to go on, and again He comes to carry me flailing and anxious.

Am I always the atheist in Arms, me the believer who doesn't believe?

And He soothes His own restless child in arms with the whisper, law of the universe that He's writing deep into this heart: Eucharisteo *always precedes the miracle, child.*

And the chin trembles and I stroke her cheek, her body leaning back against mine, and I tentatively open the hand to receive the gift of now ... I name the now gifts and I await miracle.

That button nose. I touch a finger to its tip and smile. I gaze long, memorizing.

That sprinkling bridge of freckles. I brush my finger across them. These, these I will remember.

The way that singular curl spirals over her ear. The way it winds like silken staircase, on and on and on. And I lean over and the lips seal the delicate spot on her forehead with a long kiss, her skin berry wine and I feel Him, His kiss of tender truth:

All fear is but the notion that God's love ends. Did you think I end, that My bread warehouses are limited, that I will not be enough? But I am infinite, child. What can end in Me? Can life end in Me? Can happiness? Or peace? Or anything you need? Doesn't your Father always give you what you need? I am the Bread of Life and My bread for you will never end. Fear thinks God is finite and fear believes that there is not going to be enough and hasn't counting one thousand gifts, endlessly counting gifts, exposed the lie at the heart of all fear? In Me, blessings never end because My love for you never ends. If My goodnesses toward you end, I will cease to exist, child. As long as there is a God in heaven, there is grace on earth and I am the spilling God of the uncontainable, forever-overflowing-love-grace.

I wrap a thread of her curls around a finger. I stare into that face conceived in love, reflecting love, and I feel His fall soft on me. I am child in His arms and His breath falls warm upon my face and what I feel for this daughter He feels for me, and the gifts, all these gifts I keep counting, they are His love gifts and they're slowly waking me up to the tenderest, fiercest Love of all.

Cradling this child, her eyelashes fluttering, her breath

rising and falling in sure and steady rhythm, I know it in the pulsing, real, surest kind of way: "Perfect love casts out all fear." His love had done that.

The table still needs to be cleared. The bowls washed. The bread put away. Snow falls in the dark, white on a barn roof. I can't imagine what deeper layers of my wounds *eucharisteo* will gently peel back to heal, but I take her sleeping hand and trace the lines of her skin and I keep on counting blessings to keep on remembering to keep on walking out into the unknown.

I clutch soul bread and a Perfect Love that knows no end.

go lower

God created the world out of nothing,
and as long as we are nothing,
He can make something out of us.
Martin Luther

I'm taking photos of light sliding across a wall, light lying out
lazy along the pine-planked floor and pouring into the old
bottles, when she asks for my camera. She's not three and a
half feet tall. I press the shutter on light seeping into the grain
of the hewn beams, into that wood that stood as a tree under
sun in the fields two hundred years ago. It's like the rays are
looking for a way in along the beam's century-old cracks, light
looking to revive the long-dead, to raise the cut down. I'm
capturing beauty on a Tuesday morning in a farmhouse, giving
thanks for now by reverencing it with a frame and the sacred
eyes, but how could I have known it would be the child who
would hand me the light?

"I take some pictures too, Mama? I won't break anything, I
won't. *Promise.*" Her eyes are the oldest dawn, an otherworldly
morn. She's cupping her dimpled hands, showing me how
she'll cradle the lens. This child churns me to butter and her
voice spreads me out and I slip the neck strap over her head.

"Which button do I press again?" She looks up at me. How do her eyes widen to catch that much unadulterated joy?

"Just press this one." I could inhale her, fragrance of peonies in June.

She presses the shutter.

Vase. Click.

Doorway. Click.

Cupboards. Click.

Her laughter makes me laugh too and I can hear her going through the house, flagrantly recording all time and space. Child and mother, we've exchanged places, her seeking wonder, me with hands of pencils and LEGO bits and books, and I try to return order to chaos and she too returns to Eden, naming each moment with a frame.

Eventually she comes looking for me, her face filled with lens, her every step activating another click. I'm separating whites from darks in the laundry room.

"Can you show them back to me now?" She holds the camera out to me, as long as the neck strap will allow. Nothing can restrain her giddiness.

Settling into a pile of laundry, our heads lean toward each other and touch. Her arm around my neck, we scroll through her photos on the glowing screen. A picture of me bent over her, showing her which button to press. I'm mountain over her lens. I can feel the laughter rising up in her, and she cups her hand over her mouth to catch the bubbling pleasure. She's enchanted by her photos. I grin.

Frame of a table. A doorknob. A bookshelf skewed on a tilt.

Yet her photos surprise, every single one. Why? It takes me a moment to make sense of it. It's the vantage point. At thirty-six inches, her angle's unfamiliar to me and utterly captivating:

the study ceiling arches like a dome, her bed a floating barge. The stairs plunge like a gorge.

She's Alice in Wonderland all the world grown Everestlike around and above her.

"Do you like them, Mama?" She pats my cheek with her laughter-drenched hand.

I can only murmur, flicking through her gallery. "Marvelous ... just marvelous."

She giggles and who can resist and I lay the camera aside and tickle her soft belly and she throws the head back, bliss, and I kiss blind all up that sweet neck of hers and she laughs breathless and we roll happy. And when she scampers off into other majestic realms, I look after her longing, longing to go too, longing to go back and could I? Go with her and into the wonder? I stay. I sort laundry and thoughts.

I want that kind of crazy, happy joy, God. Jeans to the right, socks to the left. How have I lost it in the growing older, duller? How to see the world again through those eyes? To live in the wide-eyed wonder of a world that unwraps itself grandiose and larger-than-life, so otherworldly?

Those summers, my sister and I played with slippery frogs in the back ditch, creek-bottom mud squelching up through our bare toes, us sloshing through the dark of the culvert, our laughter echo-ringing off steel. We built moats and castles and all our princes really were frogs and I want those days again. Maybe that is why I curl up on the girls' bed every night and the boys pile in too, and children beg for my childhood stories. I tell gilded tales. It only takes a memory and we're the Darling children slipping off to Wonder-That-Really-Is Land and we fly.

I think of my aunt. She did fly. All over the world, an

airline steward, her whole life trotting the globe, dining in exotic locales, wandering the streets of the foreign and unusual. In her fifties, childless, she came to the farm. Sat in the living room of our farmhouse and rolled a red plastic ball across the floor to our toddling daughter. I can still hear our daughter squealing ecstasy as the ball rolled toward her and the room rang, turned inside out with the bouncing glee. We had laughed wonder. Daughter had stretched out her two little arms, clutched that giant globe in two chubby hands, and held it high over her head, her own face tilted back, the round wonders meeting. Again and again, my aunt hit replay: roll ball into purest delight, child squeals laughter, roll again. Our sides hurt happy from the laughing.

Weeks later, my aunt sent a letter. From a far-flung hotel, stamped in some post office on the other side of the ocean. It was her looping, aching epiphany that scrawled me deep: "I will never forget your daughter's wild joy in that ball—a happiness like I have never seen in all my travels through all these years. And in the simplest of experiences." I never forgot—the child-joy of that afternoon ... or my aunt's words.

Yes, otherworldly joy, *like that*. The kind you could search the world over—and find only in a child.

I pluck Little-One's pink-flowered dress from the laundry basket and hold it in hand.

It's because she's small.

Is that it? The secret to a child's language of laughter, their domain of delight, is perspective.

If the heights of our joy are measured by the depths of our gratitude, and gratitude is but a way of seeing, a spiritual perspective of smallness might offer a vital way of seeing especially conducive to gratitude.

Those child photos, that wonder I experienced firsthand through her eyes—"How much larger your life would be if your self could become smaller in it!"[1]—was that it? I had just held evidence of it.

The joy of small that makes life large.

Hadn't I personally experienced it before too, that vantage point that gave a sense of smallness before grandeur? At the lip of the Grand Canyon, peering into the carved earth, the vastness of the hewn and many-hued chasm. A late June night peering into the expanse of heavens nailed up with the named and known stars. A moon field. I hardly dare brush the limitlessness with my vaporous humanity.

But the irony: Don't I often desperately want to wriggle free of the confines of a small life? Yet when I stand before immensity that heightens my smallness—I have never felt sadness. Only burgeoning wonder. Is it because within each frame of finite flesh lies the likeness of infinite God? In all things large and spectacular, we recognize glimpses of home and the call to our own deeper chemistry. Do we writhe to peel out of our smallness and into the big life because that fits our inborn God-image?

Echo calls to echo, deep to deep.

Awe ... awe ignites joy because it makes us bend the knee and I remember a night chasing moon and we are in deepest happiness in the posture of grateful worship. Because the God-likeness within our smallness speaks to Father-God in His magnificence. I hadn't understood that in wheat under lunar light: That all wonder and worship can only grow out of smallness.

I'm standing in a mudroom, sorting children's dribbled shirts, grass-stained jeans. It's been years since I stood on the

rim of the canyon, months since I ran with the moon. I live
in laundry. How to be Little-One in now's wonderland, in
Kingdom of Heaven coming? How to *live* in a state of awe
when life is mundane and ordinary? I know layers of the
eucharisteo answer because I have felt the miracle ... but there
are layers I don't yet understand.

Light falls in gold bars across laundry.

The watch on my wrist chimes the hour, modern bells to
prayer. I stop the spinning thoughts, the probing questions,
the hands sorting, the laundry work, because God needs knees
more than hands. Bowed like Daniel, I move to the other side
of prayer with on-the-hour prayers of thanks.

Thank You, Lord, for the perspective of a child ...

Thank You for door frames and doorknobs ...

Thank You for soaring ceilings and bed barges and tables that loom
large ...

For her laughter and her wonder and her eyes that turn the world
inside out and stretch it large and leave me again in surprise ...
in awe ...

I murmur *eucharisteo* thanks in a pile of laundry and the
world expands and heightens and deepens and surges with
the glory of God and I can feel the body decreasing and the
soul increasing and joy filling the breadth between. This, *this*
is like a child happily capturing pixels, our daughter giddily
grasping the ball—the perspective of smallness that cultivates
surprised wonder, that grows gratitude, that yields joy. The
orb awe of a moon that makes the eyes see, the kaleidoscope
of a bubble that makes the time slow, this is *eucharisteo* working
its change on a life, but here, isn't this here another layer of
eucharisteo? *Eucharisteo* makes the knees the vantage point of a
life. I shake my head, my quiet laughter remembering her glee,

because isn't that how children live? Life as large surprise. A child has no expectation of a globe-trotting aunt bringing her extravagant gifts from the Orient, or a bouquet of flowers, or even a postcard. *A rolling ball? Surprise! A laughing aunt? Surprise! Again and again? Surprise!*

My mama, valley wise and grief traveled, she always said, "Expectations kill relationships." And I've known expectations as a disease, silent killer heaping her burdens on the shoulders of a relationship until a soul bursts a pulmonary and dies. Expectations kill relationships — especially with God. And that's what a child doesn't have: this whole edifice of expectation. Without expectations, what can topple the surprising wonder of the moment?

I think of it only a couple hundred times a year, that single wide-eyed night by the bed of one of our sons in the pediatric wing of a city hospital. The moaning of babes, the crying of sick children, the murmur of nurses with grim prognoses on lips and morphine in hand, these haunted through the endless hours. I did not sleep, the pain of that place begging me to pray. After our son was given the thumbs-up and the signature of release, I came home to bedrooms and bathrooms and kitchen and fridge and windows and unmerited, luxurious health and I threw up my arms in giddy gratitude. *Here? This place? Surprise!* I was a woman who saw what her life could well have been, a woman who didn't live by a deathbed or in a refugee camp or a war zone or the rubble of an earthquake. I laughed at the surprise of dishes in my sink and the wild surprise of turning on the stove to boil water and I swished toilet and I was healthy and *I got to be here and do this!* And things but forty-eight hours prior I entirely took for granted — even rather half resented as flawed and less than — I spun around: *All surprising grace!* And there has not been a single night the nearly ten years since, that my son and I haven't whispered in bedside prayers for those who cry out in the dark, for we witnessed and we remember and we will always carry . . .

Is it only when our lives are emptied that we're surprised by how truly full our lives were?

Instead of filling with expectations, the joy-filled expect nothing—and are filled. This breath! This oak tree! This daisy! This work! This sky! These people! This place! *This day! Surprise!*

C. S. Lewis said he was "surprised by joy." Perhaps there is no way to discover joy but as surprise?

The way the small live. Every day.

Yes, the small even have a biblical nomenclature. Doesn't God call them the *humble*?

The *humble* live surprised. The *humble* live by joy.

I am ear and Jesus whispers to the surprised, "God blesses those who are humble, for they will inherit the whole earth" (Matthew 5:5). The humble are the laid-low and bowed ones, the surprised ones with hands open to receive whatever He gives.

He hands them the earth.

The earth.

But is it any wonder? That word *humility* itself comes from the Latin root *humus*—the kind of earth that grows good crops. God gives *the earth* to the humus-people, the humble ones. *Humility* is that good humus that grows gratitude that yields abundant joy.

In the upside-down kingdom of heaven, down is up and up is down, and those who want to ascend higher must descend lower. And so "anyone who becomes as humble as this little child is the greatest in the Kingdom of Heaven" (Matthew 18:4). Later I read the words of F. B. Meyer. They wring me and I think about the earth and the knees and the things I never knew:

> I used to think that God's gifts were on shelves one above the other, and that the taller we grew in Christian character the easier we should reach them. I find now that God's gifts are on shelves one beneath the other, and that it is not a question of growing taller but of stooping lower, and that we have to go down, always down, to get His best gifts.[2]

To receive God's gifts, to live exalted and joy filled, isn't a function of straining higher, harder, doing more, carrying long the burdens of the super-Pharisees or ultra-saints. Receiving God's gifts is a gentle, simple movement of stooping lower.

Is this, too, why I'm often joy starved? Why a narcissistic, gluttonous world lives emaciated? But the humble joy of small child? This I had witnessed. And my aunt had never seen anything like it in all the world.

I trace the stitches of the flowers embroidered on Little-One's dress and I whisper worn words, new in revelation: "He must increase, but I must decrease" (John 3:30 NASB). I knew my soul need magnify Him, but of the flesh minimizing? And there it is bent over laundry, that humility isn't burden or humiliation or oppressive weight but humility is the only posture that can receive the wondrous grace gifts of God— God who humbled Himself and came to the feed trough and waits to be seen in light off doorknobs and the curve of vases and the mound of laundry. I shake my head, half smile, lay aside her dress because the funny thing? The moment I try to grasp for humility, she's gone. Speak of humility, shine a light shaft on it, and she's shadow-gone in the dark. "Humility is so shy," writes Tim Keller.[3] If I focus on humility, I look inward to assess if I'm sufficiently humble, and in the very act, humility darts and I'm proud, self-focused. It doesn't work. But what humbles like an extravagant gift? And hadn't I felt that joy of small, child-wonder when I paused to give thanks?

The quiet song of gratitude, *eucharisteo*, lures humility out of the shadows because to receive a gift the knees must bend humble and the hand must lie vulnerably open and the will must bow to accept whatever the Giver chooses to give.

Again, always, and always again: *eucharisteo precedes the miracle*. And you'd think I'd know that by now. But I forget. Father never forgets what I am made of, child of dust. The Wounded Warrior is achingly tender with the broken ones and He has all the patient time to gently lead those who seek and He keeps leading me back to *eucharisteo*.

Is this what is happening as I learn *eucharisteo*, to be full of grace? I humbly give God thanks for the gifts. I practice *eucharisteo*. And in that place of humble thanks, God exalts and gives more gifts and more of Himself, which humbles and lays the soul down lower. And good God responds with greater gifts of grace and even more of Himself. And I ride the undulating wave of grace, this lifting higher and higher in grace, the surging crest of joy, and this plunging lower and lower in humble thankfulness only to rise yet higher in grace and this *eucharisteo*, it offers the ultimate joyride and I don't think I ever want to get off. Is this why the oil jars of joy never run dry, but endlessly refill? He must increase and I must decrease — not because that is burden but so that my joy might increase with more of Him! I kneel down to toss in the laundry.

I set the dial to extra dirty. I stay on my knees and watch the water run into the washer, watch it splash against the circular glass of the washing machine's front door, hear its gurgling fall. Down it flows. Down, always down, water runs, always looking for yet lower and lower places to flow. I watch water run and spiritual water must flow like this ... always seeking always the lowest places—and the washtub begins to rock. I must go lower. I tell myself this, watching water run. That whenever I am parched and dry, I must go lower with the water and I must kneel low in thanks. The river of joy flows down to the lowest places.

I get up off my knees.

⁓

I hang socks. Across the rack, white flags of surrender. My thoughts, they're hung up on humility and smallness and receiving all as surprising grace and how this *eucharisteo* has layers that lead deeper into the kingdom, lead deeper into my truest, fullest self, the one He intended. Children play in the basement below my domestic choreography, thunder of feet and crazy laughter. Swoop and drape, quotidian work, familial cadence constant as rising and setting sun and God fills the common moments. A shatter of glass splinters the rhythm.

A child screams.

I wince eyes tight and the arteries tighten in mother-distress.

"*You* did it!"

"*You* pushed me right into it! *I* didn't do a thing!"

"Moooooom! Mommmmm?"

I exhale. I take each step down the stairs slow, methodical, a climber descending deliberately because they're at the brink and the precipice is black. A day of attempting to restore domestic order has already racked up a tally of highlighter scribbled on a sleigh bed frame, a CD cracked in half, a paint stain on a bedroom carpet, and an endless drone of sibling squabbles. When I get to the bottom of the stairs, blades of glass meet me, carpet of shards in front of the stereo unit.

"The glass in this door is still good." A daughter swings the remaining cabinet door. I think I am supposed to be pleased. "He just broke this one."

"*I* broke?" Son whips his hand to chest, throws arms in the air. "I was just running after you. It was *your* shoulder that slammed into the cabinet."

I'm wound tight. I'm pressing my molars together, compressing the jaw. Clenching the hands tight. Ten minutes ago and that theoretical exploration of a theology of joy? Well, theories and theology stillbirth unless they can take on some skin, breathe in the polluted air of this world, and make it happen. And my knees are stiff and it's jarring, how peace can shatter faster than glass, the breakneck speeds at which I can fall—and refuse to bend the knees at all.

Can I just be David, and evening and morning and at noon, complain and murmur, mourn the mother's lament of dependent faith that God *will* hear my voice (Psalm 55:16–17)? Can I hold the tongue from the Israelite complaint with its ungrateful discontent and bitter accusations, complaint that kindles God's anger (Numbers 11:1)? I dare not let loose my tongue for I know which cry is more likely. But I can't seem to hold her back, that tail of the heart, the tongue, she springs anyway.

"What in the world were you thinking? How many times have we said no running? I am just ..." I'm spewing and it's ugly and the words are so frazzled with frustration, they fray midstream. I can feel the slow smothering, the tight choking, and I can feel it in the throat, rising ... this moan, this baying bawl ... an injured animal wild, the trapped mad, and this is not a David lament. But I carry these David words memorized, grace for when I can't get the David lament right: "I was so foolish and ignorant—I must have seemed like a senseless animal to you" (Psalm 73:22).

God holds us in the untamed moments too.

I breathe deep, look at them. I remember: *Lament* is a cry of belief in a good God, a God who has His ear to our hearts, a God who transfigures the ugly into beauty. *Complaint* is the bitter howl of unbelief in any benevolent God in this moment, a distrust in the love-beat of the Father's heart. God's anger kindles hot when the essence of the complaint implies doubt in His love and I rub my forehead and shake my head. Lament is this long learning, hard like *eucharisteo*. And this I know like I am coming to know my name, Ann, "full of grace": the more I learn *eucharisteo*, the more I learn His love, the less likely I am to Israelite complain and the more I genuinely lament, complaint that trusts His heart.

I look into the faces of the guilty and a son arcs his eyebrow, shrugs his shoulders nonchalant and doesn't God Himself express righteous indignation, wounded deep with His own sinning Israelite children? Didn't God's heart often break? Didn't He grieve and rage and feel rejection (Genesis 6:6; Exodus 4:14)? I read it in the pages of Scripture, lines of His own story, the Joy-God owning His own grief, so I won't be Naaman and I won't pretend I don't feel any pain. Army chief

Naaman (2 Kings 5:1), Naaman with the grotesque leprosy that thickens the skin numb. Numbness, too, can twist the body beastlike. In the end, it's the numbness that kills you.

I lean against the stair wall. I will be real and I will feel life and I will be Naaman who bends the knee, enters the muddy waters of the emotions. True lament is the bold faith that trusts Perfect Love enough to feel and cry authentic.

Holding my head in my hands, I ask it honest before God and children and my daily mess: "Can we really expect joy all the time?"

I know it well after a day smattered with rowdiness and worn a bit ragged with bickering, that I may feel disappointment and the despair may flood high, but to *give thanks* is an action and *rejoice* is a verb and these are not mere pulsing emotions. While I may not always feel joy, God asks me to give thanks in all things, because He knows that the *feeling* of joy begins in the *action* of thanksgiving.[4]

True saints know that the place where all the joy comes from is far deeper than that of feelings; joy comes from the place of the very presence of God. Joy is God and God is joy and joy doesn't negate all other emotions — joy *transcends* all other emotions. Though my marriage tree may not bud and though my crop of children may fail and my work produce little yield, though there is no money in the bank and no dream left in the heart, though others may choose different ways to live their one life, till my last heaving breath, I will fight to the death for this: "I will take joy" (Habakkuk 3:18 ESV). I will struggle to heed this until I am no more: "Dear brothers and sisters, when troubles come your way, consider it an opportunity for great joy" (James 1:2), and I will listen and again I will listen and I will wrestle to put skin on it: "*Rejoice* in the Lord *always*. I will say it again: *Rejoice!*" (Philippians 4:4 NIV, emphasis added).

I gnaw my lip. The body howls when joy is extinguished. The face shrivels pain, the voice pitches angry cry. "No man can live without joy" is what Thomas Aquinas wrote.[5] And I confess, it is true, I have known many dead waiting to die.

The glass lies everywhere broken. But this isn't about this glass but old glass, about glass to God, about glass to my life as a whole. I see right through to what I am.

Only self can kill joy.

I'm the one doing this to me.

The theology I've been turning over, it comes now clear windowpane and I can see, holy vision.

Joy is a flame that glimmers only in the palm of the open and humble hand. In an open and humble palm, released and surrendered to receive, light dances, flickers happy. The moment the hand is clenched tight, fingers all pointing toward self and rights and demands, joy is snuffed out. Anger is the lid that suffocates joy until she lies limp and lifeless. And for me, it's a cosmic-numbing notion that far eclipses this domestic moment. It speaks to the whole of my life and the vision brands me: The demanding of my own will is the singular force that smothers out joy—nothing else.

Pride, mine—that beast that pulls on the mask of anger— this is what snaps this hand shut, crushes joy. When I would read Henry Ward Beecher's words later, I'd take it for my own story, so familiar his thoughts: "Pride slays thanksgiving ... A proud man is seldom a grateful man, for he never thinks he gets as much as he deserves."[6] Dare I ask what I think I deserve? A life of material comfort? A life free of all trials, all hardship, all suffering? A life with no discomfort, no inconveniences? Are there times that a sense of entitlement—*expectations*—is what inflates self, detonates anger, offends God, extinguishes joy?

And what do I really deserve? Thankfully, God never gives what is deserved, but instead, God graciously, passionately offers gifts, our bodies, our time, our very lives. God does not give rights but imparts responsibilities—response-abilities— inviting us to respond to His love-gifts. And I know and can feel it tight: I'm responding miserably to the gift of this moment. In fact, I'm refusing it. Proudly refusing to accept this moment, dismissing it as no gift at all, I refuse God. I reject God. *Why is this* eucharisteo *always so hard?*

I look down at shattered glass, glass that brings memories, glass that gives me eyes to see in. And I see: I had thought joy's flame needed protecting.

All these years, these angers, these hardenings, this desire to control, I had thought I had to snap the hand closed to shield joy's fragile flame from the blasts. In a storm of struggles, I had tried to control the elements, clasp the fist tight so as to protect self and happiness. But palms curled into protective fists fill with darkness. I feel that sharply, even in this ... and this realization in all its full emptiness: My own wild desire to *protect* my joy at all costs is the exact force that *kills* my joy.

Flames need oxygen to light.

Flames need a bit of wind.

The theology's putting on skin.

All light seen is light from the past and light now old from the sun streams through the window, glints off the glass shards. Broken glass ignites in light and there it is, the secret of joy's flame: *Humbly let go.* Let go of trying to *do*, let go of trying to control ... let go of my own way, let go of my own fears. Let God blow His wind, His trials, oxygen for joy's fire. Leave the hand open and *be*. Be at peace. Bend the knee and be small and let God give what God chooses to give because *He only gives love* and whisper surprised thanks. This is the fuel for joy's flame. Fullness of joy is discovered only in the emptying of will. And I can empty. I can empty because counting His graces has awakened me to how He cherishes me, holds me, passionately values me. I can empty because I am *full* of His love. I can trust.

I can *let go*.

I hadn't known that joy meant dying.

What did I think hard *eucharisteo* and the table of the Last Supper meant?

But dying to self demands that I might gratefully and humbly receive the better, the only things that a good God gives. To be nothing in the flesh and Christ might be everything in the soul, to follow after Jesus who "humbled himself and became obedient to death ..." (Philippians 2:8 NIV), to follow Christ to the table of *eucharisteo*, the table of surrender that gives thanks for what is given—this is *joy*! True humility is self-smallness to the point of "blessed self-forgetfulness" and what could bring more happiness than emptying of self-will and being wholly immersed in the will of God for this moment? Joy—it's always obedience.

I know it deeper now: This *eucharisteo* is no game of Pollyanna but the hard edge of blade.

Only self can kill joy.

I take a long deep breath. I step from the stairs, stairs that have led all the way down into this.

I kneel down into a mess of glass.

I have known this place. I remember the red tears and the cutting away pain, and was this careless breaking of glass really about all the cares that made me break glass long ago? This time, I know healing. *Eucharisteo* makes the knees the vantage point of a life and I bend and the body, it says it quiet: "Thy will be done." *This* is the way a body and a mouth say thank you: *Thy will be done.* This is the way the self dies, falls into the arms of Love.

This is why. This is why the fight for joy is always so hard.

"No one who ever said to God, 'Thy will be done,' and meant it with his heart, ever failed to find joy—not just in heaven, or even down the road in the future in this world, but in this world *at that very moment*," asserts Peter Kreeft. "Every other Christian who has ever lived has found exactly the same thing in his own experience. It is an experiment that has been performed over and over again billions of times, always with the same result."[7]

I am kneeling in glass and my memories of shattered glass and Jesus comes soft, "Thy will be done is My own joy story, child, from beginning to end."

And I think of Jesus' beginning, His supernatural conception. His mother bends the knee and submits her will to God's: "Let this happen to me as you say!" (Luke 1:38 NCV). This is a woman, a womb, a hand humbly opening to the perfect will of God. Jesus' mother sings over the dividing cells of His divinity: "How my spirit rejoices in God my Savior! For he took notice of his lowly servant girl.... He has brought down princes from their thrones and exalted the humble. He has filled the hungry with good things." (Luke 1:47–48, 52–53). In Mary's humility—her willingness to die to her expectations and plans—God exalts her. In her submissiveness to His will, He fills her emptiness with fullness of Himself.

Her refrain of humble, surrendered gratitude quietly sings through all ages.

I think of the end of His earthly life. Jesus Himself bends the knee in a garden and weeps His own song: "Father, if you are willing, take this cup from me; yet not my will, but yours be done" (Luke 22:42 NIV). He opens wide His mouth and accepts; He will drink this cup of suffering too. Why? For the greater joy. Joy now, joy forever. Conceived in grateful humility, Jesus faces death in grateful humility. And I hear it soft too, what all His life speaks: Joy is in the acquiescing.

A circle of children stand around me, watching, waiting. Long slivers of transparency, blades, lie before me, catching light.

I humbly open my hand.

Without a word, one by one, they come to the outer edges and they kneel too.

And I humbly open my hand to release my will to receive His, to accept His wind. I accept the gift of now as it is — *accept God* — for I can't be receptive to God unless I receive what He gives. Joy's light flickers, breathes, fueled by the will of God — fueled by Him.

A shaft filters through an afternoon window and the cracks of the aged wood revive in sun.

I pray.

I let go. Lay the hand open. The sun slides across old hairline scars.

My palm holds light.

empty to fill

> Use me then, my Savior,
> for whatever purposes and in whatever way you may require.
> Here is my poor heart, an empty vessel;
> fill it with your grace.
> *D. L. Moody*

I wake to rain in October, water upon panes.

Autumn comes quietly to wed the countryside. The maples all down the lane blush and silently disrobe. I make beds, smooth out sheets.

In the kitchen, I light a candle and the wick bows, a willing flame. A fire flickers in the hearth, slow warmth in slow time for a slow rain.

On the rim of the world, edge of a cornfield gilded, I listen to rain fall shy on the roof, on the corn's rustling leaves, leaves of the dead still standing. Dead leaves of cornstalks, thousands, touch, like bows across strings, making music like water. Like running water. Fields make music with sky, with that sea come looking for dry land, and rivulets course quiet down glass. Gray clouds track low, head east. I lay breakfast bowls out on the table.

Soon those children, that fine man, will come in hungry

from the barn. Silver spoons, stainless steel cups, enamelware pitcher of milk, farm honey. I stand for a moment by the table, looking out a wet window to the south. One comes now, a son with his hood pulled up against early morning rain. I watch him, love of ours, meandering up the back walk. His head is bent low, feet finding all the puddles. He's splashing through ancient water, water from the beginning that has cycled through all centuries, puddle-jumped by a thousand young boys through the ages and I wonder if the water Adam knew falls here.

The clothesline strings across the back walk. Droplets reel out, a jeweled necklace, framing now. From one forgotten clothespin hangs a singular raindrop. And I see: the clothesline is the beam, the wooden clothespin an upright post. I see a cross in the clothespin. Son looks up, sees me at the window, and he waves, all a smile.

The droplet falls from the cross clothespin, grace upon us.

And for a moment, longer, long, I blaze.

This child, this time, this day, we are all here, grace, all grace, and this fountain of Great Grace falls all around and it could flow through us and on into the world, and with borrowed breath I am fueled, a torch in October rains.

I am blessed.

I *can* bless.

So this is happiness.[1]

I set the honey down on the table laid out and I wave back at my son and he laughs in the rain. I am a flame to light other flames.

In the October mist, *eucharisteo* opens the eyes, the heart, to the grace that falls upon us, a drop, a river, a waterfall of blessing filling our emptiness. It falls into the open hand and makes life a paradise again. We wonder: If *eucharisteo* had led us to let go and open the hand to receive all His shimmering river of gifts, how can we now close the hand?

If I close these fingers, try to hold, hoard the river—dam up the grace—won't the water grow stagnant? Long the children and I once looked at photos of the dead Dead Sea, and we read how the Jordan River streams into the sea and nothing flows out of the sea and the salt content rises and everything dies. I think of this. That fullness grows foul. Grace is alive, living waters. If I dam up the grace, hold the blessings tight, joy within dies ... waters that have no life.

I turn my hand over, spread my fingers open. I receive grace. And through me, grace could flow on. Like a cycle of water in continuous movement, grace is meant to fall, a rain ... again, again, again. I could share the grace, multiply the joy, extend the table of the feast, enlarge the paradise of His presence. I am blessed. I *can* bless. A life *contemplating* the blessings of Christ becomes a life *acting* the love of Christ.

I listen to wind in the corn, rain on the pane, and I find my place. All the lost pieces are finding their place.

The name I had lost back at the beginning—Ann, full of grace—weren't these a few more of the pieces? *Eucharisteo* was laying bare my realest self, revealing my true birthright— the endless riches of His grace. *The endless riches of His grace.* I am naming grace and I am finding my name and over the course of months, years, I am becoming, I am returning. I am Ann, full of grace, and I am blessed and couldn't I bless and couldn't this fullness flow on and on and on and this could be happiness? Are these the long lost pieces of name with three letters?

Skies clear.

A Thursday morning, I flip pancakes and the phone rings. The youth pastor. I don't have children old enough to even be in youth group. He wonders if I'm interested in serving with our youth group for a weekend on the streets of Toronto. I remember the streets of Toronto. My first panic attack was on those streets, city that choked me tight. I was then the age of many of the kids in youth I'd be chaperoning. Could I go back, live full on those same streets, now be full of His grace? Was this the way I might bless? And is any opportunity we are given to let the fullness of grace flow on, the opportunity we always should take? The pieces lie uncovered, ready for the taking. The call seems from God. I say yes. *Yes!*

This is my place, openhanded.

Who could have known how grace would fall and on whom?

The youth group walks down Yonge Street, Toronto's main drag, toward the Yonge Street Mission, a bit of November stealing into an October night. Last of the light seeps out of the gold of the trees and I linger behind, dig hands deeper into pockets, look for a vestige of warmth. A grey chill is creeping up the wet pavement. Cars hiss by in thickening twilight. It's going to be a long night out here.

A long night doing what we've come to do, to bless Christ in the other. A night not walking wide of the crumpled hurt, not looking the other way like we normally do, not a night about us and our agendas and getting to wherever we're going because isn't the place we always really want to go to, the place of seeing God? But I still almost miss him standing there, there in the shadows, a wild mane of graying hair, back to me, in front of the mission's front entrance. I'm focused on the kids. Trying to ignore the cold. It's easy to forget the how of happiness, to shift the focus and forget to let the stream flow on. And it's him, his tribe, we've come to bless, be blessed by. Before I reach the entrance of the mission, the bulk of a man steps out in front of me, walks toward our cluster of kids on the street. His buddy stays in the shadows, swigging long out of a one-liter pop bottle. Something inside tightens fear, twists hard.

Marisa and Hadassah and Erica are up ahead, kids from the country huddled together, hands drawn up into warmth of coat sleeves, waiting for staff from the Center for Student Missions to meet us, give us directions. Tyler and Dan and J. D. are closer to the street, checking out models of cars flashing by. I can hear Dan's voice above the others, "Catch that little bimmer? Sweet." Kids mingle, joke, laugh, wait.

I'm a few steps behind this bulk of back and tangled hair when I see the man raise his hands to his face. He pulls down a mask. He's pulling down a mask, walking into the center of our youth group. I walk faster.

From behind, I can see the man's hands wildly gesticulating, and he must be saying something, but I can't make out his words, words muffled under the mask. For a moment, he turns and I see clearly the garish plastic of a clown's mask. Over his shoulder, I can see the uneasiness of our group standing outside the mission, Marisa's eyes, Hadassah's ashen face. My blood courses fast and I try to remember: trust. *No matter what unfolds here, He is always good and we are always loved. Let go.*

I catch a phrase.

"Why you think I'm wearing this %*$& mask? Hey? Why?"

Hadassah steps back. The raspy voice yells louder, leans into these farm kids.

"Why would I wear a *$% mask like this?"

Erica scuffs her shoe at the crack in the sidewalk. None of us know what to do with this. It's not on the itinerary. One never knows what it will cost to bless.

Then the man rips the mask from his face and the blade of his howl slashes at us all stiffened to this spot here.

"I'm wearing the &%$& mask to mask my feelings."

He shakes the painted rubber face in his hand. "I'm masking the real me! Know what I mean?"

The heart jolts. I have never heard the whole human condition spoken so baldly, and from the unexpected lips, and I want to raise a hand to my own face, see if I can peel off mine.

There are words, drifting ones, but I can't hear them. Only see his wide shoulders shudder. Erica looks up. Tyler chews his lip. And the night air on Yonge Street fills with this guttural moan, this pitched wail.

It's the exposing of a naked soul.

He's crying. Sobbing. I catch snatches ... "I'm so *&$** up ... Jesus ... Savior ... need ... know what I mean?... Just so ... Jesus ... Lord ... know what I mean?"

Bared, he writhes, storms past me, a flurry of tears, hair, hands. A chaperone from our group calls softly after: "Jesus loves you ..."

He stops. Half turning, he tries to steady his voice between the wracking of sadness, tries to find the face that went with that voice. "Yeah, He does. And He loves you too, lady."

I don't know what any of this means. The wind whips at his hair. He blusters down the street. Has any grace fallen from our presence in this place?

When the staff from the mission, our drivers, arrive, our group is quieted, shaken. They direct us to enter the mission. And at the door, there he is, mask still in hand.

He has unfinished business.

His eyes dart, desperate, driven. His buddy keeps guzzling it down. But there's more to this story, lines he's got wrong, parts we haven't understood. I study his face, I read his eyes, eyes asking what eyes silently plead: "Do you have time to really listen?" The traffic whistles by. Yes, we have time. What is time for if not to bless?

"Hey, I'm sorry, OK?" the man bellows. "I've got issues, know what I mean? I'm like, bipolar."

His buddy spews his drink, mocking. "You're not bipolar." Like graffiti, he smears the words across the coming dark. But the scoffing doesn't deter. It's us he's got to say something to, whatever *this* is.

"Hey, I'm *&%$* messed up, man. Look at me!" He steps into the company of young people. Some look away. "Look at me!" His rage shakes us. Shakes the drowsy, shakes the slumbering, shakes us to look at what we really came to see, to look straightway into it and really open the soul wide *to see* and it terrifies.

His nose is crooked, busted up somewhere, healed all wrong. His mouth clings to a few brown teeth. His skin is pocked, ruddy, and his eyes look like a childhood friend's. Maybe he's my age.

"I'm a **%$& retard. Fried my brain on crack, know what I mean? Got a pacemaker in here." He pounds his chest. "OD'd just down there," he waves his hand toward a side street, "and it took them five hours to find me. Don't do crack, know what I mean?" His eyes are fiery, searching the faces of these country kids. "Don't get &*%*$ messed up like I did. Love your mom and dad cuz they love you, know what I mean?" He is choking back emotion. So am I.

I wonder where they are, his parents, if they know he's here, like this, if they care that he's in all this strangling torture. I care. I think I do. What do you do with all this grizzled pain? What do you do to dress these oozing, gory wounds, what do you do to be a healing grace to a soul mangled in skin with a fried brain? I stuff my hands deeper in pockets and I am the one who feels utterly bankrupt before a homeless man and I give all I really have. I pray. He rummages in his duffel bag, looking for something. What's he trying to do? What's He trying to do?

My arms stiffen hard and the pockets don't go deep enough. The kids search each other's eyes. Nobody knows what comes next in a night, a life, unscripted.

He straightens. He has something in his hand. He shoves it at Erica.

It's a dog-eared Bible. A Gideon Bible.

"Read Romans 7 to 8." He shakes his finger at the grubby cover.

I can hardly hear over the traffic, the rumble of the city.

"Louder. So they hear you!"

Then comes Erica's voice, calmed by these words she knows and the Person in them.

" … I do not understand what I do. For what I want to do …"

And a low bass throbs.

It's his voice. He's mumbling the words from memory, his eyes penetrating, his hand keeping beat with each word Erica reads. "… but what I hate I do."

It's like he's directing an orchestra with those grimy hands, the refrain of his life, beating out the Words that reverberate with his brokenness. The traffic blurs by blind and the night sets in cold and I am stilled inside, rapt, freeze-framing this image in my mind, this scene on life's stage of a man whose cerebellum is scalded with fraudulent relief but he knows the lines, the God-words branded deeper, right into his core. His fingernails are so dirty.

" ... I know that nothing good lives in me, that is, in my sinful nature." He slurs some of the words, stumbles. Erica reads on and he marks each word with a swaying hand, his voice echoing hers: "For I have the desire to do what is good, but I cannot carry it out."

He's rocking his whole body to the cadence of ancient words, this cry that his flesh weeps. He turns my way and I look into tearing eyes, his begging eyes, " ... *What a wretched man I am!*"

He has torn it off like a rind. The masks. Those words say who he is. Who we are. Here stands the cold, bare skin of a soul. Can I, just my eyes, hold him?

I know these last lines of the chapter, for they are mine too, and I speak them with them: "Who will rescue me from this body of death? Thanks be to God—through Jesus Christ our Lord!"

Grace.

The mission worker speaks to him in low tones. Our group spills past and into the mission, escapes. He holds open the door. I am the last one to trickle by.

I can't walk by without looking into him. I turn and we are face-to-face. I feel no panic, no attack of anxiety. His eyes implore and his gravelly voice begs, "Did I get it right this time?"

I'm busted open.

Do I do any of the good I long to do?

Did I bless?

Am I blessing?

We are two looking into the other. All the world falls away. I know. *I know. This is happiness.*

I speak *eucharisteo*, the only words I can muster.

"Thank you."

I say the words slowly, hope they soak into his pores, broken man who yearns to bless, and I am him and he is me and behind the masks we are all the same. All, we only find joy in the blessings that are taken, broken, and given.

I nod and smile and somewhere find the courage to say it slow again, sure, so he knows.

He is broken and he has given.

"Thank you."

Our eyes do hold the other.

On Yonge Street, we enact *eucharisteo*.

On a Toronto street corner, he has begged for grace.

The grace to be the blessing.

And on a Toronto street corner, I have been more of my true name.

His face, his voice, his story, they saturate me. When I open my Bible later, to read of Jesus at the Last Supper, again I am with him, an untamed mane on Yonge Street who took off all our masks and howled our collective cry to not just take the blessing, but *be the blessing.*

The snow flies. The amaryllis blooms in the windowsill. Life buds tender in winter, and I read:

> The evening meal was being served.... He got up from the meal, took off his outer clothing, and wrapped a towel around his waist. After that, he poured water into a basin and began to wash his disciples' feet, drying them with the towel that was wrapped around him....
>
> When he had finished washing their feet, he put on his clothes and returned to his place. "Do you understand what I have done for you?" he asked them. "You call me 'Teacher' and 'Lord,' and rightly so, for that is what I am. Now that I, your Lord and Teacher, have washed your feet, you also should wash one another's feet. I have set you an example that you should do as I have done for you." (John 13:2, 4, 12–15 NIV)

Jesus is about to let flesh be broken with nail, heart be broken with rejection, the chains be broken with bleeding love. And in His last hours before His earthly end, He doesn't run out to buy something or catch a flight to go see something, but He wraps a towel around his waist and kneels low to take the feet of His forsakers gently in hand and wash away the grime between their toes.

This is the full-bodied *eucharisteo*, the *eucharisteo* that touches body and soul: hands and knees and feet awash in grace.

At the last, this is what will determine a fulfilling, meaningful life, a life that, behind all the facades, every one of us longs to live: gratitude for the blessings that expresses itself by *becoming the blessing*.

Eucharisteo is giving thanks for grace. But in the breaking and giving of bread, in the washing of feet, Jesus makes it clear that *eucharisteo* is, yes, more: *it is giving grace away. Eucharisteo* is the hand that opens to receive grace, then, with thanks, breaks the bread; that moves out into the larger circle of life and washes the feet of the world with that grace. Without the breaking and giving, without the washing of feet, *eucharisteo* isn't complete. The Communion service is only complete *in service*. Communion, by necessity, always leads us into community.

I hadn't fully seen it until after that night on Yonge Street: *Eucharisteo* means "to give thanks," and *give* is a verb, something that we do. God calls me *to do* thanks. *To give the thanks away.* That thanks-*giving* might literally become thanks-*living*. That our lives become the very blessings we have received.

I am blessed. I *can* bless. *Imagine!* I could let Him make *me* the gift!

I could *be* the joy!

I scour pots and grin silly: I can wash feet here by washing dishes. My heart can enter into communion anywhere and anywhere my hands can enact the Eucharist! The tap water runs hot over my hands and I rinse steel. The world gleams. Christ's ministry began with His miracle of turning water into wine at the marriage feast in Cana. And at the close of His earthly ministry, Christ turns from the wine of the Last Supper back to the water, the water for the washing of feet.

Always and again: *Eucharisteo* precedes the miracle.

This is one of His miracles too: the taking of a life and making it a blessing.

Scratching a stubborn pot furiously with a wire scrubby, I remember it again, what I once read of liturgy. That *liturgy* has its roots in the Greek word *leitourgia*, meaning "public work" or "public servant." The meaning! This life of washing dishes, of domestic routine, it can be something wholly different. This life of rote work, it is itself public work, a public serving — even this scrubbing of pans — and thus, if done unto God, the mundane work can become the living liturgy of the Last Supper. *I could become the blessing, live the liturgy!* I rinse pots and sing it softly, "This is my song of thanks to You ..."

In the moment of singing that one line, dedicating the work as thanks to Him, something — the miracle — happens, and every time. When service is unto people, the bones can grow weary, the frustration deep. Because, agrees Dorothy Sayers, "whenever man is made the centre of things, he becomes the storm-centre of trouble. The moment you think of serving people, you begin to have a notion that other people owe you something for your pains.... You will begin to bargain for reward, to angle for applause."[2]

When the laundry is for the dozen arms of children or the dozen legs, it's true, I think I'm due some appreciation. So comes a storm of trouble and lightning strikes joy. But when Christ is at the center, when dishes, laundry, work, is my song of thanks to Him, joy rains. Passionately serving Christ alone makes us the loving servant to all. When the eyes of the heart focus on God, and the hands on always washing the feet of Jesus alone — the bones, they sing joy, and the work returns to its purest state: *eucharisteo.* The work becomes worship, a liturgy of thankfulness.

"The work we do is only our love for Jesus in action," writes Mother Teresa. "If we pray the work ... *if we do it to Jesus, if we do it for Jesus, if we do it with Jesus* .... that's what makes us content."[3]

That is what makes us content — the contented, deep joy is always in the touching of Christ—in whatever skin He comes to us in.

I want the contentment, the real happiness, the touching of Christ in the work and I look for Him. We invite a young woman in an abusive relationship to come to live at our place for a season. I write words that line themselves into books and four times a year we give away the proceeds from those projects to Africa to supply a medical clinic, fill a stable, dig a well, more. We give the blessing of presence to elderly in nursing homes. Ten years, all eight of us, we don't exchange Christmas gifts but give sewing machines, chickens, coats, food, hope to those in need in our global family. We write letters, share ourselves, with our sponsor children through relief organizations. I become an advocate for Compassion International, a Christian child development ministry, and I campaign for the sponsorship of more children. We gather bikes and eight of us ride in Ride for Refugees, raising awareness and funds for displaced families around the world. Our children laugh and pump the air with happiness that they've given more of their lives away and I feel the smile that spreads across a life.

~)

> Christian hands never clasp
> and He doesn't give gifts for gain
> because a gift can never stop being a gift—
> it is always meant to be given.

~)

In an endless cycle of grace, He gives us gifts to serve the world. This is how to make a life great and *eucharisteo* embarks us on the path: "Whoever wants to be a leader among you must be your servant, and whoever wants to be first among you must become your slave" (Matthew 20:26–27).

Outside my window, the whole of creation chooses just this. The leaves of the maple tree freely unfurl oxygen, clouds overhead grow pregnant with rain to bless, the soil of our fields offer up yield. All His created world throbs with the joy in *eucharisteo*: "It is more blessed to give than to receive" (Acts 20:35).

This is the way Jesus Himself chose. "That is what the Son of Man has done: He came to serve, not be served—and then to give away his life in exchange for the many who are held hostage" (Matthew 20:28 MSG).

It's the astonishing truth that while I serve Christ, it is He who serves me. Jesus Christ still lives with a towel around His waist, bent in service to His people ... in service to me, as I serve, that I need never serve in my own strength. Jesus Christ, who came into this world "not to be served but to serve others and to give his life as a ransom for many" (Mark 10:45), will one day come again and "put on an apron, and serve them as they sit and eat!" (Luke 12:37), and even this very day He faithfully serves that we might say, "The LORD is my helper" (Hebrews 13:6).

Every day for a month we as a family read together Isaiah 58 and we can't get over it and we come to know it in the marrow and the fiber:

> *Feed the hungry,*
> *and help those in trouble.*
> *Then your light will shine out from the darkness,*
> *and the darkness around you will be as bright as noon.*

> *The LORD will guide you continually,*
> *giving you water when you are dry*
> *and restoring your strength.*
> *You will be like a well-watered garden,*
> *like an ever-flowing spring. (Isaiah 58:10– 11)*

It's the fundamental, lavish, radical nature of the upside-down economy of God.

Empty to fill.

While the Deceiver jockeys to dupe us into thinking otherwise, we who are made in the image of God, being formed into Christ's likeness, our happiness comes, too, not in the having but in the handing over. Give your life away in exchange for many lives, give away your blessings to multiply blessings, give away so that many might increase, and do it all for the love of God. I can bless, pour out, be broken and given in our home and the larger world and never fear that there won't be enough to give. *Eucharisteo* has taught me to trust that there is always enough God. He has no end. He calls us to serve, and it is Him whom we serve, but He, very God, kneels down to serve us as we serve. The servant-hearted never serve alone. Spend the whole of your one wild and beautiful life investing in many lives, and God simply will not be outdone. God extravagantly pays back everything we give away and exactly in the currency that is not of this world but the one we yearn for: *Joy in Him.*

In early spring, the trees that were losing their leaves when I drove away to Yonge Street now come again to bud. It rains. I drive into town, the windshield wipers rocking back and forth in the rain. I'm gathering with a women's small group at Roberta Fryers' bungalow, one with the sign "The

Thai Trio" hanging over the mailbox, home to three elderly women who spent the whole of their lives being the blessing, missionaries in Thailand. Women meet in Roberta's entrance with embraces. Nancy Martin has interceded in prayer for me for years, calls me her other daughter, and makes these honey-dripping, old-fashioned doughnuts that are ravishing. Anne Peterson and Ann Van den Boogaard, mothers to a collective tribe of eighteen, both smile, nod, and I take my place at the table and now we are complete, The Trio of Anns seeking to be full of grace. The rain is falling harder on the windowpanes. We circle together with Effie Struyk and Mary Cook, and as a community, we take Communion. I bow and pray over bread. And when I break it, I remember a body broken and His heart torn open, and I break open. Love falls, a tear. I pass the bread. For a long while we are stilled and deeply moved.

Then, quietly, I fill the basins with water warm.

Circled together as a community, we give communion. We bare our toes, soles, and I bend with sisters in Christ, dip my hands into water, and touch shy skin. We wash feet, all around, we wash feet. We lap water across skin and I hold a woman's heel and I gently bathe and as group facilitator, I ask each of us in the room to think about this washing of feet as symbolic of our lives on a grand scale, of how we are called to complete the Communion service in service. I tilt my head to look into her face and I ask it quiet in a quiet room: "Do you, in your day-to-day life, feel served? How might we as a community better serve you?"

And she, mother of eight, an elder's wife, children's ministry leader, one who pours her life out in unending ways, she whispers, haltingly through emotion. "But I'm the one who needs to ask if I've been a blessing."

I hear the echo of a voice on Yonge Street.

"But you—*oh, how you have blessed*." With the tepid water, I wash her toes, these beads between fingers, and I recount the long string of ways she's intimately blessed me: "The day you took me for a walk through the woods and you listened to the faint heartbeat of my faith. The countless words you have sent me, a hand of friendship." I take the cloth and wash her heel. "The way you have been real with me, transparent and authentic, and we have been mothers and we have been sisters and we have wept." And I look up into her face, her wet feet in my hands, and again the chin wobbles all feeling. In this room of women, washing feet, it overflows. With memories of the ways each has become the blessing. Unmasked, we wash our faces in tears of joy. Hands cupping dripping soles, I see how it is our very presence in each other's lives that makes us the gift. It is by the very function of our being, *not our doing*, that we are the beloved of God. And so we *become* the love of God, blessing those He loves.

The God of Abraham is the God of Yonge Street is the God of the women bent over basins, God who answers our pleas for a fulfilling life with His promise: "I will bless you ... *and you will be a blessing*" (Genesis 12:2 NIV, emphasis added).

I walk out to the street through rain, grace falling all around, and I drive home thinking of my brother-in-law, John. John, who had buried his two sons, who let me into his healing through crazy grief when he said, "The way through the pain is to reach out to others in theirs." I have known ache and becoming the blessing is what deeply blesses us and this is the way He binds up our wounds.

Empty to fill.

I walk in our back door to candlelight still flickering, hang the keys on the hook, and look around at the steep mountain of laundry there in the mudroom, the shoes scattered, a coat dropped. The mudroom sink is grime ringed. Fingerprints smear across the mirror. I laugh the happiest wonder. In the afternoon's drizzle, I give happy thanks for the daily mess with a smile a mile wide, because this is again my chance to wholeheartedly serve God, to do full-bodied *eucharisteo* with the hands and the heart and the lips. I can count each task a gift, pure *eucharisteo*. *Grace!* This work — the thousand endless jobs — they each give the opportunity for one to *become* the gift, *a thousand times over*! Because with every one of the thousand, endless jobs, I become the gift to God and to others because this work is the public God serving, the daily liturgy of thanks, the completing of the Communion service with my service.

Eucharisteo wakens me wide-eyed and nodding to the words of Tagore that I, a mother of six, now own, bought with the practice of *eucharisteo*, "I slept and dreamt life was joy, I awoke and saw life was service, I acted and, behold, *service was joy*."[4]

I reach out and touch the reflection in the splattered mirror over the sink and whisper into those eyes: Yes, today, *again*, yes, *you can bless!* Here you can enact *eucharisteo*; here you can become a current in a river of grace that redeems the world!

Here I can become the blessing, a little life that multiplies joy, making the larger world a better place.

God can enter into me, even me, and use these hands, these feet, to be His love, a love that goes on and on and on forever, endless cycle of grace.

I am nearing the wonder of Communion.

the joy of intimacy

I think we delight to praise what we enjoy
because the praise not merely expresses
but completes the enjoyment;
it is its appointed consummation.

C. S. Lewis

I fly to Paris and discover how to make love to God.

It's June, after all—Paris in June. I had long felt the stirrings of something more, but how could I have known what a love like this will really mean? It's June and the wheat heads are filling out right to the ends.

My friend Linda, the same who had first dared me to jot down one thousand gifts, now over eighteen months ago, she's rented a flat in Paris for six weeks in early summer, right on the Seine, across from the Louvre, down from Notre Dame. Would I like to come and stay a week with her?

The agoraphobic farm hick who has spent a lifetime wrestling fears? Jetting off to Paris? Flying solo to a foreign country to stay a week with a woman she knows only as a voice at the other end of a telephone line? My sister laughs, uncertain, and my mama raises her eyebrows. "You may never have a chance to see Paris again, Ann. We'll be good. Just go!"

He had smiled, winked, a farmer telling his wife to fly. And if I have a panic attack? And if I miss one of the connections between here and the nearly four thousand miles to there? Or if the plane crashes? I have no idea what those seven days in Paris could hold. I think that's the point.

Wasn't it time to fully live?

Hadn't counting one thousand gifts, counting on endlessly, counting on *eucharisteo*, hadn't it begun to deep heal the soul holes so I could be the wing that takes to the sky in peace? Eagerly celebrate His gifts wherever I find them?

The wind blows through the fields and those heads of wheat, they murmur, old wives whispering *go, go.* I do.

I go and they stand under the shade of the maple, all six of the love-children, and that chiseled Dutch man stands tall behind them, and with hand that has held me he holds our youngest. They all wave, wave like banners in the wind, and I'll carry the memory of the ocean-blue eyes all across the Atlantic. I watch them long in the rearview mirror and I am an amnesiac being healed, for I really remember that *eucharisteo* has taught me to trust. I leave crops in the field and a husband with half a dozen children. There are a thousand ways to humbly let go.

At the airport I wait with pocket Bible in hand, wait for the boarding of Flight TS788, that plane that will wing me away from their faces with the freckles sprinkled, hair with the cowlick and the curl. *Could I please have a few good verses, Lord— something to hang on to?* Just a few to calm the jittery nerves, for that, oh, stomach lurching up into throat, that crazed, bloodshot panic that wants to scream, "What in the world was I thinking?" Planes explode and people die and the man next to me, two days' growth and long hair hanging in eyes, he

strums a guitar, melodic strains. *OK, Lord—a psalmist's song?*
A David sent for a Saul vexed in spirit? That'll do fine. I read
the open Scripture, lean back into notes soothing and a divine
sense of humor. When the shaggy shepherd stands, slings the
guitar case over his shoulder, our eyes meet. I whisper, "Thank
you." He accepts the gift.

I board, breathe, buckle, bow my head, and murmur thanks
to Him who never takes leave. It's impossible to give thanks
and simultaneously feel fear. This is the anti-anxiety medicine
I try to lay in my wide-open palm every day. *Thank You, God,*
for surprising songs.

The plane flies; I cocoon in God.

It's an hour or two of blackness, a brief layover, and a long
stretch of darkness before I can see it out of the plane's portal
window: sun rising red over Greenland. The world tilts scarlet.
We fly into the light splitting back the dark. I press my cheek
into the cold of the windowpane, wanting the whole of the
erupting horizon. Happiness burns like a longing, and over
the wing and the whir of the propellers, forty thousand feet
over earth, I can hear Him, singing, waking the world. He's
singing that song! The one I really didn't believe He sang! "He
will take delight in you with gladness. With his love, he will
calm all your fears. He will rejoice over you with joyful songs"
(Zephaniah 3:17).

He sings love! In the air, over the world, I can *see* the song,
the ardency of the notes pulsing in colors. The curve of the
world burns ruby, a jewel prying open the day. And I can
see in: Love is the face at the center of our universe. A sacred
Smile; Holiness ready to die for intimacy. Light and waves and
land and sky crescendo in passion and He serenades, "How do
I love thee?"

I count the ways.

Memory of their freckled noses crinkled in laughter
Flying through black (we fly!) into celestial radiance
A window seat and eyes for this

In *eucharisteo*, I count, count, count, keeping the beat of His song, the love song He can't stop singing, this long song of longing. That He sings love *over me*?

What else can all these gifts mean?

Crazy, I know, but until *eucharisteo* had me write the graces on paper, in my own handwriting, until it alerted my mind to see the graces in the details of my very own life, I hadn't really known. With every grace, He sings, "You are precious to me. You are honored, and I love you" (Isaiah 43:4). "For you are a chosen people ... God's very own possession" (1 Peter 2:9).

I was afraid? I would have let fears that He wasn't close, wasn't passionately caring, wasn't tenderly tending, keep me from seeing this sunrise bleeding love up over all the world? Now that would have been crazy! Look at that love that orchestrates red over water, that arranges light to play ocean in shimmering lines, that composes sky to gradate, scale of luminosity. And all for us — in this moment! He chose me — us! To be His bride! True, that's the intellectual premise of the Christian life, but only as the gifts are attended, not as ends but as means to gaze into the heart of God, does the premise become personal, God's choosing so utterly passionate. *So utterly fulfilling.*

It's a new voice, this endless stream of grace, one I never get over. This love song He is singing, it is the antithesis of life's theme song, that refrain of rejection I know so well. That mental soundtrack of condemnation and criticism that I've let run on continuous replay, lyrics I learned from the grade three boys huddled on the ice, exploding laughter when my skates slid east, west, and I fell south, from the trendy city girl moved to the country who snickered at my thrift store shirts, from the critical eye of every evaluator, judge, assessment, grade. That heavy beat of failure, a pounding bass of disappointment, it has pulsed through my days and I've mouthed the words, singing it to myself, memorizing the ugly lines by heart. They become the heart. For years, I tried medication, blade, work, escape, all attempts to drown out that incessant, reverberating drum of self-rejection. All futility, acidic emptiness.

But here on a plane over black waters, I hear it well: the only thing to rip out the tape echoing of self-rejection is the song of His serenade. One thousand gifts tuned me to the beat. It really is like C. S. Lewis argued: that the most fundamental thing is not *how we think of God* but rather *what God thinks of us*: "How God thinks of us is not only more important, but infinitely more important."[1] Years of Christian discipleship, Bible study, churchgoing had been about me thinking *about* God; practicing *eucharisteo* was the very first I had really considered at length what God *thought of me*—this ridiculous and relentlessly pursuing love, so bold. Everywhere, everything, Love!

Giving thanks awakens me to a God giving Himself, the naked, unashamed passion, God giving Himself *to me*—for me—a surrender of love. "Gratitude is the most fruitful way of deepening your consciousness that you are ... a divine choice," wrote Henri Nouwen.[2] A divine choice! He chooses His children to *fully* live! Fully live the fullest life: the astonished gratitude, the awed joy, the flying and the free. The discipline of giving thanks, of unwrapping one thousand gifts, unwraps

God's heart bare: *I choose you. Live!* Over Greenland, I hear the beat of his heart, that song, crystal clear: "I have loved you," says the LORD (Malachi 1:2 NIV), "I have loved you with an everlasting love; I have drawn you with loving-kindness" (Jeremiah 31:3 NIV).

In a thousand ways He woos.

In a thousand ways I fall in love.

Isn't falling in love always the fullest life?

How can I know what this Love will really mean?

The plane descends and from my seat I can spot fields of wheat and they wave here too, a welcome. *A welcome.* I take a deep breath and smile. *Gift.*

When we land, I find the baggage claim and I wait and this is all I can think: I am falling in love. Falling into being fully alive. I tuck a lost strand behind my ear; the heart beats loud in the ears.

In the airport, in the street, the voices are foreign, exotic, thick with travel and miles and I can't understand, can't respond. People stream, move me along, but everywhere I go, I'm accompanied by this Voice whispering to me new words, new love — urging me, *Respond, respond.*

Linda, in a black sweater and smile that warms straight through, she finds me in the melee and leads the way back to her flat, woman forging a way. I had caught a red-eye flight across the Atlantic, had flown into red sun rising, hadn't slept in over thirty-six hours, but when she asks if I'd like to stroll down to the city center, I nod yes, *yes*! Leaving bags up on the loft bed, we stroll to the traditional center of France, point zero of Paris marked in stone on the cobbled courtyard of Notre Dame. The Dame's perched gargoyles eye us. In the shadow of the church towers, not far from a statue of Charlemagne mounted on steed, old Parisian men sit watching the world stream by. Under our feet lie ruins of a Roman building, bits of stone from a long-buried medieval road, a crumbled wall that failed to keep the invading Franks out in AD 497. Tourists in black patent heels and Nike running shoes descend steps down into the crypt one hundred yards below the shadow of Notre Dame. But for me, it's those open doors calling.

Ornately carved, the massive doors of the Notre Dame lie open, arms receiving the weary and I am that. Even in the touristic whir of the courtyard, I can hear the singing. It's that song I've been hearing all day, all over the world. We thread through the crowd, drawn.

Under the carved central portal with its statues of the enthroned Christ, I crane the neck over the crowd and I can see a choir robed in white, ethereal, standing in Notre Dame's central nave. This air is old, the ground, holy. A triad of windowpanes, dark reds, vibrant blues, kaleidoscope of shifting shades, break out of the blackness behind the choir and all the light reverberates, shimmers. I can *see* this song. It fills all the vaulting space.

Their voices echo His love song.

Somewhere in the heights, the notes and spirits mingle.

Aria ascends and heads, they bow, and Linda and I shift for a clearer view into the light of the cathedral. Behind us a tourist bus grinds down the street and teens talk on cell phones. All around, screens glow with text messages, digitalized images. Bulbs flash. And where the crossbeams of the cross-shaped cathedral intersect, at Notre Dame's center, at Paris's center—at my center—on the altar table, I can see it and the breath lodges hard in the chest.

Bread and wine.

On the table in gold chalice, gold cup, gold circling all round, the Eucharist.

"While they were eating, Jesus took bread, gave thanks and broke it . . ." (Matthew 26:26 NIV).

How many miles have I traveled around this spinning planet and what does God again reveal as preeminent, as always the first step of entering in, the thing He can't stop calling me to do? Had I left the farm, left my small world, got on a plane to fly a whole night over watery depths, landed in Paris, the romance of France, traveled, yes, even to one of those thousand places you must see before you die, for God to speak to me the *exact* same word He had spoken to me back at the farm, had been speaking to me for months, a year and a half now — the same word He speaks everywhere?

Eucharisteo.

In the central nave, the cup is lifted high and my rusty French can't easily unravel the words but I'd know that inflection anywhere, that universal language, language we'll speak forever in heaven but could learn already here: gratitude, gratitude, *always eucharisteo.*

Do I know what this Love will really mean?

My eyes follow the stone arches rising over us, granite hands clasped in prayer over souls. I think of all who have gone before, the hands of medieval peasants who chiseled the stone under which I now stand. I think of those long-ago believers who had a way of entering into the full life, of finding a passage into God, a historical model of intimacy with God. I lean back to see the spires. I think how lives, whole generations, were laid down to build this edifice, to find a way in. But they thought the steps to the God-consummation were but three: purgation, illumination, union. Had my own

journey of transformation into the full life taken me on the
same pilgrimage of the ancients who had built and passed
under these stone arches?

Purgation was the first step toward full life in God,
according to ancients. Awakened to the chasm separating
from God, one prays for divine assistance to *purge* the soul
of self-will. And for me too, *eucharisteo* had gently slowed
me down, opened my hand to purge me of my hold, my
control, on the world. With each gift I had accepted and given
thanks for, I let go of my own will and accepted His. But my
purgation, this releasing of sin and self, wasn't an act of will
or effort, but the act of *Christ* and His grace all-sufficient.
Overwhelming grace drew me to the Christ full of glory that
I might empty of the self.

I empty to become full. Full of grace ... *to fully live.*

Illumination, the intermediary step in the path to full life
in God, so said the ancients. The seeker sees. What the ancient
saints called a vision of heaven, a way of seeing that draws one
closer to God. *Eucharisteo* had been *exactly* this for me, opening
my eyes to a way of seeing, to a realization that belief is, in
essence, a way of the eyes. The one thousand presents wake me
to the presence of God—but more so, living *eucharisteo*, living
in thanks, had done the far harder work of *keeping* me awake
to Him. I began to see that nothing I am counts for anything,
but all that I count of Him counts for everything—seeing eyes
might *illuminate* the glory of Christ in all.

I am all eye, seeing through life as glass to God.

Union, the medieval Christians thought, was the final and
culminating step in the hungry pursuit of the full life, the
mystical oneness achieved by only the most devout. *Union.*
Yet don't all the true believers, the ardent see-ers, have union

from the first moment of repentance, becoming *one with Christ* in His death, burial, and rising from the dead? Union is actually and always the first step of the Christ journey. And yet attending to grace upon grace ushers into an ever deepening union, one we experience on the skin and in the vein, feel in the deep pit of the being, an ever-fuller realization of the Christ communion.

Endless thanksgiving, *eucharisteo*, had opened me to this, the way of the fullest life. From initial union to intimate communion—it isn't exclusively the domain of the monastics and ascetics, pastors and missionaries, but I, domestic scrubber of potatoes, sister to Brother Lawrence, could I have unbroken communion, fullest life with fullest God? "To be a saint is to be fueled by gratitude, nothing more and nothing less," writes Ronald Rolheiser.[3]

Little had I known that counting one thousand gifts would launch me on a thousand-year-old journey of transformation. Would it really give me, the empty-handed and close-fisted, the gift of becoming fully alive, fully one? Do I even know what that really means?

Pigeon wings clap the air, land somewhere overhead, unafraid of the gaping mouthed gargoyles. My eyes fall upon the abutments of this door of the center west portal, carved with the five wise virgins and the five foolish virgins. Will I be one of the waiting, watching ... one longing for the Bridegroom? For the union? That feeling under the gothic door arches ... This feeling. I remember this feeling. The way my apron billowed in the running, the light, the air. The harvest moon. I remember. The yearning. To merge with Beauty Himself. But here ... now? Really? With Him utterly pure and me so soul ugly? I hold the side seam of my skirt in fingers clenched tight, Linda and I walking along the Seine in the warmth of June twilight.

I am not at all certain that I want consummation.

We pass the stalls that line the quays of the Seine, tourists browsing the old books, shelves of penciled sketches, the faded prints offered by *les bouquinistes*. Lovers hold hands. Everywhere, lovers in Paris. All I can think: real communion terrifies. And who wouldn't cower at the invitation to communion with limitless Holiness Himself? When I read the words of Walter Brueggemann, I nod fervently, my sentiments encapsulated exactly: "The shock of such a partner destabilizes us too much. The risk is too great, the discomfort so demanding. We much prefer to settle for a less demanding, less overwhelming meeting. Yet we are haunted by the awareness that only this overwhelming meeting gives life."[4] Yes, God as partner shocks and I'm too ugly, spiritually, physically, too filthy, too ... *low* to be courted by God and He lavishes His love, the uncontainable riches, and can I trust His love and part of me is right anxious to flee. Yet I *am* haunted. *Only* this overwhelming meeting gives the fullest life: the holy and hallowed communion. Do I know what that means?

Monday morning dawns. Quiet click of heels on the cobblestone of Rue Mazarine. Church bells intone morning. From the belfry of Saint-Séverin? — those ancient ones cast in 1412? He just can't stop singing, can He? I stir, reach for my pocket Bible.

"But the person who is joined to the Lord is one spirit with him," reads 1 Corinthians 6:17. I run my hand along the beams over my loft bed, wood hewn by a hand several hundred years ago. I can hear Him. He's calling for a response; He's calling for oneness. *Communion.*

Jesus says there is no other way to take up the faith but complete union: "I am in my Father, and you are in me, and I am in you" (John 14:20). I am stilled. I think on being in Christ and Him being in me and He is wind whisperer and I am leaf and He stirs and I tremble: "Remain in me, and I will remain in you" (John 15:4). He's calling me to graft on, become one with the True Vine, the vine the biblical symbol of joy, festivity . . . *fullness*. He's calling to come and *celebrate* being made one, and in Him, by Him, to bear the fruit of the full life round.

I see it clear, June coming in bright on the breeze through open window: there is no real reality, no full life, outside of the relationship with Love, because God Himself wraps Himself eternally in relationship: God the Father, God the Son, and God the Holy Spirit existing in relationship, an encircling dance of communion sweetest. God is love—*everywhere! everything!*—and He can only be love because He exists in triune *relationship*. Before I ever breathed or the earth ever spun, the love within the Godhead orbited, Father loving Son "before the creation of the world" (John 17:24 NIV) and when I am in union with Christ, I too am lavished with the love the Father has for the Son. *In union, that love is mine—ours!* I can't simply ignore His serenade because I'm unsure, uncomfortable, uninterested, thinking I've claimed Christ as my Savior already anyways. God *is* relationship and He woos us to relationship and there is nothing with God if there is no relationship.

I can hear Paris waking.

Cars humming down the Quai de Conti. The hushed whir of a bicycle, the closing of doors out on the street. I lay thinking. This invitation to have communion with Love—is this the edge of the mystery Paul speaks of? "'A man leaves his father and mother and is joined to his wife, and the two are united into one.' This is a great mystery, but it is an illustration of the way Christ and the church are one" (Ephesians 5:31–32). The two, Christ and the church, becoming one flesh—the mystery of that romance. Breath falling on face, Spirit touching spirit, the long embrace, the entering in and being within—this is what God seeks? With each of us?

Is this the apex of the dare to fully live?

I would later read the words of John Calvin, Protestant Reformer, and wonder fresh at the meaning of the mystery: "God very commonly takes on the character of a husband to us. Indeed, the union by which he binds us to himself when he receives us into the bosom of the church is like sacred wedlock."[5] And again, "Therefore that joining together of head and members, that indwelling of Christ in our hearts—in short that mystical union—are accorded by us the highest degree of importance."[6]

Mystical union. This, the highest degree of importance. God as Husband in sacred wedlock, bound together, body and soul, fed by His body, quenched by His blood—this is where *eucharisteo* leads. Lover bestows upon the Beloved gifts, the Beloved gives thanks for those gifts and enters into the mystical love union. If God, who could have any life of His choosing, finds the most satisfying joy in communion within the Trinity, wouldn't I?

I know and don't know why I am afraid.

How receptive to God do I really want to be?

"Morning ..." Linda's voice floats up to the loft. She's folding the blankets of her futon. First light is falling from the floor-to-ceiling balcony windows. "So, what's on your itinerary for Paris?"

Linda maps it out and over a handful of days, one by one,
I stroke off items on the penciled itinerary in my Moleskin:
the glass sanctuary of thirteenth-century Sainte-Chapelle,
the millions of fragments of colored transparency, suspended
like a delicate ornament, midair. (No one dare speak lest we
fall.) A day wandering the mirrored halls, groomed gardens,
of Versailles, gold shimmering in sun. (My heels bleed blisters
we walk so far.) The Eiffel Tower pierces the night sky, a
lightning rod electrified, and I snap too many photographs.
(Everywhere, shutters capturing, this the perfect backdrop for
lovers kissing in June dusk.) We walk streets of perfumiers,
boutiques, book shops, restaurants with full-size pigs on spits
slowly rotating in front windows. Everywhere, cathedral spires
penetrate sky. Each evening, I lie in my loft bed and across the
narrow blue lines of my come-with-me-everywhere gratitude
journal, under the title "June Gifts" I write a few more ...

> White-haired women lined at the grocery, baguettes dangling out
>   of baskets
> French waiters
> Pigeons on peaks of copper-green roofs
> Rusting bicycles with wire baskets, pedaling down narrow streets
> Blue-knickered boys digging in a sandbox in the shadow
>   of Notre Dame
> Keys jingling in the pocket of the janitor of Saint-Germain-des-Prés
>   as he bows to pray before the altar
> Blooming weeds in the cracks between cobblestone
> Tolling church bells

I think about union and what I'm skirting, what I'm drawn
to ... I turn out the light. I lie in the dark, waiting for sleep.
Waiting to know what this all means.

It is late on Friday afternoon when Linda and I wander the

Louvre, brave a whirring circus of shutters to catch a hint of
Mona Lisa's smile. But for me, the aura of the *Mona Lisa* isn't
how I will remember the Louvre. It's the mystery we enter into
in the upper chambers, heavy with the scent of God.

The notes lure. Throughout the galleries of the second
story, we can hear it faint, high and lilting, music drifting like
a fragrance. Aren't art galleries to be hushed, quiet affairs?
Where's the music coming from? The enigma of it keeps me
seeking, peering anxious around every corner. The beat grows
stronger, the words clearer, and then there in a large gallery,
entirely unexpected, I stumble clear into it: a choral ensemble
gathered in formal attire, black bottoms, white tops, their
perfectly formed mouths singing Wolfgang Amadeus Mozart's
Nocturnes 1 and 2.

A crowd fills the room; the man beside us in the doorway,
his head, shoulders, swaying the music indwelling. Jean
Restout's painting, *Pentecost*, hangs massive on a wall in front
of the ensemble and the director raises her hand for their voices
to scale heights. Listening to harmony, I attend to the canvas
before the choir: the Holy Spirit descending as flame upon the
heads of life-sized apostles. It's a vivid, dramatic imaging of
words I remember from Acts 2:4: "And everyone present was
filled with the Holy Spirit." God falling. God filling. *Union.
Fulfilling.* The notes pitch high and the heartstrings tremor.

Dare I respond?

The ensemble's striking upper octaves echo and I wander
reluctantly on, find myself in an adjacent gallery standing before
a gilded frame, a diminutive and unassuming work, directly at
eye level. A Rembrandt. The chorus holds a note long. These
brushstrokes, gold light soaking canvas, these glorious Rembrandt
strokes, they illuminate two sojourners leaning in awe at a table.

It's a Rembrandt of strangers at Emmaus eating with Christ.
Am I in the shadows behind the young servant, oblivious to the
miracle unveiling? Do I recognize Christ here, enter into Emmaus
epiphany? "When he was at the table with them, he took bread,
gave thanks, broke it and began to give it to them. Then their eyes
were opened and they recognized him" (Luke 24:30–31 NIV).

Eucharisteo—communion—that hound of heaven, He
won't relent, *always, everywhere, eucharisteo,* opening the eyes to
God.

Notes and song and that wooing love and He can't stop the
intimate pursuit, the passionate love and I dare the response, a
barely tremor, a hardly song. "Bless the LORD, O my soul: and
all that is within me, bless his holy name" (Psalm 103:1 KJV).

I peer at His hands holding bread. Then the crescendo.

Bless "the LORD, who daily loadeth us with benefits"
(Psalm 68:19 KJV). "Bless the LORD at all times: his praise shall
continually be in my mouth" (Psalm 34:1 KJV). "Enter into
his gates with thanksgiving, and into his courts with praise: be
thankful unto him, and bless his name" (Psalm 100:4 KJV).

I could bless very God.

Not take anything. Not ask anything, demand anything,
petition anything. *I could simply give something to God.* A gift to Him!
Like He had given one thousand, countless, gifts to me! This I could
do! I look into the face of the painting, of Christ giving thanks and
breaking bread.

God, He has blessed—caressed.

I could bless God—caress with thanks.

It's our making love.

God makes love with grace upon grace, every moment a
making of His love for us. And He invites the turning over of
the hand, the opening and saying the Yes with thanks. Then

God lays down all of His fullness into all the emptiness. I am in Him. He is in me. I embrace God in the moment. I give Him thanks and *I bless God* and we meet and couldn't I make love to God, making every moment love for Him? To know Him the way Adam knew Eve. Spirit skin to spirit skin.

This is what His love means. I want it: *union*. This is the one gift He longs for in return for His unending gifts, and this even I could give Him, and anywhere. *Anywhere*—in the kitchen scrubbing potatoes, in the arching cathedrals, in the spin of laundry and kids and washing toilets—anywhere I can have intimate communion with Maker of heaven and earth. I can't help myself here. Inches from the canvas, strains of Mozart carrying, I whisper *eucharisteo*:

Thank You, God, for the bread of now ...

for Your Son and sacrifice ...

for the love song You keep singing, the gift of Yourself that You keep giving ...

for the wild wonder of You in this moment.

A stranger on the road, my cold heart burns (Luke 24:32) and He is bone of my bone and flesh of my flesh and I am His and He is mine and I want to touch the paint. I want to run my fingertips across oils, let the colors saturate my skin, let them run into my blood. I want to be in the painting, *Supper at Emmaus*, the painting to be in me. I want to be in God and God to be in me, to exchange love and blessings and caresses and, like the apostle-pilgrims, my eyes open and I know it because of this burning of the heart: this moment is a divine interchange. I raise my hand slightly, finger imperceptibly the air before the canvas and this is intercourse disrobed of its connotations, pure and unadulterated: a passing between. A connection, a communicating, an exchange, between tender Bridegroom and His bride.

The intercourse of soul with God is the very climax of joy.

The scrolling gold frame holds what I long for and I feel this burn too, flush of embarrassment up the face. And yet … we're called to do more than *believe in God*; we're called *to live in God*. To enter into Christ and Christ enter into us — to cohabit. Is this why it is His will for us to always give thanks in all things — the unbroken communion (1 Thessalonians 5:18)?

The choir sings; on a mauve wall Rembrandt's Christ breaks the bread, Communion, and the words of Teresa of Avila play in my head, a beckoning refrain:

> *Just these two words He spoke*
> *changed my life,*
>
> *"Enjoy Me."*
>
> *What a burden I thought I was to carry —*
> *a crucifix, as did He.*
>
> *Love once said to me, "I know a song,*
> *would you like to hear it?"*
>
> *And laughter came from every brick in the street*
> *and from every pore*
> *in the sky,*
>
> *After a night of prayer, He*
> *changed my life when*
> > *He sang,*
> *"Enjoy Me."*[7]

That's His song! *I rejoice in you. Come rejoice in Me.* The song that plays the world awake, the song that fuels joy: *Enjoy Me. Enjoy Me!*

Is there a greater way to love the Giver than to delight wildly in His gifts?

I hand Linda my camera. Will she record this moment, me before Rembrandt's *Supper at Emmaus*? I would carry it back home across the Atlantic, that photo of me in a long black dress, me with head bowed slight, smiling shy. I would hold that time captured and know that this was the holy moment I knew the warmth of union with Christ, not union only positionally, but communion with Christ *experientially*. I'm a celebrant! Officiating at the endless Eucharist of thanksgiving, a celebrant celebrating Christ, anywhere I could take up the elements of the moment and I might *live eucharisteo*, experiencing and enjoying Christ! (Might the world split with joy if all were celebrants celebrating Communion?)

"Would a soul continually eye His everlasting tenderness and compassion ... [then] it could not bear an hour's absence from Him; whereas now, perhaps, it cannot watch with Him one hour," writes John Owen, Puritan theologian.[8] "Every other discovery of God, without this, will but make the soul fly from Him; but if the heart be once much taken with the eminency of the Father's love, it cannot choose but be overpowered, conquered, and endeared unto Him."[9]

Linda hands me the camera, the one who dared in the beginning now witnessing the full leap into Arms and I nod grateful, turn to those painted hands holding bread, holding me. Will I remember this, not wanting to spend an hour's absence from Him?

My last day in Paris we do what we've done every day: touch her past, taste her breads and cheeses, listen to her sounds on every street corner, violins, guitars, cellos, watch her international faces and vibrant colors. I'm alive with His scent.

Off Rue de Rivoli across the street from the church, St-Gervais-et-St-Protais, I find an island of quiet in a monastic bookstore. A spray of blushing heritage roses creep up the sun-washed stone along the back wall. Hand-hewn beams span the low ceiling and light floods in from the wall of paned windows facing the empty street. A young nun in a long blue robe serves browsers in hushed, lilting French, her fawn eyes inviting, welcoming. I, too, drift through the stacks of Bibles, French titles, crosses. Back by old wooden stairs climbing up stone wall, standing in a pool of afternoon sun, I pick up a CD of hymns. I read and I shake my head in wonder. Can that really be the title?

Eucharistique.

I lay my hand over the word. Why do I even wonder? I read the title again to be sure. Yes, *eucharisteo always, everywhere, right where you are* and I can't shake the question from my love-drunk head: How badly do I want the deep communion? The dappled light shifts on the stone wall. I trace the letters "e-u-c-h ..." Communion with God, what was broken in the Garden, this is wholly restored when I want the God-communion more than I want the world-consumption. What that first and catastrophic sin of ingratitude ruptured, what that one bite of the forbidden fruit stole from those fully alive — *union* — can be repaired by exact inverse of the Garden: lifestyle gratitude and a willingness to eat of the bread He gives in this moment. How badly do I want to return to perfect Paradise, walk with God in the cool of the evening, *be fully alive*?

"O my soul, thou art capable of enjoying God, woe to thee if thou art contented with anything less than God," Francis de Sales gently, rightly urges.[10] Does earth have anything I desire but Him? I have to ask it. And I know the answer: When I remember the gifts and how He loves me ... I am moth drawn again to His ardent flame.

My finger underlines the CD title whispering *eucharisteo*. I have underlined my life and one thousand times I have practiced the language of *eucharisteo* and I now know this song. I step out into the street, ready to return, to listen to the song, to set a print of Rembrandt's *Supper at Emmaus* in the farm kitchen sill and live fully, hand wide open. I now testify: Counting His graces makes all moments into one holy kiss of communion and communion comes in the common. He will break bread and I will take and the world is His feast! and He is love! and nothing will keep my hand from filling with His.

Into a sun-orb sky, I fly home.

And into the heart of God.

afterword

It is spring, the farm in spring. Dust devils blow gritty vortexes across tilled fields and a single crow sits high in an apple tree abloom in the orchard, an iridescent black silhouette in a cloud of delicate white. A morning dove is sitting on a clutch of blue eggs under the leaves of the sunburst locust by the porch. I take a load of sun-dried laundry off the line.

Balancing the basket of fresh towels on one hip, I step in the back mudroom door into a still-teetering pile of jeans dirty from the stone picking out in the fields, into the shoes strewn, the LEGOs scattered, the half-baked experiment in the mudroom basin that involved green dye and too much sand, the kitchen sink always filling, the pantry always emptying, and I can see it and who could miss it, that herd of dusty footprints tracking mud across the kitchen floor? The washing machine groans. The oven timer beeps frantic. I have no idea where half a dozen kids are.

I step over the darks and lights sorted. Why doubt the dare to fully live? Now and right here. Why not let all of life be penetrated by grace, gratitude, joy? This is the only way to welcome the Kingdom of God.

I drop the basket on the wooden ironing board in the mudroom, pick my way through to the oven. Every breath's a battle between grudgery and gratitude and we must keep thanks on the lips so we can sip from the holy grail of joy. Nowhere else in the whole tilting universe lies the joy of the Lord but in that one word. I silence the siren of the oven, of me.

Out the kitchen window the sky rolls out. Apple blossoms fill all the orchard. The morning dove warms her bluing hope. I can hear Him, what He is telling the whole world and even me here: this is for you. The lover's smile in the morning, the child's laughter down the slide, the elder's eyes at eventide: this is for you. And the earth under your feet, the rain over your face upturned, the stars spinning all round you in the brazen glory: this is for you, you, you. These are for you—*gifts*—these are for you—*grace*—these are for you—*God*, so count the ways He loves, a thousand, *more, never stop*, that when you wake in the morning you can't help turn humbly to the east, unfold your hand to the heavens, and though you tremble and though you wonder, though the world is ugly, it is beautiful, and you can slow and you can trust and you can receive each moment as grace. *Eucharisteo. Eucharisteo. Eucharisteo.*

Isn't that the music playing? The playing in the stereo, playing the world alive. The music from Paris, *Eucharistique*. Did Hope-Girl put it in while she washed down bathrooms? It's her favorite CD since she smoothed out the page of a fresh journal and began her own One Thousand Gifts list the day after her baptism, day after she claimed the full life. She has left the CD case on the counter.

I pick it up, run my hands across the letters again. And the moment opens unexpectedly. I'm in the cemetery kneeling, tracing the only five letters carved deep in that slab of granite laid down in the dirt.

"A-I-M-E-E." *Loved one.*

I remember her silken hair. I still don't know why He took her. I don't know why her children don't run free on spring days with mine, laugh with my sister's. Don't know why my parents' hearts were left to weep, eroding all away. Though I cry, this I know: *God is always good and I am always loved* and *eucharisteo* has made me my truest self, "full of grace." Doesn't *eucharisteo* rename all God's children their truest name:

"Loved one."

Me, my dad, my mama, all the children, all the broken ones, all the world, He sings us safe with the refrain of our name, "Loved one."

In the window next to the stove, the porcelain dove soars. In the sill a framed print of Rembrandt's *Supper at Emmaus* invites. How many times a day do I look at this print in my kitchen and return to that sacred moment of soul communion in a still gallery? How many times a day do I again reach to embrace Him in communion thanks? It comes again now like it does every day, what I had read after I had already counted thousands of gifts: that this discipline of counting graces is as old as God's people themselves, the seriously devout Jews of today still giving thanks to God one hundred times a day. The words of the rabbis have been impressed deep into my skin, my being, their words beckoning the way into joy:

> Blessings keep our awareness of life's holy potential ever present. *They awaken us to our lives.... * With each blessing uttered we extend the boundaries of the sacred and ritualise *our love of life. One hundred times a day, everywhere we turn, everything we touch, everyone we see.* The blessings can be whispered. No one even need hear. No one but the Holy One. "*Holy One of blessing, Your presence fills the Universe. Your presence fills me.*"[1]

My gratitude journal is lying open on its permanent home on the counter, enumerating moments, making a ledger of His love. It is Chesterton who encapsulated the truth of my numbering life: "The greatest of poems is an inventory."[2] I grin happy in the midst. No, I'll never stop the counting, never cease transcribing the ballad of the world, the rhyme of His heart. He and I, a couplet. Count one thousand gifts, bless the Holy One one hundred times a day, commune with His presence filling the laundry room, the kitchen, the hospital, the graveyard, the highways and byways and workways and all the blazing starways, His presence filling me.

This is what it means to fully live.

In the dark of the next morning's dawn, I receive a dashed-off note from Shelly, her seven-year-old daughter still heavily sedated in the operating recovery room after reconstructive surgery for a shattered elbow that threatens to render her right hand useless. Shelly who testified how The Gift List had changed me. Shelly who has lived *eucharisteo* with me and the List unwraps the same in her too and she writes: "*God is good. Always.*" I nod yes, think of Aimee's name engraved in stone, all our names, all of us, the loved ones. My fingers over the keyboard, I think of that letter from my father-in-law asking who is ready. That mother, her daughter with cancer, full of questions. And now I think I have the beginning of an answer. I write Shelly prayers and love and sign my name with what I have come in the end to wholly believe. Who I am and always have been.

All is grace,

Ann

I press Send and my clenched fists open to a clutch of faith that warms into the coming light. In the orchard, the day's first wind blows a thousand apple blossoms from the trees. They shower earth's dark breast.

I watch them fly. A snow of endless beauty.

And I feel His caress.

acknowledgments

To these, I humbly offer up the two most profound, potent words I know:

Thank you.

Laura Barker for pioneering and breaking ground, Laura Boggess and Marybeth Whalen for generously believing, Bill Jensen for surest faith and tireless championing, Leslie Leyland Fields for wise, girding words, and Andy Meisenheimer for the unlikely yes.

For Mick and Sheri Silva, who were the gift.

For the Zondervan team, Mike Salisbury and Dirk Buursma who go the extra mile in their kingdom work, for Sandy Vander Zicht the consummate professional who graciously took this project under her experienced wing to make a fledgling fly. I am indebted.

For every single blog reader—and you know your beautiful names—for every thoughtful note, for every kind prayer, for every time you read, offered your friendship, passed on a post to a friend, and invited one more to the circle of friends ... these pages are because of you and I will never be able to thank you enough. I love community with you—appalling grace!

For Marlene Fitch, Sherri Martin, Anne Peterson, Annette Weber, Megan Modderman, Linda Chontos, Lydia Bower, Shannon Woodward, L. L. Barkat, Sally Clarkson, Elizabeth

Foss, Bobbie Wolgemuth, Shannon Lowe, and the fellowship of GBF, the unwavering friends who held the hands up when I was faint-weary. Life in the Love Body with you heals, gives life, multiplies joy. For Shelly Kearns, biblical scholar, who kept true pastoral company through the early draft words. For Holley Gerth who received pages so fresh with such faith. For Tonia Peckover, *for everything*, these years and the together pilgrimage. For you all, I will always be grateful.

For Linda Sunderland who dared me to count to one thousand. You change lives. *How to thank you?*

For John and Tiffany Voskamp who have courageously trusted God's goodness, and for David, Noa and Mya, Lia and Ana, the faithful five. I am so thankful we have the gift of doing life together.

For Molly, the sister who has been one, a safe, strong place; for John, the brother who has prayed and come the whole long way; for my dad who has loved through hard times, the highest of compliments; and for my mama who has shown me how to live into the God-strength with beauty, grace, and astonishing joy.

Caleb, Joshua, Hope, Levi, Malakai, Shalom, six who have swollen me, shaped me, and birthed me into love. I weep for the grace of each of you, the six crowning gifts. Mama loves you from here to eternity and back.

Darryl, the far better, wiser half, who daily takes my hand and tenderly leads into living fully for Him. I am so glad you asked for forever and I said yes. I never expected so much joy.

For God the Father, God the Son, and God the Holy Spirit ... who draws the whole beautiful world into communion's embrace and the dance of the Holy Fulfilling.

Bible translations

Scripture quotations marked NIV are taken from the Holy Bible, *New International Version®, NIV®*. Copyright © 1973, 1978, 1984 by Biblica, Inc.™ Used by permission of Zondervan. All rights reserved worldwide.

Scripture quotations marked KJV are taken from King James Version of the Bible.

Scripture quotations marked NASB are taken from the *New American Standard Bible*. Copyright © 1960, 1962, 1963, 1968, 1971, 1972, 1973, 1975, 1977, 1995 by The Lockman Foundation. Used by permission.

Scripture quotations marked ESV are taken from *The Holy Bible, English Standard Version*, copyright © 2001 by Crossway Bibles, a division of Good News Publishers. Used by permission. All rights reserved.

Scripture quotations marked AMP are taken from *The Amplified Bible* Copyright © 1954, 1958, 1962, 1964, 1965, 1987 by The Lockman Foundation. All rights reserved. Used by permission.

Scripture quotations marked MSG are taken from *The Message*. Copyright © 1993, 1994, 1995, 1996, 2000, 2001, 2002. Used by permission of NavPress Publishing Group.

Scripture quotations marked NCV are taken from the *Holy Bible, New Century Version*. Copyright © 1987, 1988, 1991 by

notes

chapter 2: a word to live ... and die by

1. "How Much Oxygen Does a Person Consume in a Day," *How Stuff Works*. *http://health.howstuffworks.com/question98.htm* (accessed April 20, 2010).

2. Augustine, *Confessions of Saint Augustine*, book 10, chapter 21, Christian Classics Ethereal Library, *http://www.ccel.org/ccel/augustine/confess.xi.xxi.html* (accessed April 20, 2010).

3. Albert Schweitzer, *Reverence for Life*, trans. Reginald H. Fuller (New York: Harper, 1969), 41.

4. Alexander Schmemann, *For the Life of the World: Sacraments and Orthodoxy* (Crestwood, N.Y.: St. Vladimir's Seminary Press, 1973), 18.

5. Ibid., 61.

chapter 3: first flight

1. Jean-Pierre de Caussade, *Abandonment to Divine Providence*, book 1, chapter 1, section 4, Christian Classics Ethereal Library, *http://www.ccel.org/ccel/decaussade/abandonment.ii_1.i.i.iv.html* (accessed April 20, 2010).

2. Martin Luther, quoted in Bob Kelly, *Worth Repeating: More than 5,000 Classic and Contemporary Quotes* (Grand Rapids: Kregel, 2003), 379.

3. John Piper, *When I Don't Desire God: How to Fight for Joy* (Wheaton, Ill.: Crossway, 2004), 124.

4. Erasmus, quoted in Andy Zubko, *Treasure of Spiritual Wisdom* (New Delhi, India: Motilal Banarsidass, 2003), 219.

5. Alexander Schmemann, *For the Life of the World: Sacraments and Orthodoxy* (Crestwood, N.Y.: St. Vladimir's Seminary Press, 1973), 15.

6. C. S. Lewis, *God in the Dock* (Grand Rapids: Eerdmans, 1994), 52.

7. Julian of Norwich, quoted in Richard Foster, ed., *Devotional Classics* (San Francisco: HarperSanFrancisco, 1993), 71.

chapter 4: a sanctuary of time

1. Mark Buchanan, *The Rest of God: Restoring Your Soul by Restoring Your Sabbath* (Nashville: Nelson, 2007), 45, emphasis added.

2. Evelyn Underhill, quoted in Martin H. Manser, ed., *The Westminster Collection of Christian Quotations* (Louisville: Westminster, 2001), 270.

3. Elisabeth Elliot, *Through Gates of Splendor* (Carol Stream, Ill.: Tyndale House, 1986), 20.

4. See Abraham Joshua Heschel, *The Sabbath* (New York: Farrar, Straus and Giroux, 2005).

chapter 5: what in the world, in all this world, is grace?

1. G. K. Chesterton, *Orthodoxy* (Rockville, Md.: Serenity, 2009), 138.

2. Augustine, *Confessions of Saint Augustine*, book 7, chapter 12, Christian Classics Ethereal Library, *http://www.ccel.org/ccel/augustine/confess.viii.xii.html* (accessed April 20. 2010).

3. Julian of Norwich, *Revelations of Divine Love*, trans. Elizabeth Spearing (London: Penguin, 1998), 59.

4. G. K. Chesterton, *Collected Works of G. K. Chesterton: Collected Poetry: Part 1*, ed. Aidan Mackey (Fort Collins, Colo.: Ignatius, 1994), 38, emphasis added.

5. Teresa of Avila, quoted in Amy Welborn, *The Loyola Kids Book of Saints* (Chicago: Loyola, 2001), 87.

6. See Gregory Wolfe, "The Wound of Beauty," *Image* 56 (Winter 2007–8), *http://imagejournal.org/page/journal/editorial-statements/the-wound-of-beauty* (accessed April 20, 2010).

chapter 6: what do you want? the place of seeing God

1. Amy Carmichael, "Immanence," in *Mountain Breezes: The Collected Poems of Amy Carmichael* (Fort Washington, Pa.: Christian Literature Crusade, 1999), 19.

2. J. I. Packer, *Rediscovering Holiness: Know the Fullness of Life with God* (Ventura, Calif.: Regal, 2009), 69.

3. Gerard Manley Hopkins, "As Kingfishers Catch Fire," in *Gerard Manley Hopkins: The Major Works*, Catherine Phillips, ed. (New York: Oxford University Press, 2002), 129.

4. A. W. Tozer, *The Pursuit of God* (Camp Hill, Pa.: Christian Publications, 1982), 73.

5. C. S. Lewis, *The Great Divorce* (New York: Macmillan, 1946), 77.

6. Irenaeus, quoted in *Letters of Faith through the Seasons*, James M. Houston, ed. (Colorado Springs: Cook, 2006), 1:152.

7. C. S. Lewis, "The Weight of Glory," in *The Weight of Glory and Other Addresses* (Grand Rapids: Eerdmans, 1965), 12–13.

chapter 7: seeing through the glass

1. Jean-Pierre de Caussade, quoted in *A Guide to Prayer for All God's People*, Rueben Job and Norman Shawchuck, eds. (Nashville: Upper Room, 1990), 244.

2. Annie Dillard, *Pilgrim at Tinker Creek* (New York: HarperPerennial, 1998), 33.

3. John Piper, "From His Fullness We Have All Received, Grace Upon Grace," Desiring God, *http://www.desiringgod.org/ResourceLibrary/Sermons/ByDate/2008/3394_From_His_Fullness_We_Have_All_Received_Grace_Upon_Grace/* (accessed April 20, 2010).

4. G. K. Chesterton, quoted in James M. Houston, *Joyful Exiles: Life in Christ on the Dangerous Edge of Things* (Downers Grove, Ill.: InterVarsity, 2006), 140.

5. "People generally do not make efforts to actively infuse their daily experiences with greater emotional quality," posits scientific researcher and professor Rollin McCraty. "Although most people definitively claim that they love, care, appreciate, it might shock many to realize the large degree to which these feelings are merely assumed or acknowledged *cognitively*, far more than they are *actually experienced* in their feeling world. In the absence of conscious efforts to engage, build, and sustain positive perceptions and emotions, we all too automatically fall prey to feelings such as irritation, anxiety, worry, frustration, self-doubt and blame" (Rollin McCraty, "The Grateful Heart," *The Psychology of Gratitude*, ed. Robert A. Emmons [New York: Oxford University Press, 2004], 241, emphasis added).

6. James H. McConkey, *Life Talks* (Harrisburg, Pa.: Fred Kelker, 1911), 103.

chapter 8: how will he not also?

1. *The Strongest NIV Exhaustive Concordance*, 2nd ed. (Grand Rapids: Zondervan, 1999), 1583.

2. Quoted in Robert A. Emmons, *Thanks! How the New Science of Gratitude Can Make You Happier* (New York: Houghton Mifflin, 2007), 89.

3. Brennan Manning, *Ruthless Trust* (New York: HarperCollins, 2002), 24.

4. Dennis Linn, Sheila Fabricant Linn, and Matthew Linn, *Sleeping with Bread: Holding What Gives You Life* (Mahwah N.J.: Paulist, 1995), 1.

chapter 9: go lower

1. G. K. Chesterton, *Orthodoxy* (Rockville, Md.: Serenity, 2009), 19.

2. Quoted in G. B. F. Hallock, "The Cultivation of Humility," *Herald and Presbyter* 90 (December 24, 1919): 8.

3. Timothy Keller, "The Advent of Humility" *Christianity Today*, December 22, 2008, *http://www.christianitytoday.com/ct/2008/december/20.51.html* (accessed January 24, 2010).

4. I am indebted to Tonia Peckover for her thoughtful insights.

5. Thomas Aquinas, quoted in Peter Kreeft, *Catholic Christianity* (Fort Collins, Colo.: Ignatius, 2001), 357.

6. Henry Ward Beecher, *Life Thoughts, Gathered from the Extemporaneous Discourses of Henry Ward Beecher* (New York: Sheldon, 1860), 115.

7. Peter Kreeft, "Joy," *http://www.peterkreeft.com/topics/joy.htm* (accessed April 12, 2010), emphasis added.

chapter 10: empty to fill

1. *My body of a sudden blazed;*
   And twenty minutes more or less
   It seemed, so great my happiness,
   That I was blessed and could bless. (W. B. Yeats, "Vacillation")

Quoted in Richard J. Finneran, *Yeats: An Annual of Critical and Textual Studies*, vol. 6 (Ann Arbor: University of Michigan Press, 1998), 147.

2. Dorothy Sayers, *Letters to a Diminished Church* (Nashville: Nelson, 2004), 143.

3. Mother Teresa, quoted in *A Guide to Prayer for All God's People*, Rueben Job and Norman Shawchuck, eds. (Nashville: Upper Room, 1990), 228.

4. Rabindranath Tagore, quoted in John Shea, *The Spiritual Wisdom of the Gospels for Christian Preachers and Teachers* (Collegeville, Minn.: Liturgical Press, 2006), 193.

chapter 11: the joy of intimacy

1. C. S. Lewis, "The Weight of Glory," in *The Weight of Glory and Other Addresses* (Grand Rapids: Eerdmans, 1965), 10.

2. Henri Nouwen, *Life of the Beloved* (New York: Crossroad, 2002), 60.

3. Ronald Rolheiser, *The Holy Longing: The Search for a Christian Spirituality* (New York: Random House, 1999), 66.

4. Walter Brueggemann, *Finally Comes the Poet* (Minneapolis: Fortress, 1989), 45.

5. John Calvin, *Institutes of the Christian Religion*, ed. John T. McNeill (Philadelphia: Westminster, 1960), 2.8.18 (2:385).

6. Ibid., 3.11.10 (2:737).

7. Teresa of Avila, "Laughter Came from Every Brick," in *Love Poems from God*, ed. Daniel James Ladinsky (New York: Penguin, 2002), 276. Copyright © 2002 by Daniel Ladinsky. Used by permission of Daniel Ladinsky.

8. John Owen, *Communion with the Triune God* (Wheaton, Ill.: Crossway, 2007), 124.

9. Ibid., 128.

10. St. Francis de Sales, *Introduction to the Devout Life* (New York: Kessinger, 1997), 299.

afterword

1. Dennis Lennon, *Fuelling the Fire: Fresh Thinking on Prayer* (Queensway, UK: Scripture Union, 2005), 43, emphasis added.

2. G. K. Chesterton, *Orthodoxy* (Rockville, Md.: Serenity, 2009), 55.

one thousand gifts

DEVOTIONAL

To the Oregonian Three

*who have always believed that standing straight into wind
is how to fly on His wings of grace*

contents

your journey by grace

It all began quite spontaneously, unintentionally. One of those things God grows up in the most unexpected places.

A friend dared me to start counting one thousand things I loved. I took the dare, accepted the challenge, kept track of one thousand things, one thousand gifts—a thousand *graces*—on a quiet, unassuming blog. Before I knew it, thankfulness to God began to fully change me.

What I actually found—startling!—was more daily wonder and surprising beauty than I ever expected. And in a few short years, this daily hunt for God's grace, His glory, *had* ushered me into a fuller life. A life of joy! Over the past several years, I've listed over four thousand gifts ... and I continue. Once one has begun, has tasted and known He is God, who can stop giving Him glory? Thousands more have begun their own lists—in jail cells and by death beds, in third-world slums and by faith alone—and it's not overstatement to say that giving Him thanks has made me—and innumerable others—overcomers.

How did all this happen?

A few years ago, I decided to try to live this giving thanks as I believe Jesus did each day, regardless of His circumstances. And what I found was that in giving thanks for each moment and savoring it as bread from His hand, I'd find sustenance and the grace of God Himself in it. I wrote a book about this gratitude journey called *One Thousand Gifts*. I didn't start with any specific steps, but through this intentional, daily practice of giving thanks, I found myself on a transformative journey that affected every aspect of my life—including all the broken places. God began to show me the graces, the love gifts, that were right before me, waiting to be noticed, waiting to be received. This easily overlooked stuff, the small—and especially the hard—became for me a life-giving stream of *joy in Him.*

Even when I am sometimes impatient or unwilling, when I face conflict and heartache, I've begun to accept that even the impossible is a possible opportunity to thank God, to experience the goodness and grace of the Giver of all!

There is always only more grace.

And it's always more than I expect.

And you? You in the midst, you in the mire, are you too thinking about counting one thousand gifts, about making your life all about joy in Christ, about loving God and enjoying Him forever? There is so much joy in seeing how He uses our simple act of *noticing* the blessings He bestows all around us to transform our lives and the lives of those we touch.

So here is how I suggest you begin this journey by grace, begin your own gift list, count all the ways He loves you:

Pray. Start with a simple request, making it the refrain of your day: "God, open the eyes of my heart." This journey must be Spirit-led, every day.

Receive. Open your hand to the simple, daily gifts, writing down all the unique and ordinary things you notice, from the grand and obvious to the humble and hidden.

Praise. Praise Him for the unexpected and the unlikely, for the daily and the difficult, and the graces in disguise. The more you count, the more gifts you will see. Do not disdain the small. The moments add up, and we might come to believe it—*the whole earth is full of His glory!*

Beyond that, there is no method or formula. There is simply a willingness to bend to receive, to begin to take note of the daily love God unfurls.

What could be simpler, more glorious, than doing what we were made for?

It could be like this: I found setting a goal of one thousand gifts over a few months beneficial—it kept me attending to all the ways He whispers, "I love you." Some folks count ten graces a day, others just three a day to total one thousand in a year, while still others spend one day a week intensely, wildly counting, a jarring wide-awake. Whatever you do, the practice is intended to be a way of cultivating a habit, of learning to live praise, to make gratitude and joy your default, to move thanksgiving away from a holiday to a *lifestyle*—that all the days might be holy and set apart for real joy.

These sixty reflections chronicle my discovery, each one like a singular tree in a lush forest of graces. While every journey is unique, my humble prayer is that sharing these glimpses will companion and encourage you in your own prayerful discovery of a lifestyle of Christ-focus and communion. Of how extravagantly God loves you and how desperately you need Him every moment. Most of all, I hope these entries expand your view of the endless and matchless grace of an overflowing God. Just turn to the back of this book, press open that journaling space, and begin your own list of one thousand gifts— *take the dare to fully live!*

Oh, let the gift-hunt begin! God is waiting to reveal so much through your desire to know Him more deeply and completely—but His grace is only experienced *directly*. The most important thing is simply to begin.

May God bless your journey with the greatest gift of all—more and more of Himself!

All is grace.

Ann

surprising grace

This is what the LORD says:

"In the time of my favor I will answer you,
    and in the day of salvation I will help you;
I will keep you and will make you
    to be a covenant for the people,
to restore the land
    and to reassign its desolate inheritances."

Isaiah 49:8

That field of beans west of the barn, it looked gaunt come October, bean pods all hanging like bony ribs.

Whenever the wind sighed, the whole field just rattled skinny.

That's how my dad always spoke of a railish man, that you could count his ribs. Nothing in me wanted to count those beans, know the yield, from that spare field.

When my husband, the Farmer, rolled the combine in and lowered the combined head to bring those beans in, I sat beside him, raised my voice to ask it above the combine's working engine: "Is it possible that something that doesn't look like anything—can still amount to something?"

The field, it was hard to even look at it. I've known a face in a mirror much like that.

"Well—it isn't much to look at, is it?" The Farmer looks up from the combine's steering wheel, looks across the field to the north. "Weedy. And thin."

The white of the sow thistle seeds mingles with the dust. This field had no rain in July, and a man can't make a sky give. He can just make the knees bend and the hands raise. The harvest looked like a failure. I've known this, been this, am this.

The first time thanksgiving is ever mentioned in Scripture, this is what we read:

> And this is the law of the sacrifice of peace offerings that one may offer to the LORD. If he offers it for a thanksgiving, then he shall offer with the thanksgiving sacrifice unleavened loaves mixed with oil, unleavened wafers smeared with oil, and loaves of fine flour well mixed with oil. With the sacrifice of his peace offerings for thanksgiving he shall bring his offering with loaves of leavened bread.
>
> *Leviticus 7:11–13 ESV*

The first time thanksgiving is mentioned in Scripture, the thanksgiving offering was part of the peace offering. Could that be the thing?

Could it be—no one receives the peace of God without giving thanks to God? Is thankfulness really but the deep, contented breath of peacefulness? Is this why God asks us to give thanks even when things look a failure? When there doesn't seem much to give thanks for?

The beans rattle through the combine, the auger filling the bin with golden beans like bread rising slow.

There were to be ten offerings of bread in every thank offering of the Israelites.

The first were like crackers. The second like wafers. These were known for their thinness. This was the order of thanks.

The thanks began for the thin things, the wafer things that almost weren't, and the way the people of God give thanks is first to give thanks for even the meager and unlikely.

Then it came, thanks for the leavened bread. Why would leaven, yeast—that which is seen in Scripture as impure, unwanted—why would leaven be included as part of the thanks offering?

Authentic thanks is always for *all* things, because our God is a God kneading *all* things into a bread that sustains. Paul gave "glory in tribulations" (Romans 5:3 KJV) and took "pleasure in infirmities, in reproaches, in necessities, in persecutions, in distresses for Christ's sake" (2 Corinthians 12:10 KJV), and he knew that which didn't look like anything good might yield good, all in the hand of a good God.

To bring the sacrifice of thanksgiving means to sacrifice our understanding of what is beneficial and thank God for everything because He is benevolent. A sacrifice of thanks lays down our perspective and raises hands in praise anyways—*always*. A sacrifice is, by definition, not an easy thing—but it is a sacred thing.

There is this: We give thanks to God not because of how we feel but because of who He is.

"See it on the monitor?" The Farmer points to the screen to the right of the combine's steering wheel. "See the numbers, how many bushels an acre? If you didn't see the numbers, you'd never guess it, would you? It's yielding higher than it looks." He's shaking his head in happy wonder.

"Really? How can that be?" The numbers on the screen defy the seemingly sparse and stunted crop, and I'm laughing incredulous.

"I know! I know ..." The Farmer smiles, glances down at the beans feeding into the combine head, one eye still watching number of bushels on the screen.

He who is grateful for little is given much laughter ... and it's counting the ways He loves, *this* is what multiplies joy.

The life that counts blessings discovers its yielding more than it seems.

Why don't I keep more of an eye on the number of His graces? Why don't I want to know that even though it doesn't seem like there's been enough rain, He reigns and He is enough and the bounty is greater than it appears?

The thin places might be the places closest to God and the skinny places might be fuller than they seem, and who isn't full when they have Christ?

"Look how many seeds were really hiding in this pod!"

Little Shalom, she calls to me walking back across the field. "Count them, Mama."

"Yes," I say. "Yes, let's count."

And there's this counting the ribs of the field, graces filling unexpectedly, thanksgiving always this walking toward peace, and I see it.

See it—how the Farmer waves to me from the harvest seat, his hand turned willingly up to the sky.

God, cause me to know it afresh today: the life that counts blessings discovers its yielding much more than it seems. And my life yields most when I yield most to You.

choosing grace

His secret purpose framed from the very beginning
[is] to bring us to our full glory.
1 Corinthians 2:7 NEB

They lay her gravestone flat into the earth, a black granite slab engraved with no dates, only the five letters of her name. Aimee. It means "loved one." How she was. We had loved her. And with the laying of my sister's gravestone, the closing up of her deathbed, so closed our lives.

Closed to any notion of grace.

Really, when you bury a child—or when you just simply get up every day and live life raw—you murmur the question soundlessly. No one hears. *Can there be a good God?* How can He be good when babies die, and marriages implode, and dreams blow away, dust in the wind? Where is grace bestowed when cancer gnaws and loneliness aches and nameless places in us soundlessly die, break off without reason, erode away? Where hides this joy of the Lord, this God who fills the earth with good things, and how do I fully live when life is full of hurt? How do I wake up to joy and grace and beauty and all that is the fullest life when I must stay numb to losses and crushed dreams and all that empties me out?

Is this the toxic air of the world, this atmosphere we inhale, burning into our lungs, this *No, God? No, God, we won't take what You give. No, God, Your plans are a gutted, bleeding mess, and I didn't sign up for this and You really thought I'd go for this? No, God, this is ugly and this is a mess and can't You get anything right and just haul all this pain out of here and I'll take it from here, thanks. And God? Thanks for nothing.* Isn't this the human inheritance, the legacy of the Garden?

Everywhere, a world pocked with scarcity.

I hunger for filling in a world that is starved.

But from that Garden beginning, God has had a different purpose for us. His intent, since He bent low and breathed His life into the dust of our lungs, since He kissed us into being, has never been to slyly orchestrate our ruin. And yet, I have found it: He does have surprising, secret purposes.

I open a Bible, and His plans, startling, lie there barefaced. It's hard to believe it, when I read it, and I have to come back to it many times, feel long across those words, make sure they are real. His love letter forever silences any doubts. He means to rename us—to return us to our true names, our truest selves.

He means to heal our soul holes.

From the very beginning, that Eden beginning, that has always been and always is, to this day, His secret purpose—our return to *our full glory. Appalling*—that He would! Us, unworthy. And yet since we took a bite out of the fruit and tore into our own souls, that drain hole where joy seeps away, God's had this wild secretive plan. *He means to fill us with glory again.* With glory and grace.

Grace, it means "favor," from the Latin *gratia*. It connotes a free readiness. A free and ready favor. That's grace. It is one thing to choose to take the grace offered at the cross. But to choose to live as one *filling* with His grace? Choosing to *fill* with *all* that He freely gives and fully live—with glory and grace and God?

I know it but I don't want to: it is a choice.

Living with losses, I may choose to still say yes.
Choose to say yes to what He freely gives.

God of all gifts, thank You. Thank You! For the grace to choose to see. I choose to say yes today to all You give. Do the work in me — I want to more fully live.

first grace

But the basic reality of God is plain enough.
Open your eyes and there it is!
By taking a long and thoughtful look at what God has created,
people have always been able to see
what their eyes as such can't see: . . .
the mystery of his divine being.
Romans 1:19 - 20 MSG

It's after I cut the squash right open.

The two halves split and quartered there on the cutting board.

After the paintbrushes are washed out, after the pawns of the chess game are all returned to their squares, after the potatoes are baked and served, the dinner plates are pushed back empty. The Farmer splits the Word right open then and that's when I'm cut to the quick.

"First, I thank my God ..." That's what it reads, right there in Romans 1. The Farmer reads it slow—what should always come first in everything. And Paul writes more, peels back the hot holiness of God. I hold it there in my hands. The holy words that hollow me out.

> The wrath of God is being revealed from heaven against all the godlessness and wickedness of people, who suppress the truth by their wickedness, since what may be known about God is plain to

them, because God has made it plain to them. For since the creation
of the world God's invisible qualities — his eternal power and divine
nature — have been clearly seen, being understood from what has
been made, so that people are without excuse.

For although they knew God, they neither glorified him as God
nor gave thanks to him ... as they did not think it worthwhile to
retain the knowledge of God, so God gave them over to a depraved
mind, so that they do what ought not to be done.

Romans 1:18–21, 28

The light fills the drinking cups still on the table. I can feel its
warmth on the nape of my neck. Spring coming. The heat of it
melting everything cold.

One of the best writers I've read and a kind friend, pastor, and
fellow Canadian, Mark Buchanan, asked the most critical questions of
them all: "What initially sparks God's anger? What is the root sin, the
molten core of wickedness and godlessness — that convinces God to
turn us over?"[1]

Isn't that what we have to figure out? It's right there in Romans 1.
It's not the sinfulness you'd think it'd be: It's the thanklessness — that
we do. It's our thanklessness that first stirs the full wrath of God.

The beginnings of Genesis and Romans 1 pivot on the same point:
Eve's thanklessness for all God does give and her resentfulness of the
one fruit He doesn't give, this is the catalyst of the fall. Which Romans
1 confirms: "For although they knew God, they neither glorified him
as God nor *gave thanks* to him, but their thinking became futile, and
their foolish hearts were darkened."

Our fall is always first a failure to give thanks.

The pride of thanklessness always comes before the fall. God makes
Himself plain and there's no excuse — but they did not give Him
thanks.

I have done this and just this morning, there spooning potatoes. The house upended with ridiculously messy and wondrous living. Paint smeared on a shirt, across a table. The chess loser in loud tears. The stringy innards of squash all over the counter. Instead of falling on my knees in thanks, I fall into sin and anger.

When I refuse to give God thanks? God lets our very lives become refuse.

I'd do well to stitch it into the fabric of me: *A lack of doxology leads to depravity.*

That is what Buchanan discovers in Scripture, right there in Romans: "The heart of wickedness and godlessness is that: a refusal to glorify God. It's the refusal to thank Him."[2]

Wickedness isn't rooted primarily in some ghetto, on some shady backstreet. No, as Buchanan states, "All the wickedness in the world begins with an act of forgetting."[3]

I nod slow.

In a thousand infinite ways God turns His glory around for us to see, but we can shrug; we can turn a blind eye. And so He lets it come, what we want — and everything, us, it all goes black.

There is light at the table, these open pages filling with it.

Isn't that what Paul is saying? When, in light of everything, we don't turn to God in thanks, God gives in to what we want — and turns us over to the dark ...

Turn in thanks and everything turns — and God doesn't turn away.

And there is this: If all the dismembering wickedness in the world begins with an act of forgetting — then the act of literally counting blessings literally re-members us to God. This is the making whole.

After lunch, I clean off the counter, gather up the halved squash and their inners, and afterward turn to the journal and jot down another note of thanks, for the time and the light to see by.

For all these halves, they are finding their wholes.

Father God, You are the Begetter of grace. Forgive me for being a forgetter of thanks. This is no trivial thing. It leads to wicked things. Hear the cry of my heart: Forgive me for not giving You thanks. If thanks is the highest form of thought—make it my first thought. Turn me toward thanks first—so my life doesn't turn into the last thing I'd hoped for. Turn me toward You first—first things first means to give You thanks first.

thinking grace

Through Jesus, therefore,
let us continually offer to God a sacrifice of praise—
the fruit of lips that openly profess his name.

Hebrews 13:15

When the rope pulls tight, Levi holds on—and it looks like happy wonder might right split him.

The kid, he's all snow-caked—all celebration.

He's making me grin. Life could be like that—giving way to the celebration of fully living.

He's making me the child—the laughter falling like snow and his cheeks all red, winter and wonder right in him, and his father winks at me and I lay on the snow and this moment right here, it warms right through.

Who can't laugh with him, this sledding straight to the sheer edge?

He does go down more than once or twice.

I wait for tears.

And I'm the fool not knowing what it's all about. It's there in his eyes: the thrill is in the trying what doesn't seem possible.

Isn't that always the place where fear meets faith and the face of God?

The snow's bluing in twilight. The dog's panting happy. The boy's all full of life, wonder-filled.

The sun is doing its own sliding down. I try to memorize all this wonderful—the faith and the falls and the fully living.

Robert Frost is right: "An hour of winter day might seem too short."[4] And there are Eden days—days you want the boy to stay freckled and laughing loud and the light to linger longer and the dog to keep running you young.

It's not trite, this waking to wonder, giving thanks for all this.

Thanks isn't shallow Pollyanna-ism. Didn't Chesterton suggest that?

"I would maintain that thanks are the highest form of thought, and that gratitude is happiness doubled by wonder."[5]

And I wonder if this is why thanks is the highest form of thought—because this is always the right order of things: Us laid low. Before God on High.

Isn't this what's partly awry in the world? The world needs fewer complaints and more thanks—those engaged in the highest thoughts.

The world needs more men and women living thanks, thinking loftiest.

Why would we ever tire of bending low in thanking—*thanking*—this highest form of thinking?

This is what all the great artists and thinkers do—they stay awake to the wonder of God's world. Great thinkers are the grateful thankers—the real greats live gratefully.

And is this the art of life—to keep awake to the wonders in His Word and this world?

Isn't it wonder that sparks love?

Levi swings round on his sled, chasing joy, that thing that swings open everything.

He yells at me as he flies by. "Isn't this great?"

And I smile thanks for the wonder of here. Thanks, that thing that makes you the child full of wonder, the great thinker, the kingdom of heaven belonging to those who are like the children.

And the trees at sunset, they're lit aflame right down there in the woods.

~

Father God, make me never tire of the highest form of thinking—thanking. Make today great—by causing me to think gratefully. Engage me in the highest thoughts—gratefully laid low before You.

here-now grace

And he took bread, gave thanks and broke it,
and gave it to them ...
Luke 22:19

I remember once sitting at the hairdresser's. The woman beside me reads, and I read her title in the reflection of the mirror: *1,000 Places to See Before You Die*. Is that it? Are there physical places I simply must see before I stop breathing within time, before I inhale eternity?

Why? To say that I've had reason to bow low? To say that I've seen beauty? To say that I've been arrested by wonder?

Isn't it here? Can't I find it *here*?

These very real lungs will breathe in more than 11,000 liters of air today, and tonight over our farm will rise the Great Hexagon of the blazing winter stars—Sirius, Rigel, ruby Aldebran, Capella, the fiery Gemini twins, the Procyon, and in the center, scarlet Betelgeuse, the red supergiant larger than twice the size of earth's orbit around the sun.

Isn't it here? The wonder? Why do I spend so much of my living hours struggling to see it? Do we truly stumble so blind that we must be affronted with *blinding* magnificence for our blurry soul-sight to recognize grandeur? The very same surging magnificence that cascades over our every day here. Who has time or eyes to notice?

I don't need more time to breathe so that I may experience more locales, possess more, accomplish more. Because wonder really could be here—for the seeing eyes.

The face of Jesus flashes. Jesus, the God-Man with his own termination date. Jesus, the God-Man who came to save me from prisons of fear and guilt and depression and sadness. With an expiration of less than twelve hours, what does Jesus count as all-important?

"And he took bread, *gave thanks* and broke it, and gave it to them" (Luke 22:19, emphasis added).

I read it slowly. In the original language, "he gave thanks" reads "*eucharisteo.*" I underline it on the page.

The root word of *eucharisteo* is *charis*, meaning "grace." Jesus took the bread and saw it as grace and gave thanks. He took the bread and knew it to be *gift* and gave thanks.

But there is more, and I read it. *Eucharisteo*, thanksgiving, envelopes the Greek word for grace, *charis*. But it also holds its derivative, the Greek word *chara*, meaning "joy." *Joy*. Ah ... yes. I might be needing me some of that. That might be what the quest for more is all about —that which Augustine claimed, "Without exception ... all try their hardest to reach the same goal, that is, joy."[6]

I breathe deep, like a sojourner finally coming home. This has always been the goal of the fullest life—joy. And my life knew exactly how elusive that slippery three-letter word, *joy*, can be. My whole being responded to that one word. I longed for more life, for more *holy joy*.

That's what I was struggling to reach, to seize. Joy. But where can I seize this holy grail of joy? I look back down to the page. Was this the clue to the quest of all most important? Deep *chara* joy is found only at the table of the *euCHARisteo*—the table of thanksgiving. I sit there long ... wondering ... is it that simple?

Is the height of my *chara* joy dependent on the depths of my *eucharisteo* thanks?

So then as long as thanks is possible—I think this through—as long as thanks is possible, then joy is always possible. *Joy is always possible.*

Whenever, meaning—"now"; *wherever,* meaning—"here."

The holy grail of joy is not in some exotic location or some emotional mountain peak experience. The joy wonder could be here! Here, in the messy, piercing ache of now, joy might be—unbelievably—possible! The only place we need see before we die is this place of seeing God, here and now.

I whisper it out loud, let the tongue feel these sounds, the ear hear their truth.

Charis. Grace.

Eucharisteo. Thanksgiving.

Chara. Joy.

A triplet of stars, a constellation in the black.

This search for the constellation in the dark—grace, thanksgiving, joy—it might be like that—a reaching for stars.

God, thank You for showing me the beauty in all these here-now wonders that You've placed before me—to do good and right work in me. Cause me to see all that encircles me today with new eyes of thankfulness.

anti-anxiety grace

Surely I have composed and quieted my soul;
Like a weaned child rests against his mother,
My soul is like a weaned child within me.

Psalm 131:2 NASB

There are birds at the feeders, chickadees. They flit, nervous. I watch the light in the trees, the way it falls across the walls. Across the calendar and to-do lists, and I try to remember to breathe.

John Calvin and I, we both remember the year we were four.

The year I was four, my sister was crushed under the wheels of a truck in our driveway. That is my first memory, the day Aimee was killed.

Fears have formed me.

John Calvin's mother died the year he was four. Scholar and historian William Bouwsma describes Calvin as "a singularly anxious man."[7] Calvin buried all three babies born to him and his wife. He said he found in the Psalms "all the griefs, sorrows, fears, doubts, hopes, cares, perplexities, in short all the distracting emotions with which the minds of men are wont to be agitated."[8] The man understood fear.

Clouds have skirted in heavy from the west. The walls in the kitchen have fallen gray and silent. Joshua's playing it quietly, up and down the piano this morning, the *Music Box Dancer*. A friend laid out in great detail this weekend how the economy is about to implode. Chronic illness flares. Teenagers ask big questions. I keep smoothing out calendar pages, pushing things back. *How do you remember how to dance?*

What is the answer to anxiety? Joshua's playing so sure, the house lilting, tilting with happiness. That's what Calvin wrote. "The stability of the world depends on this rejoicing of God in his works." And again, "If on earth, such praise of God does not come to pass, ... then the whole order of nature will be thrown into confusion."[9]

Our worlds reel unless we rejoice. A song of thanks steadies everything.

The answer to anxiety is the adoration of Christ.

My Bible lays open beside my gratitude journal. There are piano lessons today and already a little brother's in tears, word-bruised by a big brother, and sisters are arguing loud over whose turn it is to make the bed, and I've snapped, exasperated, ugly, at a whining middle kid who doesn't want to stomp through snow and cold to get eggs from the henhouse. Anxiety can wear anger's mask. Fear of failing, of falling, of falling behind, it can make us fierce. Life can be messy before nine in the morning.

Joshua's tripping on notes. The thermometer out on the tree, its mercury is sluggish and heavy. Hard frost lines windows. How to breathe and dance?

"We are cold when it comes to rejoicing in God!" wrote Calvin. "Hence, we need to exercise ourselves in it and employ all our senses in it—our feet, our hands, our arms and all the rest—that they all might serve in the worship of God and so magnify Him."[10]

That's it. When exasperation mounts, *exercise* our song, employ all our senses.

I use my hand, pick up the pen, and write down a few more gifts —*employ* the senses to see and magnify God in that gratitude journal.

I warm. Joshua's practicing the chorus. Exercise. Employ. *Exalt.*
The answer to anxiety is always to *exalt Christ.*

The chickadees scuttle at the feeder and fly, warmth on the wing. I watch from the window. A child presses into me and the window and we have time. There is wonder. Everything absorbs into thanksgiving.

Calvin said that. "If we compare a hawk with the residue of the whole world, it is nothing. And yet if so small a portion of God's work ought to ravish us and amaze us, what ought all his works do when we come to the full numbering of them?"[11]

Ravish and amaze? Did Calvin number too? Come to the full numbering, the one thousand, the endless numbering of the infinite grace of God? My pen is on the counter.

Joshua's playing perfect joy now, the *Music Box Dancer,* finding all the right notes, exercising all this exaltation. And I'm thinking no one sees me in the kitchen spinning around, exercising feet and hands and arms and all the rest, smiling happiness anyways.

Dancing brave and unafraid anyways.

Holy Father, John Calvin said that the stability of the world depends on the rejoicing in Your works. Doesn't my world also stabilize when I rejoice in Your works? I'm echoing Calvin today: "What ought all Your works do when we come to the full numbering of them?" I too might dance. Cause me to remember it today, Lord: adore Christ to combat anxiety.

trusting grace

Do not be anxious about anything,
but in every situation,
by prayer and petition,
with thanksgiving,
present your requests to God.

Philippians 4:6

Anxiety has been my natural posture; stiffness, my default. The way I curl my toes up, tight retreat. How I angle my jaw, braced, chisel the brow with the lines of distrust. How I don't fold my hands in prayer, how I weld them into tight fists of control. *Always control—pseudopower from the pit.* How I refuse to relinquish worry, like a babe a mother won't forsake, an identity.

Do I hold worry close as this ruse of control, this pretense that I'm the one who will determine the course of events as I stir and churn and ruminate? Worry is the facade of taking action when prayer really is. And *stressed*, this pitched word that punctuates every conversation, is it really my attempt to prove how indispensable I am? Or is it more? Maybe disguising my deep fears as stress seems braver somehow.

An untroubled heart relaxes, trusts, leans assured into His ever-dependable arms. Trust, it's the antithesis of stress. "Oh, the joys of those who trust the LORD" (Psalm 40:4 NLT). But how to learn trust like that? Can trust be conjured up simply by sheer will, on command?

I can't fill with joy until I learn how to trust: "May the God of hope fill you with all *joy* and peace as you *trust* in him, so that you may overflow" (Romans 15:13, emphasis added). The full life, the one spilling joy and peace, happens only as I come to trust the caress of the Lover, Lover who never burdens His children with shame or self-condemnation but keeps stroking the fears with gentle grace.

If I believe, then I must let go and trust. Belief in God has to be more than mental assent, more than a clichéd exercise in cognition. What is saving belief if it isn't the radical dare to wholly trust?

Pisteuo is used more than two hundred times in the New Testament, most often translated as "belief." But it changes everything when I read that *pisteuo* ultimately means "to put one's faith in; to trust." *Belief is a verb, something that you do.*

Then the truth is that authentic, saving belief must be also? The very real, everyday *action* of trusting ... Then a true saving faith is a faith that gives thanks, a faith that sees God, a faith that deeply trusts? How would *eucharisteo* help me trust?

I read the verse several times in the Amplified Bible on an afternoon while young hands work scales up and down the piano keys. "Jesus replied, 'This is the work (service) that God asks of you: that you believe in the One Whom He has sent [that you cleave to, trust, rely on, and have faith in His Messenger]'" (John 6:29 AMP). That's my daily work, the work God asks of me? To trust.

Sometimes, too often, I don't want to muster the energy. Stress and anxiety seem easier. Easier to let a mind run wild with the worry than to exercise discipline, to rein her in, slip the blinders on, and train her to walk steady in certain assurance, not spooked by the specters looming ahead. Are stress and worry evidences of a soul too lazy, too undisciplined, to keep gaze fixed on God? To stay in love? I don't like to ask these questions, sweep out these corners where eyes glare from shadows.

Stress brings no joy. Isn't joy worth the effort of trust?

"This is the work (service) that God asks of you: that you believe in the One Whom He has sent [that you cleave to, trust, rely on, and have faith in His Messenger]."

And I know and haltingly confess: Much of the worry in my own life has been a failure to believe ... a wariness to thank and trust the loving hand of God.

I make soup and I bake bread, and I know my supreme need is joy in God and I know I can't experience deep joy in God until I deep trust in God. I shine sinks and polish through to the realization that trusting God is my most urgent need.

He who did not spare his own Son, but gave him up for us all— how will he not also, along with him, graciously give us all things?

Romans 8:32

He gave us Jesus. *Jesus! Gave Him up for us all.* If we have only one memory, isn't this one enough? Why is this the memory I most often take for granted?

He cut open the flesh of the God-Man and let the blood. He washed our grime with the bloody grace. He drove the iron ore through His own vein. Doesn't that memory alone suffice? Need there be anything more? If God didn't withhold from us His very own Son, will God withhold *anything* we need?

If trust must be earned, hasn't God unequivocally earned our trust with the bark on the raw wounds, the thorns pressed into the brow, your name on the cracked lips? How will He not also graciously give us all things He deems best and right? He's already given the incomprehensible.

Christ our Crossbeam.

The counting of all blessings is ultimately summed up in One.

The radical wonder of it stuns me happy, hushes me still: *It's all Christ.* Every moment, every event, every happening.

It's all in Christ and in Christ we are always safe.

~~~

Lord, cause me to take a deep breath right now and really trust in my Savior—that He really saves. Thank You, Lord; in my Savior I am always safe.

urgent grace

As a father has compassion on his children,
   so the LORD has compassion on those who fear him;
for he knows how we are formed,
   he remembers that we are dust.

Psalm 103:13–14

God gives us time. But who has time for God? This may not make any good sense.

A well-known pastor was once asked what his most profound regret in life was: "Being in a hurry." That is what he said.

> Getting to the next thing without fully entering the thing in front of me. I cannot think of a single advantage I've ever gained from being in a hurry.
>
> But a thousand broken and missed things, tens of thousands, lie in the wake of all the rushing.... Through all that haste I thought I was *making up time*. It turns out I was *throwing it away*.[12]

In our rushing, bulls in china shops, we break our own lives. Haste makes waste. The hurry makes us hurt.

Whatever the pace, time will keep it and there's no outrunning it, only speeding it up and pounding the feet harder; the minutes pound faster too. Race for more and you'll snag on time and leak empty. Hurry always empties a soul.

In a world with cows to buy and fields to see and work to do, in the beep and blink of the twenty-first century, with its "live in the moment" buzz phrase that none of the whirl-weary seem to know how to do, who actually knows how to take time and live with soul and body and God all in sync?

Life is so urgent it necessitates living slow.

It's only the amateurs—and this I have been, and it's been ugly —who think slow and urgent are contradictory, opposite poles. Is this the secret that all the life experts know? That in Christ, urgent means slow. That in Christ, the most urgent necessitates a slow and steady reverence. That in Christ, time is not running out. This day is not a sieve, losing time. In Christ, we fill—gaining time.

We stand on the brink of eternity. So there is enough time. Time to breathe deep and time to see real. Time to laugh long, time to give God glory and to rest deep and to sing joy. And just enough time in a day not to feel hounded, pressed, driven, or wild to get it all done. There is time to grab the jacket off the hook and time to go out to all air and sky and green. And time to read and wonder and laugh with all of them in all this light.

All this time refracting in prism.

All this time that could refract in praise ...

> *So what if we really paid attention*
> *and nickel-and-dimed life away*
> *on afternoon tag by the cedars.*
> *A string of bare toes with a stack of old books.*
> *This one lone bowl filling with morning light.*
> *Day after day, shelling out slow mindfulness*

on whatnots of amazing grace,
collecting pieces of God-glory.
This buying a bit of medicine
that cures ADD of the soul.

~~~

Lord, I can't fully express my gratitude for the time You've given.
So I want to spend my life really living today.

silk grace

... the heavens are the work of your hands ...
Like clothing you will change them
  and they will be discarded.
But you remain the same,
  and your years will never end.
The children of your servants will live in your presence ...

Psalm 102:25 – 28

It's a scant harvest of sweet corn this year.

The rains deluging in spring, then giving up its obsession with us come about mid-June.

From my post at the stove, out the window to the south, there the Farmer bends and bows over the cornstalks like an offering, the only way a life can reap a harvest.

The Farmer brings in cobs and the kids husk it back to kernels, to the nuggets of gold.

This takes time.

"Dad, can you tell Levi to stop going so fast?"

Joshua is cutting corn at the table under the spruce trees. Shalom is carrying the pans of corn to Hope and me at the stove. Malakai hauls and Caleb cuts too, on the far side of the table, with his own mountain of gold.

"Look—Levi's husking the cobs alright, but there are way too many hairs still left on these cobs." Joshua runs his hand over a cob, testifying.

"See all the corn silks he's left behind?" He holds his palm right open to all these hairs, blonde threads, summer's tassels.

"Levi …" The Farmer sets a stack of sun-warm cobs on the table and turns. "Just slow down—take your time on each cob. Do it well." He runs his fingers slowly across all the kernels of gold. "Just go slow —so you can get it all."

"Josh?" The Farmer leans over the table. "Watch how many kernels you're losing here." He smiles, winks. "We could all do that—slow down."

There was that sign in the yard of the Mennonites to the north: "Slow: Children at Play."

I could put a sign like that over the sink.

I blanch the next batch and there are the kernels of moments I've lost. How if I'd just gone slow, I could have multiplied all that He's given.

It's strange how the mind works.

The mind would rather fret about the future or pine over the past —so the mind can cling to its own illusion of control. But the current moment? It cannot be controlled. And what a mind can't control, it tends to discount. Brush past … over.

It's the battle plan of the enemy of the soul—to keep us blind to this current moment, the one we can't control, to keep us blind to Him, the One who controls everything.

There is that: What if instead of discounting the current moment, the uncontrollable, the simply given—what if I counted it—and on the God who controls it all?

What if all our running around is only our trying to run away from God—the great I AM, present in the present moment?

What if I woke to now and refused to hurry because I didn't want to refuse God?

What if I didn't discount this moment but counted it for what it is —God here?

It is only the present moment alone that holds the possibility of coming into the presence of God. Look around, breathe deep, enter into this one moment.

Now could be an altar. *This time* could be a tabernacle.

In God, there is no time, only eternity—or more simply, only now. His name is I AM. Here—*wherever my feet are*—is where I can love Him.

All these multiplying moments . . .

The steam curls up out of the pot like a prayer ascending and the windows fog and I can only see what is here, now.

Levi carries one cob to me, his witness, and all I can see is his smile.

The way he has slowed.

The way his hands now fill with this harvest of silk . . .

Lord God, forgive all running around that is merely a running away from You. Today, cause me to refuse to hurry because I don't want to refuse You. Instead of discounting the current moment, the uncontrollable, cause me to count it—and on the God who controls it all. This present moment holds the possibility of coming into Your presence—and I am slowing for the silk of now.

recognizing grace

What I mean, brothers and sisters, is that the time is short ...
For this world in its present form is passing away.

1 Corinthians 7:29, 31

They tramp in loud and fling themselves out of their coats like cicada splitting skins, leave boots a trail of droppings.

The Tall-Girl lets the door swing loose and it slams the fingertips of Little-One and she yelps a pain dance of salty tears.

In the tussle out of a stubborn sleeve, a big brother swipes hard the head of a little brother and Small-Son wails the mad fists and there are coats and boots and books and who has time for all this *more*—more work, more mess, more stress?

I can feel my pulse quicken fierce. Entering fully into the moment can overwhelm, a river running wild. I will forget again, and again, and again.

But today I do remember. I breathe and I reel and I hold my ground and my tongue in this torrent coming down. I've staked my claim to the miracle.

I know the way to the Promised Land.

I do what I always need to do. I preach it. I preach it to the person I need to preach to the most. I preach to me. The skin's tugged hard by

the rush of time and I say it aloud in current pounding past, words
I need like water:

Calm. Haste makes waste. Life is not *an emergency. Life is brief and it is
fleeting, but it is* not *an emergency.*

I pick up a coat and thank God for the arms that can do it.

*Emergencies are sudden, unexpected events—but is anything under the sun
unexpected to God?*

I call a son back and hand him a hanger and thank God that he can
do this too.

Stay calm, enter the moment, give thanks.

I thank God for boots and we line them straight and the little hands
help.

And I can *always give thanks because an all-powerful God has all these
things—all things—always under control.*

I breathe deep and He preaches to me, soothing the time-frenzied
soul with the grace river in whisper.

Life is not an emergency.

I soothe the cheek of the mad-fisted child. I give thanks for that
one curl that always lies on his forehead beckoning. He lays his head
on my shoulder. I stroke his hair, wind my finger round that curl. I
can feel the heat of his cheeks. I can feel time's current in my blood
ease ... meander. For a moment, longer, I hold him—and life—and
I hold it mindfully, attentively ... thankfully.

Life at its fullest is this sensitive, detonating sphere, and it can be
carried only in the hands of the unhurried and reverential—a bubble
held in awe.

I carry the Small-Son boy to the table.

When those hungry eyes and empty tummies circle round the
table, smiles big just like their daddy's when he's eyeing something
good heaping high on a platter, they are all story and loud talk and

hardly able to restrain the waiting for the nod, and I grin it too. "You may ..."

They dive.

I watch them feast. They quiet. Taste buds savor it long. It's that same recipe my mama baked up when I was a kid, cowlicks sliding up the front of my hair, just like theirs.

The Boy-Man mumbles, his mouth sticky full. "I am not eating mine fast." His tongue licks chocolate off lip. "Wanna taste it all."

A boy takes a big bite, too big, smiles knowingly. I look around at their faces, their taste buds all alive, eyes shining delight in the sweet.

When did I stop thinking life was dessert?

Only in the slowing, the sitting down at the table, when His hands held the bread and the thanks fell from His tongue, do the open-eyed, the wide-eyed, see the Face they face. The fast have spiritually slow hearts.

It takes a full twenty minutes after your stomach is full for your brain to register satiation. How long does it take your soul to realize that your life is full?

I weigh the moment down with full attention here.

Life is dessert — too brief to hurry.

Time is not running out. This day is not a sieve, losing time. With each passing minute, each passing year, there's this deepening awareness that I am filling, *gaining* time. We stand on the brink of eternity.

The Small-Son pauses between bites, wiggles his tooth with tip of his tongue. I watch him and I smile. He sees me watching and he grins. He takes that last bite of chocolate-melt and with mouth still full of gooey good, he serenades soft, "I love you, Mom ... and all this."

And all this.

This cathedral moment, this time before it bursts.

All this.

Father, with all the gifts I count, You are filling me, giving me more time to recognize the significance of the story You are writing on these days. Cause me to see more of these beautiful cathedral moments You place in my life every day. I want to slow down today—and truly taste of Your goodness.

singing grace

... always giving thanks for all things
in the name of our Lord Jesus Christ ...
Ephesians 5:20 NASB

So we stand there and listen long, and neither one of us can stop smiling and I almost forget to breathe.

The frogs have returned, the frogs and their song.

Why does the trilling in the throat of a frog do this wondrous thing inside of me?

The oldest boy, he and the dog go crashing off through that worn carpet of leaves all rustling, boy and lab questing for big things.

But Littlest One and I?

We've already found it.

That sound.

A symphony of sound, trilling low and deep, fills the spaces between the trees, lifts us too. It is like the water, a looking glass of trunks and limbs, like the water itself croons.

With the everyday eyes I can't see the singers at all. It takes time for eyes to adjust to stillness, and only the slow really see.

Then—there they are, on the far side. *There!* These glinting eyes flickering up through waters. The peepers are back, and we can see them, see the source of the song. Who doesn't want front-row seats to glory?

Can we pick our way across the swamp—can we get any closer?

She squeezes my hand tight and we splash across the bog and in a flash, the pond snaps shut.

All is soundless. Just this glassy reflection of maple branches pointing up to that curve of muted moon come early.

She and I swish-swash farther out, as far as we can go. Then wait.

On this isle of tangled grass, the water slowly rises up to our boot ankles. A red-tailed hawk swoops and soars, his wings motionless on the currents. The moon rides higher, tailing sun dipping. We say nothing, this Little One and I, but watch the swamp's mirror, waiting stock-still for the singers to surface.

The dog, loud and large, charges up, smashing our reflection of anticipation.

"Go, Boaz," she whispers too loud at the dog. "We're waiting for the frogs to sing!"

From within the woods somewhere, a brother whistles, and Boaz ricochets off.

We wait. Then one by one, they pop to the light. We catch our breath. Dare not move.

Tentatively it comes, this chorus, then crescendo, throaty yet gilded, and she squeezes my hand and we're spellbound, smiling silly.

I could sit here forever, listening.

Doesn't all the hurry make us hurt?

Slow never killed time. It's the rushing and racing, the trying to catch up, this is what kills time—ourselves.

Why in the world do we keep wounding ourselves?

Life is not an emergency.

And this, this is the only way to slow down time ...

Long, so very long, she and I, we just sit. We just soak in frog songs

on golden pond. When our toes are cold and the shadows stretch,
I stand slow, not wanting to.

"We leaving the frogs, now?" she whispers up to me.

I nod ... reluctant.

So Littlest One, she swings round and two splashing steps into it,
all falls quiet.

The sudden hush turns our heads.

The swamp's soundless, blinked silent by hurried sloshing.

I scoop up one wide-eyed little girl and whisper into her the ways
of God:

"You can only hear your life sing—when you still."

~⁀○

*Father God, You tell me to still. For the very best of reasons. So today—
I will. I've been missing the songs far too long.*

ugly grace

For God was pleased to have all his fullness dwell in him,
and through him to reconcile to himself all things.

Colossians 1:19 – 20

The wrinkled man in the wheelchair with the legs wrapped, the girl
with her face punctured deep with the teeth marks of a dog, the mess
of this world, and I *see*.

In German, it's *hübsch-hässlich*. In French, *d'un beau affreux*. What
the impressionist painter Paul Gauguin encapsulated as, "*Le laid peut
être beau*" — the ugly can be beautiful.

The *ugly-beautiful*.

And I nod it soft. *Yes, Father, You long to transfigure all, no matter how
long it takes. You long to transfigure all.*

In Christian circles, we elevate what we deem beautiful, endeavor
to create spheres of pristine beauty, and perhaps rightly so, for
"whatever is good, pure, lovely, think on these things." But I wonder
if maybe in the upside-down kingdom of God, what we regard as
unlovely is, in Jesus, lovely. Because somewhere, underneath the
grime of this broken world, everything has the radiant fingerprints of
God on it. Seeing the world with Jesus' eyes, we have the astonishing
opportunity to daily love the unlovely into loveliness.

And, funny thing, I'm discovering that when I lean deep into my secrets, when I draw the lens up close to the ugly in my life, examining the weave, the texture, the shadows, it too is beautiful.

When I deeply see:

- bedsheets painted with highlighter?... *children live here!*
- dead rose left too long in vase?... *lingering memories of a brother's gift.*
- Great-grandma's wicker laundry basket overflowing in the mudroom?... *we had a full, rich weekend!*
- vehicle souvenirs—a collection of shoes, Sunday school paper, Lego pieces?... *we'll gather them up too.*
- study table spread out with thoughts and ideas?... *we're thinking now.*
- a pile of tossed shoes on a shelf in the garage?... *worn days of a good summer.*
- stack of tattered books?... *stories that have become real.*

Aren't these ugly things, in their own way, part of the gift list too?

God is always good and we are always loved ... even when what He gives may appear ugly.

Up close, touching the unexpected comeliness in these domestic messes, I can't help but wonder ...

Does all the ugliness in my life look this beautiful?

It would, if I got closer.

Is that why God stays so close to us?

Lord, draw me nearer to the scratched situations in my life, the scarred places. Get me close enough to You to see the beauty in them.

graffiti grace

Fear not, for I have redeemed you;
I have called you by name, you are mine. . . .
Because you are precious in my eyes, and honored,
and I love you, I give men in return for you,
peoples in exchange for your life.

Isaiah 43:1, 4 ESV

When I find out what a teenager's done, I'd like to ring one slender neck. Dirt rings the mudroom sink like nasty vandalism.

To-do lists keep scrawling ugly, longer and longer. I can't find my watch anywhere. The bathroom mirror is splattered and smudged.

The weather forecast makes it impossible to know if we should plant our next field or wait until the next rain or what to do. We watch the sky for a sign. We pray, *we pray these begging prayers.*

I go a whole week watchless, not knowing what time it is.

I can't make sense of anything and this lump in my throat burns.

A high school friend, one who knew the thick glasses and the crush on the Dutch farm boy and the blessed scent of the library stacks, she and I are an impossible twenty years older and we go for a walk.

I listen to her talk of career changes and photography and marriage maybe someday soon? She has all these questions of her own. I can only nod.

We're walking down a side street in town when I stop. I stop and reach for my camera.

Rachel—she keeps talking about mortgage rates, about the Gospels and Jesus and speech pathology and the meaning of life, and her mind has always been this mushrooming wonder holding me rapt.

I aim the camera at the sidewalk. Fiddle for the shutter. The lens works to focus.

And Rachel stops midsentence. She reads the words chalked on asphalt out loud, words I'm focusing on. She reads them slow, like a decoding of everything.

"Hey beautiful, you are loved ☺" scrawled right there on the sidewalk, happy face chalked there grinning too.

"Oh." She says it like an awakening. "And here I just thought it was graffiti."

I nod in the middle of an epiphany.

The graffiti can be grace.

What seems a defacement may be a glimpse of His face. *All the writing on the wall could be love notes.*

I turn to Rachel, the camera, the capturing, still in hand, and the wind gusts, and I cheer it into the wind, into her—

"Hey beautiful, you are loved!"

And she laughs loud and we're carried.

Everything could make sense. And the real mystery of grace is that it always arrives in time. Like the wind, grace finds us wherever we are and won't leave us however we were found.

I take another picture. So I'll remember.

"This deciphers everything, doesn't it?" I say it to myself, only half asking. The other half of me knowing with a certainty I've not felt before. Love always deciphers everything.

And the dialect of God is the day just as it comes—and whenever I slow down and shift perspective, it's possible to read the impossible: the divine language of love written on all the walls. This smiling, startling alphabet of grace.

That's what jolts me, right there on the sidewalk: Grace isn't a mere Pollyanna feeling. It's a force. It's a powerful force. As startling as the power of electricity. Grace is the power of God pulsating with this passionate love of God, this jolting, blazing, dangerous love that pierces all of humanity's pitch-black.

Grace always shocks.

Grace always stuns.

Grace is always what we need.

It's what everyone groping around lost in the dark has to know: turn toward grace and you turn on all the lights. The whole black asphalt at our feet torches with the revelation.

And there is more than enough light to see it.

How the day's fresh mercies make even here clean enough.

Clean enough for all these chalkings of His love.

Lord God, there will be walls I run into today, walls that seem to box me in, walls that have writing on them that I long to decode. When I rightly read Your Word, I can rightly read the world: the graffiti of this world is grace in Your hands.

coded grace

I have learned how to be content with whatever I have.
I know how to live on almost nothing or with everything.
I have learned the secret of living in every situation,
whether it is with a full stomach or empty, with plenty or little.

Philippians 4:11 – 12 NLT

Sitting there before the window, I'm struck.

All these years I was saved. I had said my yes to God, but I was really living the no.

I may have always known that change takes real intentionality, like a woman bent over her garden beds every day with a spade and the determined will to grow up something good to strengthen the heart.

I may even have known that change requires more than merely thinking the warm and fuzzy thoughts about a door and a way through and that Greek word, *eucharisteo*, holding the mystery to the full life and ever after.

But none of that at all meant that I knew what to do.

To live — at all — I needed to know.

I begin the list. Not of gifts I want, but of gifts I *already have*. That is the beginning, and I smile. I can't believe how I smile. I mean, they are just the common things, and maybe I don't even know they are gifts, really, until I write them down and see what they look like.

Writing the list, it makes me feel ... happy. All day. I can hardly believe how it does that, that running stream of consciousness, river I drink from and am quenched in, a surging stream of grace and it's wild how it sweeps me away. And I add one more to the list. To feel it all again. I can't understand why it does that. And yet ... too ... the list, it feels foreign, strange. Long, I am a woman who speaks but one language, the language of the fall—discontentment and self-condemnation, the critical eye and the never satisfied.

This thanks that I am doing—it seems so ... crude. Trivial. If this list is the learning of the language of *eucharisteo*—this feels like ... guttural groanings. But perhaps the "full of grace" vocabulary begins haltingly, simply, like a child, thankful for the childlike.

But doesn't the kingdom of heaven belong to such as these?

At first, it's the dare that keeps me going. That and how happy it makes me—giddy—this list-writing of all that is good and pure and lovely and beautiful. But what keeps me going is what I read in that Bible lying open on my prayer bench looking out the window to the snow fort. The fort with a door in the wall. It's Paul writing his letter to the Philippians. I read the fourth chapter. I almost don't see it, but Paul repeats it twice in only two sentences, so I don't miss it.

There it is—the secret to living joy in every situation, the full life of *eucharisteo*. Twice Paul whispers it: "I have learned ..." Learned. I would have to learn *eucharisteo*. Learn *eucharisteo*—learn it to live fully. Learn it like I know my skin, my face, the words on the end of my tongue. Like I know my own name. Learn how to be thankful —whether empty or full. Could the list teach me even that hard language? Over time?

I want the hunt, the long sleuth, the careful piecing together. To learn how to be grateful and happy, whether hands full or hands empty. That is a secret worth spending a life on learning.

I wake the next morning and I grip my pen, ink, to crack the code.

God, so many days have dialects I don't understand. How in the world do I learn the language of joy? One can only crack the code of contentment by learning the language of Your love. Let me count the ways.

naming grace

> He brought them to the man to see what he would name them;
> and whatever the man called each living creature, that was its name.
>
> *Genesis 2:19–20*

My list of naming God-gifts lies open on the counter ...

117. *Washing the warm eggs*

118. *Crackle in fireplace*

119. *Still-warm cookies*

Naming is Edenic.

I name gifts and go back to the Garden and God in the beginning who first speaks a name and lets that which is come into existence. This naming is how the first emptiness of space fills: the naming of light and land and sky. The first man's first task is to name. Adam completes creation with his Maker through the act of naming creatures, releasing the land from chaos, from the teeming, indefinable mass. I am seeing it too, in the journal, in the face of the Farmer: naming offers the gift of recognition. When I name moments— string out laundry and name-pray, thank You, Lord, for bedsheets in billowing winds, for fluff of sparrow landing on line, sun winter warm, and one last leaf still hanging in the orchard—I am Adam and I discover my meaning and God's, and to name is to learn the language of Paradise. This naming work never ends for all the children of Adam. Naming to find an identity, our identity, God's.

It's late, and in the lamplight when the bones finally rest, I read and turn a page and run unexpected into these words:

> Now, in the Bible a name ... reveals the very essence of a thing, or rather its essence as God's gift.... To name a thing is to manifest the meaning and value God gave it, to know it as coming from God and to know its place and function within the cosmos created by God. To name a thing, in other words, is to bless God for it and in it.[13]

I read the words again. The heart palpitates hard. I don't hear the clock or the slosh hum of the dishwasher. All I can see, think, is that my whim writing of one thousand gratitudes, the naming of the moments—this is truly a holy work.

This naming really *does* call now a gift, a gift of God. I read again: "To name a thing is to manifest the meaning and value God gave it." I look at a day, a thing, an event in front of me, and it may look manna-strange: "What is it?" But when I name it, the naming of it manifests its meaning: to know it comes from God. *This is gift!* Naming is to know a thing's function in the cosmos—to name is to *solve mystery*.

In naming that which is right before me, that which I'd otherwise miss, the invisible becomes visible.

The space that spans my inner emptiness fills in the naming.

I name. And I know the face I face.

God's! God is in the details; God is in the moment. God is in all that blurs by in a life—even hurts in a life.

GOD!

How can I not name? Naming these moments may change the ugly names I call myself.

I put a pen to a journal, to name solve, and I shake it when it runs dry, trace circles, and I coax out ink.

Lord, help me in the true work You've assigned to me today: to name the graces You give me this day. Cause me to name the ways You love — so I can own my own name: Beloved.

praying grace

I thank and praise you, God of my ancestors:
You have given me wisdom and power.
Daniel 2:23

I must never be deceived by the simplicity of *eucharisteo* and penning His love list. Frogs. Sun. Journal. Naming. Love. Here. It all feels startlingly hallowed and I breathe shallow. I should take my shoes off.

This is the other side where Daniel, man of prayer, lived. You know, change agent Daniel, mover and shaker Daniel, second-to-the-king Daniel, sleeping-in-perfect-peace-in-the-den-of-the-lions Daniel. And Daniel is a man of power prayer, not because he bends the stiff knees and makes petitions of the High Throne three times daily. Rather, his prayers move kings and lion jaws because Daniel "got down on his knees and prayed, *giving thanks* to his God, just as he had done before" (Daniel 6:10, emphasis added). Three times a day, Daniel prayed *thanksgiving* for the everyday common, for the God-love spilling forth from the God-heart at the center of all.

I am bell and He is sure wind, and He moves and I am rung and I know it for what it is: The only real prayers are the ones mouthed with thankful lips. Because gratitude ushers us into the other side of prayer, into the heart of the God-love, and all power to change the world resides here in His love. Prayer, *to be prayer*, to have any power to change anything, must first speak thanks: "In every situation, by prayer and petition, *with thanksgiving*, present your requests to God" (Philippians 4:6, emphasis added). "*First*, I tell you to pray for all people, asking God for what they need and *being thankful to him*" (1 Timothy 2:1 NCV, emphasis added). Prayer without ceasing is only possible in a life of continual thanks. How did I ever think there was another way to enter into His courts but with thanksgiving?

The gift list *is* thinking upon His goodness—and this, *this* pleases Him most! *And* most profits my own soul, and I am beginning, only beginning, to know it. If clinging to His goodness is the highest form of prayer, then this seeing His goodness with a pen, with a shutter, with a word of thanks, these really are the most sacred acts conceivable. The ones anyone can conceive, anywhere, in the midst of anything.

I am struck, a bell, and I chime long. Daniel is only a man of prayer because he is a man of thanks, and the only way to be a man or woman of prayer is to *be a man or woman of thanks*. And not sporadic, general thanks, but three times a day *eucharisteo*.

When I give thanks for the seemingly microscopic, I make a place for God to grow within me. This, *this*, makes me full, and I "magnify him with thanksgiving" (Psalm 69:30 KJV), and God enters the world. What will a life magnify? The world's stress cracks, the grubbiness of a day, all that is wholly wrong and terribly busted? Or God?

The list is *God's* list, the pulse of His love—the love that thrums on the other side of our prayers. And I see it now for what this really is, this dare to write down one thousand things I love. It really is a dare to name all the ways that *God* loves me. The true Love Dare. To move into His presence and listen to His love unending and know the grace uncontainable. This is the vault of the miracles. The only thing that can change us, can change the world, is this—His love.

"My soul doth magnify the Lord" (Luke 1:46 KJV).

So might I; yes, and even here.

Lord, You are the Giver infinitely greater than the sum of all gifts and how can I not slow and bow? Bow right now in worship. Kneel throughout the day in gratitude. Slow, wherever I am, in adoration. Could the miracle of becoming a person of prayer begin with just two words: "Thank You"?

all-here grace

Sacrifice thank offerings to God,
fulfill your vows to the Most High . . .
Those who sacrifice thank offerings honor me.

Psalm 50:14, 23

Science may explain mechanics, but how do the eyes of the soul see?

I seize the pen on the sill and I can record another one. With my hand still dribbling dishes, with the breath all caught, I etch it down in that journal always lying out flat.

362. *Suds . . . all color in sun*

I lay down the pen. Dry my hands on the dishtowel, dab at water spots transfusing into ink.

The house is a mess.

I wash up undone on an island of quiet. The loud and blur of the morning ache across my shoulders. The washing machine works, and the porcelain dove, the one with "peace" scrolled deep into wing, hangs by one clear thread. From the sink, I can see her spin, spin, this way, then that, around and around and dizzy around.

This is the way I have lived. From the time the alarm first rings and I stir on our pillows touching, stretch over his bare back and check those relentless hands keeping time on that clock. The time, always the time, I'm an amateur trying to beat time. The six kids rouse. We race.

The barn ... and hurry. The breakfast ... *and hurry*. The books, the binders ... and hurry! In a world addicted to speed, I blur the moments into one unholy smear.

I have done it. I do it still. Hands of the clock whip hard. So I push hard and I bark hard and I fall hard and when their wide eyes brim sadness and their chins tremble weak, I am weary, and I am the thin clear skin, reflecting their fatigue, about to burst, my eyes glistening their same sheer pain.

The hurry makes us hurt.

And maybe it is the hurt that drives us on? For all our frenzied running seemingly toward something, could it be that we are in fact fleeing—desperate to escape pain that pursues?

I speak it to God: I don't really want *more* time; I just want *enough* time, time to do my one life well.

The wonder right in the middle of the sink. Looking for it like this. I lay the palm under water and I raise my hand with the membrane of a life span of moments. In the light the sheerness of bubble shimmers. Bands of garnet, cobalt, flowing luminous.

I see through to the pattern. I see. The way my life, vapor, is shaping. I hadn't noticed.

Time is a relentless river. It rages on, a respecter of no one. And this, this is the only way to slow time: When I fully enter time's swift current, enter into the current moment with the weight of all my attention, I slow the torrent with the weight of me all here. When I'm looking for the glimpse of glory, I slow and enter. And time slows.

The bubble in my hand quavers, a rainbow at fringes.

And blind eyes see: It's this sleuthing for the glory that slows a life. In this space of time and sphere, I am attentive, aware, accepting the whole of the moment, weighing it down with me all here.

Full attention fills the empty ache.

Forgive me, Father, for not being all here. When Your very name is I AM and You are in the present and here is where I can love You. Today, when I race ahead—return me to all here.

hammering grace

Seek and you will find;
knock and the door will be opened to you . . .
Therefore, everyone who hears these words of mine
and puts them into practice
is like a wise man who built his house on the rock.

Matthew 7:7, 24

A contemporary and admirer of Martin Luther said, "A nail is driven out by another nail; habit is overcome by habit."[14] When I read this thought, I am surprised because I had never known, and I am sad for all that would have changed if only I had.

Do not disdain the small. The whole of the life—even the hard—is made up of the minute parts, and if I miss the infinitesimals, I miss the whole. There is a way to live the big of giving thanks in all things. It is this: to give thanks in this one small thing. The moments will add up.

I too had read it often, the oft-quoted verse: "And give thanks for everything to God the Father in the name of our Lord Jesus Christ" (Ephesians 5:20 NLT). And I too would nod and say straight-faced, "I'm thankful for everything." But in this counting gifts, to one thousand, more, I discover that slapping a sloppy brush of thanksgiving over everything in my life leaves me deeply thankful for very few things in my life. A lifetime of sermons on "thanks in all things" and the shelves sagging with books on these things and I testify: Life-changing gratitude does not fasten to a life unless nailed through with one very specific nail at a time.

Little nails and a steady hammer can rebuild a life.

Eucharisteo precedes the miracle.

I look down at the pen. This pen—this is nothing less than the driving of nails. Nails driving out my habits of discontent and driving in my habit of *eucharisteo*. I'm hammering in nails to pound out nails, ugly nails that Satan has pierced through the world, my heart. It starts to unfold, light in the dark, a door opening up, how all these years it's been utterly pointless to try to wrench out the spikes of discontent. Because that habit of discontentment can only be driven out by hammering in one iron sharper. The sleek pin of gratitude.

I hammer.

How much is my tongue, tail of the heart, learning the real language of *eucharisteo*? I forget Eden and naming and nails, and it all seems just a bit ... juvenile. Contrived. This is the whole of the secret learning? I confess, even after all that I've seen and tasted and touched, I do scoff. I yearn for the stuff of saints, the hard language, the fluency of thanksgiving in all, even the ugliest and most heartbreaking. I want the very fullest life. I wonder, even just an inkling—is this but a ridiculous experiment? Some days, ones with laundry and kids and dishes in sink, it is hard to think that the insulting ordinariness of this truly teaches the full mystery of the all most important, *eucharisteo*. It's so frustratingly common—it's offensive.

Driving nails into a life always is.

I pick up the journal. Paul had twice said it and I mustn't forget it. He said he had to learn. And learning requires practice—sometimes even mind-numbing practice. C. S. Lewis said it too, to a man looking for fullest life: "If you think of this world as a place intended simply for our happiness, you find it quite intolerable: think of it as a place of training and correction and it's not so bad."[15] It might even be good. So I too can be like our children and the everyday training, memorizing of the Latin paradigms with the practicing chants: *amo, amas, amat*. The washing machine dings and I light up. This is why I had never really learned the language of "thanks in all things"! Though pastors preached it, I still came home and griped on. I had never practiced. Practiced until it became the second nature, the first skin. Practice is the hardest part of learning, and training is the essence of transformation.

Practice, practice, practice. Hammer. Hammer. Hammer.

This training might prove to be the hardest of my life.

It just might save my life.

Lord God, Your Son took the ringing of the hammer and the pounding of the nails to buy my salvation. Right now I offer You up my open hands. Drive out the nails of habitual grumbling with the nails of habitual gratitude. I long to be fixed to You.

awakening grace

Give thanks in all circumstances;
for this is God's will for you in Christ Jesus.
1 Thessalonians 5:18

How could I have been dead all day and not really know it?

There had been the plugged toilet, there was no getting around knowing that. We all knew that needed attention, a toilet in a house of eight always requiring immediate resurrection.

After that, there had been the mad dash to music lessons. Lots of frantic movement, sure, and yes, flailing—but really? I'd been numbed right through, just going through the motions.

And after that, there was the burnt soup, just because I failed to stir. Is that why we die in a thousand ways every day? Because we fail to stand near the heat and stir ourselves awake?

It wasn't till our littlest, Shalom, pulled those two kitties into her arms that I knew something in me had been the walking dead all day, something in me opened wide. The way those bundles of fur purr deep into the crook of her arm, so quiet. She turns to them and laughs, so full of life, and something stirs in me, so loud.

Maybe it's the way her tendrils fell that made me see it—that I had fallen asleep all day to the glory, and everywhere. That I had missed my life because I had missed the graces, and I didn't want to live like this, and isn't that what Robert Louis Stevenson had written?

"The man who forgets to be thankful has fallen asleep in life."[16]

The toilet fail, the music fumbling, the soup founder—a woman can forget in a thousand ways.

Our youngest, she says it tickles, the way his tail flicks her nose. She says it and her eyes, they laugh with all this light.

She tilts her head so the kitten is in the crook of her neck, tail waving happy—and the way she half smiles, it upholds everything. And this purring. It's all so perfectly loud.

She's tickling me awake. A heart can murmur gratitude with its every wide-awake beat.

I have known it, and I know it again, the love crawling all up and over her: intentionally look for ways to give thanks, purpose to give thanks, dare yourself to give thanks anyways—and it's the setting of an alarm and you could wake up to nothing less than your life.

Set out a gratitude list and there it goes again: an alarm set off by the startling grace of God. Giving thanks, this is an awakening—the breath of God upon the face, close and warm.

When we fill the kitty dish, you can hear it, how they drink. Our girl lies right on her tummy so she can listen.

"Hear them, Mama?" Her eyes dance indigo sky, all uncontained, all alive.

This is what we are doing—she and I smiling over spilled milk anyways.

She and I waking up ... this lapping up of life.

⌒

Father, Awaker of the dead, awaken me again today. Tendrils of Your grace will fall today—cause me not to forget to give thanks so I don't fall asleep to my life. To the whole earth spilling over with Your glory.

all-is-well grace

Then God opened her eyes
and she saw a well of water.

Genesis 21:19

Hagar and her boy were dying of thirst with a well less than a bowshot away. How to find God in the mess?

We [actually] saw His glory ... For out of His fullness (abundance) we have all received [all had a share and we were all supplied with] one grace after another and spiritual blessing upon spiritual blessing and even favor upon favor and gift [heaped] upon gift. (John 1:14, 16 AMP, emphasis added)

That's the mystery map to the deep seeing! We saw His glory ... *because* ... we have all received one grace after another. We *have* all received one grace after another, but we only recognize the glory of God in this moment *when we wake to the one grace after another.* "If you want to be really alert to seeing Jesus' divine beauty, his glory ... *then make sure you tune your senses to see his grace,*" urges theologian John Piper (emphasis added). "That's what his glory is full of."[17] Grace — *that* is what the full life is full of, what the God-glory is full of. To see the glory, name the graces. Retune the impaired senses to sense the Spirit, to see the grace. Couldn't I do that anywhere?

Why is it so hard? Practice, practice.

What insanity compels me to shrivel up when there is joy's water to be had here? In this wilderness, I keep circling back to this: I'm blind to joy's well every time I really don't want it. *The well is always there.* And I *choose* not to see it. Don't I really want joy? Don't I *really* want the fullest life? For all my yearning for joy, longing for joy, begging for joy —is the bald truth that I prefer the empty dark?

Why do I lunge for control instead of joy? Is it somehow more perversely satisfying to flex control's muscle? Ah—*power*—like Satan. Do I think Jesus-grace too impotent to give me the full life? Isn't that the only reason I don't always swill the joy? If the startling truth is that I don't really want joy, there's a far worse truth. If I am rejecting the joy that is hidden somewhere deep in this moment, am I not ultimately rejecting God? Whenever I am blind to joy's well, isn't it because I don't believe in God's care? That God cares enough about me to always offer me joy's water, wherever I am, regardless of circumstance. But if I don't believe God cares, if I don't want or seek the joy He definitely offers somewhere in this moment—I don't want God.

In His presence is fullness of joy. *He is in this moment.*

The well is always here. God is always here—precisely because He does care.

God faithfully provides water for His people everywhere.

When you know you're Hagar and you finally come to the end of yourself and all the water in your canteen is gone and you *know* you and your son are going to *die* if you don't get some joy to the lips and down the parched throat—and now; when you can no longer stand to see those you love *die* all around you from your emptiness, pray with the eyes wide open and prayer becomes revelation. Eyes change and what we see changes in them.

You have to want to see the well before you can drink from it. You have to want to see joy, God in the moment.

Thereafter, Hagar used another name to refer to the LORD, who had spoken to her. She said, "You are the God who sees me." She also said, "Have I truly seen the One who sees me?" So that well was named Beer-lahai-roi (which means "well of the Living One who sees me").

Genesis 16:13 – 14 NLT

Hagar had known God sees, for she had met Him before, needy in the sands, yet when sent away the second time, Hagar had forgotten. She had laid her son down to die and couldn't see any well. In the domestic cloud of dust and family, I too can forget the One who sees me, but in *eucharisteo* I remember. I cup hands and all the world is water.

Love is not blind; love is the holy vision.

For a glancing moment, I am Hagar healed, Hagar who had spoken once before in a desert exile. The well, it is still there.

There is always a well — all is well.

Lord, that You would give one grace after another — tune my senses to see Your grace. Focus my sight to see the well — that all is well.

curative grace

Then the LORD told him,
"Make a replica of a poisonous snake and attach it to a pole.
All who are bitten will live if they simply look at it!"
So Moses made a snake out of bronze and attached it to a pole.
Then anyone who was bitten by a snake
could look at the bronze snake and be healed!

Numbers 21:8–9 NLT

Faith is the seeing eyes that find the gauze to heaven torn through; that, slow to witness the silent weight, feel the gold glory bar heavy in palm, no matter the outer appearance. Seeing is the spiritual life: "they might see with their eyes, hear with their ears, understand with their hearts, and return and be healed" (Isaiah 6:10 NASB). "Looking comes first," wrote C. S. Lewis.[18]

First the eyes. Always first, the inner eyes.

Looking is the love. Looking is evidence of the believing.

I remember reading it only weeks before, sitting in the surgeon's waiting room with Levi, the hospital renovation progressing slowly, the patients healing only slightly faster. (Transfiguration can be the long miracle.) Levi had daydreamed out the waiting room window, listened to the stories of car accidents and work injuries from the bandaged, and I had held my book. I'd read how the Israelites looked about and saw much to bemoan, much to complain about: "They spoke against God and against Moses, and said, 'Why have you brought us up out of Egypt to die here in the wilderness? There is no bread! There is no water! And we detest this miserable food!'" (Numbers 21:5).

I had looked around at the wounded all waiting. I had turned back to the page. And what does God send the ingrates? What came to the ingrates in the Eden beginning? A slithering blanket of snakes that coil around the complaints of the Israelites, open wide and pierce the flesh with the fang. Always, ingratitude makes the poison course.

The cure against the bite of thanklessness.

The remedy is in the retina.

How we behold determines if we hold joy. Behold glory and be held by God.

How we look determines how we live ... *if* we live.

And I had read how Jesus says, "In the same way that Moses lifted the serpent in the desert so people could have something to see and then believe, it is necessary for the Son of Man to be lifted up—and everyone who looks up to him, trusting and expectant, will gain a real life, eternal life" (John 3:14–15 MSG). I had looked up from my book and into the face of a boy with his ear bandaged and I didn't want to imagine what had happened.

I had tried to take it in. Isn't Jesus Himself saying that people need to see and then believe—that looking and believing are the same thing? That in the right inner looking we can gain the right outer life ... the *saved full* life?

I had read it and had forgotten (always!), but I remember it now. "Faith is the gaze of a soul upon a saving God."[19]

Faith is in the gaze of a soul. Faith is the seeing soul's eyes upon a saving God.

That's what makes us persevere through a life: to see Him who is invisible!

Lord, You heal every infirmity. Heal my stunted sight. Open the eyes of my heart. I long to see Your heart—even when I can't see Your hand. The remedy is in the retina.

perceiving grace

"Your eyes are windows into your body.
If you open your eyes wide in wonder and belief,
your body fills up with light.
If you live squinty-eyed in greed and distrust,
your body is a dank cellar.
If you pull the blinds on your windows,
what a dark life you will have!"
Matthew 6:22 – 23 MSG

How do we converse with a God who may not seem to honor our honor?

In the quiet, I wonder, cue card with a memory verse in hand—if I had the perspective of the whole, perhaps I'd see it? That which seems evil, is it a cloud to bring rain, to bring a greater good to the *whole* of the world? Who would ever know the greater graces of comfort and perseverance, mercy and forgiveness, patience and courage, if no shadows fell over a life? I dare flip the cue card over and I make out words on the back side, "See now that I, I am He, and there is no god besides Me; It is I who put to death and give life. I have wounded and it is I who heal" (Deuteronomy 32:39 NASB). I nod. I know. *I know.* And these truth words reconfigure the battlefield under my feet.

I grip the card and I know all our days are struggle and warfare

(Job 14:14) and the spirit-to-spirit combat I endlessly wage with Satan is this ferocious thrash for joy. He sneers at all the things that seem to have gone hideously mad in this sin-drunk world, and I gasp to say God is good.

The liar defiantly scrawls his graffiti across God's glory, and I heave to enjoy God ... and Satan strangles and I whiten knuckles to grasp real Truth and fix that beast to the floor.

It's just that the eyes are bad—my perspective. "Your eye is a lamp that provides light for your body," Jesus said. "When your eye is good, your whole body is filled with light. But when your eye is bad, your whole body is filled with darkness. And if the light you think you have is actually darkness, how deep that darkness is!" (Matthew 6:22–23 NLT). If Satan can keep my eyes from the Word, my eyesight is too poor to read light—to fill with light. Bad eyes fill with darkness so heavy the soul aches because empty is never truly empty; empty is only a full, deepening darkness. So this is what it is to be. Eve in the Garden, Satan's hiss tickling the ear. "Did God actually say ...?" (Genesis 3:1 ESV).

No Scripture glasses to read what God is trying to write through a prodigal child? Scrawl my own quick editing on the half-finished story: *failure*. Satan's tongue darts.

Not wearing a biblical lens to decipher the meaning of a doctor's ominous diagnosis? Just read Satan's slippery interpretation: *cheated*.

Not using anything to bend the light of this world so I can read my own messy days? Spray on another layer of graffiti: *worthless*.

So I have been ambushed.

Without God's Word as a lens, the world warps.

Who deserves any grace?

When I realize that it is not God who is in my debt but I who am in His great debt, then doesn't *all* become gift?

Lord, You are the only lens that can correct the vision of a life. And if I don't hunger daily for the bread of Your Word, I'll develop sight deficiency. Make me Word reflective — that I may have the right perspective.

hunting grace

My cup overflows.
Surely your goodness and love will follow me
all the days of my life,
and I will dwell in the house of the LORD forever.

Psalm 23:5 – 6

I don't think of it then.

Not then, when I raise my hands up in what isn't—well—in what it isn't, precisely, praise. Because really, the way I threw my hands up, it was more this lift of lament and exhausted surrender and end-of-the-day fatigue than any semblance of praise.

And I can't say it occurred to me right then either, throwing my hands up in the air, that it really could be that we were born with two hands because we never stop weighing the good against the bad, today against yesterday—and that I'm weighing everything all the time.

But I do know that the piles and the weeds and the to-do lists and the messiness of living—it can weigh right heavy and I can feel it in the shoulders, the back, the heart.

I can only say I thought of it after the weekly ceremony of looking for beauty to fill the vases, the crocks that have become furniture— permanent furniture—since spring, and the peonies.

Before, when a child brought in a fistful of Queen Anne's lace, summer's scattered doilies, it was only then I'd slip a vase off the shelf.

Or when boys raced in with first profusion of wild daffodils from the ditches ...

Or when the Farmer would stop the tractor at the edge of the side road on the way home from the other farms, right there by the neighbor's, and he'd fill his arms with tiger lilies growing free under the maples, him feeling no shame in greased and manly hands picking slender stems, carrying flowers home for his bride.

I'd only get a vase down then.

Because it went like this:

Have beauty.

Must get a vessel.

But when Farmer gave me these four crocks, all thrift store finds, the world spun a bit differently.

So I made these vases furniture, vases that always remained out: one on the dining room table, one by the sink, one by the hearth, one in the study — permanent fixtures in a house that could be wired for glory.

So it could go like this:

Have vessel.

Now must find beauty.

Empty containers can make us seekers, hunters of glory. I need to find grace-beauty to fill the emptiness. Not bought beauty — only beauty that can be bought with attention.

A wildflower from the roadside. A branch from the woods, grasses growing long in the ditches, zinnias from the garden, a happy round face from the sunflower patch, a flowering chive or two.

"Can I gather the flowers this week?" a son asks after the weekly cleaning, hand on the back doorknob, scissors in hand.

"Can I go too?" A little girl's already flash of blond light across kitchen.

We've become this motley tribe of beauty hunters.

So, it's when I have a vase in my hand and those black-eyed Susans are long-necked and lovely that I just plunk the bouquet of flowers directly down on the antique weight scale.

It's when the levered beam falls with a clunk.

It's only then, when the beam in my own eye falls away, that I see clear what all saints must already know ...

For those who can see, the world's beauty outweighs its burdens, its grace greater than its grime.

There is always this: pots and pans and peels. I forget to put a load of laundry in before we sit down to the dinner. I haven't taken in the load out on the line. I have to gather strewn books and take out the recycling and find a hoe for that garden.

What will I look for, to outweigh everything? *Who* will I look to, to outweigh everything?

And in the midst, my gratitude journal lies open.

It used to be that I offered generic thanks—mumble a bit of thanks before the sleep, give thanks before the meal.

Have grace.

Must give thanks—sorta (now and then).

But when gratitude journals became my permanent life furniture, white spaces opened wide, empty pages like cups to heaven, waiting to be filled with the color of His graces ... something in me shifted.

What will I look for, to outweigh everything? *Who* will I look to, to outweigh everything?

Have space to give thanks, space to chronicle a thousand gifts.

Now must *find grace.*

I become a seeker, a looker. A God-hunter—making this a daily ceremony, the gathering of grace, joy to fill the emptiness, Father-glory that never fades.

And when I look out at sunflowers, with all those sprouting weeds at their feet, I can tell just by the way they're nodding their crowning heads — the way all these flowers agree, agree.

They agree with the antique scale and here with these people in the midst of our piles.

When I go looking for glimpses of Him, when I seek to fill the empty places with more of Him who is beauty, my equilibrium recalibrates to find its center in the Judge who became grace to bestow grace and I can rightly read the scale, feel it inside, and know it's true:

If you can really see — the weight of Glory always tips the scales for joy.

I think of this, the next time I raise my hands in happy thanks ...

How light I feel — this perfect weight.

Lord God, You are the Hound of heaven who hunts the lost down and captures us with grace. Today, make me the hound of now who hunts for glory and captures joy with just that one word: Thanks.

---

beautiful grace

One thing I ask from the LORD,
   this only do I seek:
that I may dwell in the house of the LORD
   all the days of my life,
to gaze on the beauty of the LORD
   and to seek him in his temple.

Psalm 27:4

Bowed at the edge of the world, Jesus asks me soft what He asked of the man born blind: "What do you want Me to do for you?"

Jesus, I am struggling and I get turned around, but I think I know, at least in part, what I want. If I had never run, if I had never fallen here, I am not sure I would have known with blazing clarity. I may not know all that it means, but this is what I want.

I whisper with the blind beggar, "Lord, I want to see" (Luke 18:41).

This kingdom laden with glory, this, the pearl of great price, the field I'd sell everything to possess. This is the pearl that crams me with a happiness that throbs, serrated edge, pit open wide for more of His glory.

Beauty, God Himself, is the voice endlessly calling and so we see. So we reach. Doubt the philosophies, doubt the prophecies, doubt the Pharisees (especially the ones seen in mirrors), but who can doubt this

—Beauty Himself? Beauty requires no justification, no explanation; it simply is and transcends. See beauty and we know it in the marrow, even if we have no words for it: Someone is behind it. Beauty Himself completes.

This is what I'm famished for: more of the God-glory.

The only place we have to come before we die is the place of seeing God.

What is this that I feel sitting here, coursing through me relentless, hot, ardent? I *have* to seek God-beauty. Because isn't my internal circuitry wired to seek out something worthy of worship? Every moment I live, I live bowed to something. And if I don't see God, I'll bow down before something else.

How could I have forgotten how badly I wanted this?

To bow down and rightly worship.

Do I have eyes to see it is His glory and not the thing?

I am bowed like wheat, raised like grass blades, grounded and rooted to now, and from Him and through Him and to Him are all things and all is His and everything that has breath praises Him, and I whisper it again, again, again, remembering, remembering, remembering.

Eucharisteo, eucharisteo, eucharisteo.

When the purity of Jesus lies over a heart, His transparency burns the cataracts off the soul. The only way to see God manifested in the world around is with the eyes of Jesus within.

God within is the One seeing God without. God is both the object of my seeing and the subject who does the act of all real seeing, the Word lens the inner eye wears.

To sit in the theater of God and see His glory crack the dark, to open the eyes of my heart to see the fountain of His grace—thousands of gifts—I have to split heart open to more and more of Jesus.

Who can split open the eyelids but Jesus? Christ Himself tears the veil to the Holy of Holies, gives me the only seeing I have.

I have been lost and now I am found and I sing it softly, before the flying of the flocks south: "Be thou my vision, O Lord of my heart . . ."

These heavy glory-waters endlessly flood from Him and God spills. Skirts of stars swirl through black space and waterfalls canter over stones, manes of runaway horses, and lone mushroom tilts in the shadows of soundless forest, and God sees it all. This is His endless experience because this is who He is—beauty overflowing. God is happiest of all.

Joy is God's life.

Don't I yearn for it to be mine?

I was lost but now am found again, Jesus, and I know what I want: to see deeply, to thank deeply, to feel joy deeply. How my eyes see, perspective, is my key to enter into His gates. I can only do so with thanksgiving. Living in His presence is fullness of joy—and seeing shows the way in.

Our endless desires are fulfilled in endless God.

I long to know Beauty, breathe it into lungs, feel it heavy on skin. To beat on the door of the universe, pound the chest of God with the psalmist: "One thing I ask from the Lord, this only do I seek: . . . all the days of my life, to gaze on the beauty of the Lord and to seek him in his temple" (Psalm 27:4).

Faith is the gaze of the soul and I want to *see in*. So I can *enter in*. Isn't that what C. S. Lewis knew too?

What more, you may ask, do we want? Ah, but we want so much more—something the books on aesthetics take little notice of. But the poets . . . know all about it. We do not want merely to see beauty, though, God knows, even that is bounty enough. We want something else which can hardly be put into words—to be united with the beauty we see, to pass into it, to receive it into ourselves, to bathe in it, to become part of it.[20]

Isn't the longing for Beauty Himself the happiest place of all?

Lord, in Christ You name me Beloved One, and in love I call You Beautiful One. Today, turn me from seeing burdens to seeking beauty. Cause me to glimpse at the grittiness and gaze on Your glory—because could there be more joy than adoring You more?

bridge grace

Give thanks to him who alone does mighty miracles.
His faithful love endures forever.
Psalm 136:4 NLT

Count blessings and discover who can be counted on.

Isn't that what had been happening, quite unexpectedly? This living a lifestyle of intentional gratitude became an unintentional test in the trustworthiness of God—and in counting blessings, I stumbled on the way out of fear.

Can God be counted on? Count blessings and find out how many of His bridges have already held.

Had I not trusted all these years because I had not counted?

I glance back in the mirror to the concrete bridge, the one I've boldly driven straight across without second thought, and I see truth reflecting back at me: Every time fear freezes and worry writhes, every time I surrender to stress, aren't I advertising the unreliability of God? That I really don't believe? But if I'm grateful to the Bridge Builder for the crossing of a million strong bridges, thankful for a million faithful moments, my life speaks my beliefs and I trust Him again.

I fearlessly cross the next bridge.

I shake my head at the blinding wonder of it: Trust is the bridge from yesterday to tomorrow, built with planks of thanks. Remembering frames up gratitude. Gratitude lays out the planks of trust. I can walk the planks—from known to unknown—and know: He holds.

I could walk unafraid.

Is that why the Israelites kept recounting their past—to trust God for their future? Remembering is an act of thanksgiving, a way of thanksgiving, this turn of the heart over time's shoulder to see all the long way His arms have carried. Gratitude is not only the memories of our heart; gratitude is a memory of God's heart and to thank is to remember God.

I had read it this morning as I prayed the Psalms, the psalmist giving thanks for the memories. In memory, the shape of God's yesterday-heart emerges and assures of God's now-heart and reassures of His sure beat tomorrow. And for the first time I see why the Israelites are covenanted with God to be a people who remember with thanks. It is thanksgiving that shapes a theology of trust, and the Israelites bear witness and I see.

Isn't this what ultimately Jesus asks of us in the Last Supper? One of the very last directives He offers to His disciples, the one of supreme import but one I too often neglect—to remember. *Do this in remembrance of Me.* Remember and give thanks.

This is the crux of Christianity: to remember and give thanks, *eucharisteo.*

Why? Why is remembering and giving thanks the core of the Christ-faith?

Because remembering with thanks is what causes us to trust—to really believe.

Lord God, I claim Christ as my bridge back to You and I trust the Bridge Builder to hold all the moments of my life — and me. Remind me today, Lord, to give thanks to You for always holding. I am relieved of the burdens when I've believed in the Bridge Builder.

hard grace

I want to know Christ —
yes, to know the power of his resurrection
and participation in his sufferings,
becoming like him in his death.

Philippians 3:10

I can't keep myself from saying it to God, this raw sob echoing that of Teresa of Avila: "If this is how You treat Your friends, no wonder You have so few!"[21] Can I be that honest?

I am David lamenting, "Why, LORD ...?" (Psalm 10:1). Why this broken world punched through with losses? "How long, LORD?" (Psalm 13:1). How long until every baby thrives and all children sleep down the hall from a mom and dad wrapped up in love, and each womb swells with vigorous life, and every single cancer clinic sits empty and we all grow old together? How long?

I know a neighboring Mennonite woman folding away the clothes of her dead son, and I sit in a room full of the battered and busted and I lament: *Please.* And He takes the empty hands and draws me close to the thrum of Love. You may suffer loss but in Me is anything ever lost, really? Isn't everything that belongs to Christ also yours? Loved ones lost still belong to Him—then aren't they still yours? Do I not own the cattle on a thousand hills; everything? Aren't then all provisions, in Christ also yours? If you haven't lost Christ, child, nothing is ever lost. Remember, "through many tribulations we must enter the kingdom of God" (Acts 14:22 NASB).

The dark can give birth to life; suffering can deliver grace.

If all the work of transfiguring the ugly into the beautiful pleases God, *it is a work of beauty*. Is there *anything* in this world that is truly ugly? That is curse?

Can I believe the gospel, that God is patiently transfiguring all the notes of my life into the song of His Son?

What in the world, in all this world, is grace?

I can say it certain now: *All is grace.*

I see through the woods of the world: *God is always good and I am always loved.*

God is always good and I am always loved.

Everything is eucharisteo.

Because *eucharisteo* is how Jesus, at the Last Supper, showed us to transfigure all things—take the pain that is given, give thanks for it, and transform it into a joy that fulfills all emptiness. I have glimpsed it: *This, the hard eucharisteo.* The *hard* discipline to lean into the ugly and whisper thanks to transfigure it into beauty. The *hard* discipline to give thanks for all things at all times because He is all good. The *hard* discipline to number the griefs as grace because as the surgeon would cut open my son's finger to heal him, so God chooses to cut into my ungrateful heart to make me whole.

All is grace only *because all can transfigure.*

I take to heart the words of Thomas Aquinas, who defined beauty as *id quod visum placet*—beauty as that which being seen, pleases.

I wear the lens of the Word and all the world transfigures into the Beauty of Christ.

Everything could be eucharisteo.

Lord of Life, when I am between a rock and a hard place, cause me to know it full well: You make all grace because You transfigure all. Cause me today to believe, right in the midst of hard things, that You are patiently transfiguring all the notes of my life into the song of Your Son. Today, let me do hard things: live the hard discipline to give thanks in hard things. Today, I lean hard on You—who softens my heart.

this-moment grace

The life of mortals is like grass,
   they flourish like a flower of the field . . .
But from everlasting to everlasting
   the LORD's love is with those who fear him,
   and his righteousness with their children's children.

Psalm 103:15, 17

It falls unexpected in October.

A snow-white whisper hushing the trees burnt all red.

She stands at the window and I watch it fall behind her, her at the glass and the flakes so soundless, heaven on white wing.

And I don't expect it, in a room full of women and flashing laughter, the way she turns and says it quiet—

"My daughter is dying."

Sometimes grace is the way a moment unfurls into wing and something of God flutters near.

I step closer, step in, try to catch all this falling down.

Is there really anything to murmur except to just come close and stand with someone?

She says it straight out and clear. "There have been gifts."

That when the diagnosis came, the doctor said terminal and only a year more, at the most five—but then the unexpected, this wild grace of ten whole years.

How she once sang like a bird, twirled in her four-year-old spin, and then the years of slow regression, the walking giving way to the wheelchair, the songs giving way to loss of words, and now, giving way to infant beginnings.

"It's kept us always living just in this moment—because we know today is the last like this." Sometimes you know you will never forget the way the light burns in someone's eyes.

She's a flame in snow.

"Just always so grateful for every moment we've been given." It's falling straight down behind her.

I reach out, just to touch her shoulder, and she's radiant and the truth lands here in the open hands: Giving thanks to God is what ushers one into the very presence of God. And this is why He asks us to always give thanks.

He comes to those with the open, grateful hands.

In the morning the white-laced water begins its melt, these days all vapor.

Her testament, it remains, and I remember the way she flashed grace in snow, one fading moment after another, and I want to burn thanks right into me.

In the morning light coming up from the east, it's clear— everything hanging on the trees, all that is left, all the leaves ...

Still all in this open flame of bare, ardent praise ...

God, today is the last like this. This place, this people, this moment— it will never again be just like this. Cause my eyes to see everything in my life afresh. I may not pass by here again. Now is not a forever grace, but amazing grace.

small grace

"Truly I tell you, unless you change and become like little children,
you will never enter the kingdom of heaven.
Therefore, whoever takes the lowly position of this child
is the greatest in the kingdom of heaven."

Matthew 18:3 – 4

Her laughter makes me laugh too, and I can hear her going through the house, flagrantly recording all time and space. Child and mother, we've exchanged places, and I try to return order to chaos and she too returns to Eden, naming each moment with a frame.

Eventually, she comes looking for me, her face filled with lens, her every step activating another click. I'm separating whites from darks in the laundry room.

"Can you show them back to me now?" She holds the camera out to me, as long as the neck strap will allow. Nothing can restrain her giddiness.

Settling into a pile of laundry, our heads lean toward each other and touch. Her arm around my neck, we scroll through her photos on the glowing screen. A picture of me bent over her, showing her which button to press. I'm mountain over her lens. I can feel the laughter rising up in her, and she cups her hand over her mouth to catch the bubbling pleasure. She's enchanted by her photos. I grin.

Frame of a table. A doorknob. A bookshelf skewed on a tilt.

Yet her photos surprise, every single one. Why? It takes me a moment to make sense of it.

It's the vantage point.

At thirty-six inches, her angle is unfamiliar to me and utterly captivating: the study ceiling arches like a dome, her bed a floating barge. The stairs plunge like a gorge.

She's Alice in Wonderland, all the world grown Everestlike around and above her.

"Do you like them, Mama?" She pats my cheek with her laughter-drenched hand.

I can only murmur, flicking through her gallery. "Marvelous . . . just marvelous."

She giggles and who can resist and I lay the camera aside and tickle her soft belly and she throws the head back, bliss, and I kiss blind all up that sweet neck of hers and she laughs breathless and we roll happy. And when she scampers off into other majestic realms, I look after her longing, longing to go too.

Could I?

I want that kind of crazy, happy joy, God. How to see the world again through those eyes? To live in the wide-eyed wonder of a world that unwraps itself grandiose and larger than life, so otherworldly?

As G. K. Chesterton wrote, "How much larger your life would be if your self could become smaller in it."[22]

When I stand before immensity that heightens my smallness, I have never felt sadness. Only burgeoning wonder.

Dear Lord, make me decrease that You may increase and keep me small and humble. Cause me to embrace that simplest of truths — that all wonder and worship can only grow out of smallness.

humble grace

God blesses those who are humble,
for they will inherit the whole earth.

Matthew 5:5 NLT

I'm standing in a mudroom, sorting children's dribbled shirts, grass-stained jeans. I live in laundry. How to be Little-One in now's wonderland, in Kingdom of Heaven coming? How to *live* in a state of awe when life is mundane and ordinary? I know layers of the *eucharisteo* answer because I have felt the miracle — but there are layers I don't yet understand.

Light falls in gold bars across laundry.

The watch on my wrist chimes the hour, modern bells to prayer. I stop the spinning thoughts, the probing questions, the hands sorting, the laundry work, because God needs knees more than hands. Bowed like Daniel, I move to the other side of prayer with on-the-hour prayers of thanks.

Thank You, Lord, for the perspective of a child . . .

Thank You for door frames and doorknobs . . .

Thank You for soaring ceilings and bed barges and tables that loom large . . .

For her laughter and her wonder and her eyes that turn the world inside out and stretch it large and leave me again in surprise . . . in awe . . .

I murmur *eucharisteo* thanks in a pile of laundry and the world expands and heightens and deepens and surges with the glory of God, and I can feel the body decreasing and the soul increasing and joy filling the breadth between. This, *this* is like a child happily capturing pixels, our daughter giddily grasping the ball—the perspective of smallness that cultivates surprised wonder, that grows gratitude, that yields joy. The orb awe of a moon that makes the eyes see, the kaleidoscope of a bubble that makes the time slow, this is *eucharisteo* working its change on a life, but here, isn't this here another layer of *eucharisteo*? *Eucharisteo* makes the knees the vantage point of a life. I shake my head, my quiet laughter remembering her glee, because isn't that how children live? Life as a large surprise. A child has no expectations … *A rolling ball? Surprise! A laughing aunt? Surprise! Again and again? Surprise!*

That's what a child doesn't have—this whole edifice of expectation. Without expectations, what can topple the surprising wonder of the moment?

My mama, valley wise and grief traveled, she always said, "Expectations kill relationships." And I've known expectations as a disease, like a silent killer heaping her burdens on the shoulders of a relationship until the soul bursts a pulmonary and dies. Expectations kill relationships—especially with God.

I think of it only a couple hundred times a year, that single wide-eyed night by the bed of one of our sons in the pediatric wing of a city hospital. The moaning of babes, the crying of sick children, the murmur of nurses with grim prognoses on lips and morphine in hand, these haunted through the endless hours. I did not sleep, the pain of that place begging me to pray.

After our son was given the thumbs-up and signature of release, I came home to bedrooms and bathrooms and kitchen and fridge and windows and unmerited, luxurious health and I threw up my arms in relieved gratitude.

Here? This place? Surprise!

I was a woman who saw what her life could well have been. And things but forty-eight hours earlier I entirely took for granted—even rather half resented as flawed and less than—I spun around: *All surprising grace!* And there has not been a single night the nearly ten years since, that my son and I haven't whispered in bedside prayers for those who cry out in the dark, for we witnessed and we remember and we will always carry . . .

Is it only when our lives are emptied that we're surprised by how truly full our lives were?

Instead of filling with expectations, the joy-filled expect nothing—and are filled. This breath! This oak tree! This daisy! This work! This sky! These people! This place! *This day! Surprise!*

C. S. Lewis said he was "surprised by joy." Perhaps there is no way to discover joy but as surprise? This, the way the small live. Every day.

Yes, the small even have a biblical nomenclature. Doesn't God call them the *humble*?

The *humble* live surprised. The *humble* live by joy.

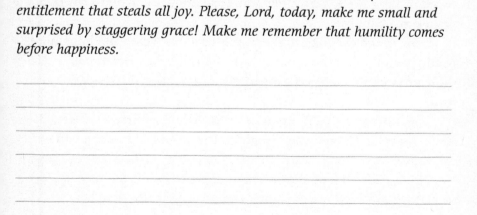

Lord, I repent of it all: the expectations that kill relationships and the entitlement that steals all joy. Please, Lord, today, make me small and surprised by staggering grace! Make me remember that humility comes before happiness.

seed grace

"Behold I have given you every plant yielding seed
that is on the face of the earth,
and every tree with seed in its fruit.
You shall have them for food."

Genesis 1:29 ESV

The two girls, they kneel in dirt, their heads near touching, and their laughter, it could be like the song of the seraphim. The dog's running in the wheat field behind the garden, gold dog breaking through green. I sort seed packets, all rattling promise. And every single one of the kids, they're all startling grimy, dirt ringing eyes like raccoons, what picking stones across the bean fields all day can do to the face, the hands, the bent back.

Now in the evening, to the bare garden, us weary and hopeful. Only one of us has shoes on. It's all a bit laughable. Bohemian. But the holy ground, isn't it always where we least expect it? I know, it's just this ...

Tomatoes at twilight. Spinach seeds. All these dirty bare feet, all their voices and ribbing and laughter. But I can feel it too, a tattered reverence ...

"Just gentle." Hope shows Shalom how to cradle the root ball of tomatoes. Do I tell the girls their rows aren't farmer straight?

"Don't drop any of the seeds." Levi leans over Caleb's shoulder.

There is light edging Caleb's knees, all his work, his gritty pants, the very bottom of his heel. It's everywhere too, the refrain of the ragamuffins: "Holy, Holy, Holy, the whole earth is full of His glory." This is what reverberates and moves me deep, the song of the wounded and washed: Holy, Holy, Holy.

"Joshua, can you bring another spade?" I call to him across the lane, him coming out of the barn, coming out from feeding all the nursing sows. We're breaking the earth open and it's making something in me heal.

And I tear open up the seed packets of zucchini, and is it this too, witnessing again this Genesis giving? That again He gives the first gift He ever gave to humanity? That again He gives the impossible gift and asks for wild faith? The seeds, they fall into my hand small, jewels. I am holding seeds, first gift He ever bestowed upon His people. Maybe this is why the bare feet? But to look at seeds and believe He will feed us? When what He gives doesn't look like near enough. When it looks like less than a handful instead of a plateful, a year full, a life full. When it looks inedible.

These seeds, they are food? It looks like a bit of a joke.

To hand someone seeds for his swelling, panging starvation, and ask him to believe in a feast—is this what everyday faith is?

Behold! For those who have learned to see—He gives, He gifts. He gifts with seeds as small as moments, grace upon grace, and the unlikely here and now, it shall sustain you, feed you. Do not disdain the small. The promise of feast is within the moments. Our enough is always in the now, because He never leaves us.

Joshua, he brings me a spade. He begins on one long row of lettuce. I plant gladioli bulbs. Levi scratches out his lines of sweet corn. Shalom pours her watering can careful over tomatoes that Hope's tucking into earth. Caleb hills up for pumpkins. We're all just ragamuffins out here hunched over our wild song of faith: *Holy, Holy, Holy* ... We pray bent not only in sanctuary but in soil, and we bow over rows, not only in pews. And if prayers are what we seed and Cross-love is what we knead, what we reap and what we eat is the harvest of God. He is enough.

Shalom, she pours the water.

The trickle making song, making clean.

This trickle making feast.

Lord, what would happen today if I saw all the not-enough, too-little in my life to be but a seed? All the hardly-things could be holy-things — small somethings You are growing into more glory for You. Cause me to believe again: All feasts began as seeds.

transplanting grace

He who was seated on the throne said,
"I am making everything new!"
Revelation 21:5

July twilight and my brother shows up at the back door.

My brother. All man. Still boy. Still freckles. Still that grin tugging at me.

"So." He rubs his hands like he's about to pull the past out of nothing. "Ya got time for a walk down the back lane?"

Shalom is already pulling at his hand, pulling hard for the back door. John and I used to go slooping up through the back ditch looking for sun-bellied frogs, and we built a base camp at the foot of the bald beech at the wood's edge and he's only a whisker younger, twelve months, thirteen days, but far older than me in adventure and spontaneity. We've come the whole long way together, a lifetime of Julys and slippery love that got away and an unexpected base of grace.

Malakai bikes ahead of us. Shalom never lets go of John's hand. The light dips the world gold and I try to open the aperture of the mind wide to snap the moment in memory. John's all talk of our Father, the first and forever One, and how he listens to Him in prayers and God leads him on in His Word. I'm right wide-open. Crazy, what wild grace can do to a guy who once boozed away everything come

Friday night. Or to an anxious girl who once twisted into a control-tight mother. Christ at the end of a cross can upend whole worlds and everything lands aright.

"There are wild raspberrrrries back heeeeeeere!" Malakai rings the woods loud and his echo peals us happy.

We're bears rustling through undergrowth, shaking down leaves to fill hungry hands with garnet clusters hanging from canes.

If you lay a hive of raspberry red on your tongue and press your tongue right to the roof of your mouth, you can squeeze the sweet right out of every cell.

Malakai and Shalom pick and giggle, fill their mouths and pucker their lips, kissing summer's juice. John laughs. Deep and happy and up into poplars. Time can only work age into skin. Within, near the soul, time's impotent and we're forever young. I feel about eight.

"Can I pick these?" Shalom has drifted farther down the patch.

"Sure! As long as they're ripe!" Malakai doesn't even look up. Bear with a mission.

"Or do you mean those daisies, Shalom?" I step out of raspberry brambles and into the field of dreams and beans so I can see her. "You can pick all the daisies you want, sweet."

"No, those are weeds." She turns her back on the billowing clouds of delicate white and she points. "I mean these."

"Just a minute ..." The soybean leaves whisper against the bare legs and I walk all the way to her. "What do you want to pick, hon?"

"These."

I follow the direct line of her very certain index finger.

Those?

"Oh, but Shalom ..." I chuckle. "Shalom, you sure you want to pick a bouquet of those?"

She's pointing to a clump of burdock.

Burrs.

The nasty hooked balls that snag you going by, Velcro to your sleeve, tangle to your hair, knot to your pant legs, your backside, your dog. Those.

"Shalom, that's a burdock, those prickly and stickly things that get stuck in your hair, remember?"

"But they're purple, Mama." She says that word *purple* like it's jeweled, like it's royal and lush. She plucks a stem.

"I like these better than daisies, because — is white even a color, Mama?" She yanks on another stalk.

"These are all *purple*." She says that word again and it's all sugar-rich on her tongue.

Malakai's got a handful of wild raspberries and Shalom's wandering ahead with her fistful of purpled burdock, and John and I follow them through the briars of our own untamed past. Out of nothing, or the real something this is, I pull now out of what was ...

A plant isn't a flower but a weed only by function of its place.

Transplant the weed to the heart and it blooms a flower, and I might function in this place.

Love is ridiculous and reconfigures everything.

Kai eats the raspberries before we get home and Shalom puts her burdock in a vase. At the end of a night of weeds and wild things, John and I stand at the back door grinning silly.

What is wilder than grace?

Lord, all that I've deemed weeds in my life are only weeds by function of whether I want them in this place or not. Cause me today to transplant all my weeds into wild wonder simply by thanking You for the grace of them in this place. How else can my life bloom?

lowest grace

He must increase, but I must decrease.
John 3:30 NASB

To receive God's gifts, to live exalted and joy filled, isn't a function of straining higher, harder, doing more, carrying long the burdens of the super-Pharisees or ultra-saints. Receiving God's gifts is a gentle, simple movement of stooping lower.

> I used to think that God's gifts were on shelves one above the other, and that the taller we grew in Christian character the easier we should reach them. I find now that God's gifts are on shelves one beneath the other, and that it is not a question of growing taller but of stooping lower, and that we have to go down, always down, to get His best gifts.[23]

I knew my soul need magnify Him, but of the flesh minimizing? And I see it then, bent over laundry, that humility isn't burden or humiliation or oppressive weight, but the only posture that can receive the wondrous grace-gifts of God—God who humbled Himself and came to the feed trough and waits to be seen in light off doorknobs and curve of vases and mound of laundry.

I shake my head, half smile, lay aside her dress because the funny thing is, the moment I try to grasp for humility, she's gone. Speak of humility, shine a light shaft on her, and she's shadow-gone in the dark. "Humility is so shy," writes Tim Keller.[24] If I focus on humility, I look inward to assess if I'm sufficiently humble and in the very act, humility darts and I'm proud, self-focused. It doesn't work. But what humbles like an extravagant gift? And hadn't I felt that joy of small child-wonder when I paused to give thanks?

The quiet song of gratitude, *eucharisteo*, lures humility out of the shadows because to receive a gift, the knees must bend humble and the hand must lie vulnerably open and the will must bow to accept whatever the Giver chooses to give.

Again, always, and always again: *eucharisteo precedes the miracle*. And you'd think I'd know that by now. But I forget. Father never forgets what I am made of, child of dust. The Wounded Warrior is achingly tender with the broken ones and He has all the patient time to gently lead those who seek and He keeps leading me back to *eucharisteo*.

Is this what is happening as I learn *eucharisteo*, to be full of grace? I humbly give God thanks for the gifts. I practice *eucharisteo*. And in that place of humble thanks, God exalts and gives more gifts and more of Himself, which humbles and lays the soul down lower. And good God responds with greater gifts of grace and even more of Himself. And I ride the undulating wave of grace, this lifting higher and higher in grace, the surging crest of joy, and this plunging lower and lower in humble thankfulness only to rise yet higher in grace.

This *eucharisteo*, it offers the ultimate joyride and I don't think I ever want to get off. Is this why the oil jars of joy never run dry but endlessly refill? He must increase, and I must decrease — not because that is burden, but so that my joy might increase with more of Him! I kneel down to toss in the laundry.

I set the dial to extra dirty. I stay on my knees and watch the water run into the washer, watch it splash against the circular glass of the washing machine's front door, hear its gurgling fall. Down it flows.

Down, always down, water runs, always looking for yet lower and lower places to flow. I watch water run and think spiritual water must flow like this ... always seeking the lowest places—and the washtub begins to rock. I must go lower. I tell myself this, watching water run. That whenever I am parched and dry, I must go lower with the water and I must kneel low in thanks.

The river of joy flows down to the lowest places.

And here on my knees I can see.

~

Lord God, today, lead me lower that I may be happier. Gifts are best found and received on bended knee. You are the Infinitely Good God who offers greater gifts of grace and even more of Yourself to those who humble themselves. Today, by Your grace let me ride that undulating wave of grace—going lower to find the lifting higher and higher in grace.

manna grace

> He humbled you, causing you to hunger and then feeding you
> with manna, which neither you nor your ancestors had known,
> to teach you that man does not live on bread alone
> but on every word that comes from the mouth of the LORD.
>
> *Deuteronomy 8:3*

I shouldn't, but I do. I look up. Into all his hardly tamed grief. I feel wild. My brother-in-law's eyes shimmer tears, this dazed bewilderment, and his stoic smile cuts me right through. I see his chin quiver. In that moment I forget the rules of this Dutch family of reserved emotion. I grab him by the shoulders and I look straight into those eyes, brimming. And in this scratchy half whisper, these ragged words choke — *wail.* "If it were up to me ..." and then the words pound, desperate and hard, *"I'd write this story differently."*

I regret the words as soon as they leave me. They seem so un-Christian, so unaccepting — so *No, God!* I wish I could take them back, comb out their tangled madness, dress them in their calm Sunday best. But there they are, released and naked, raw and real, stripped of any theological cliché, my exposed, serrated howl to the throne room.

His firstborn, Austin, had died of the same genetic disease only eighteen months prior. Now he was about to bury his second son in less than two years.

"You know ..." John's voice breaks into my memory and his gaze lingers, then turns again toward the waving wheat field. "Well, even with our boys ... I don't know why that all happened." He shrugs again. "But do I have to?... Who knows? I don't mention it often, but sometimes I think of that story in the Old Testament. Can't remember what book, but you know—when God gave King Hezekiah fifteen more years of life? Because he prayed for it? But if Hezekiah had died when God first intended, Manasseh would never have been born. And what does the Bible say about Manasseh? Something to the effect that Manasseh had led the Israelites to do even more evil than all the heathen nations around Israel. Think of all the evil that would have been avoided if Hezekiah had died earlier, before Manasseh was born. I am not saying anything, either way, about anything."

He's watching that sea of green rolling in winds. Then it comes slow, in a low, quiet voice that I have to strain to hear.

"Just that maybe ... maybe you don't want to change the story, because you don't know what a different ending holds."

The words I choked out that dying, ending day echo. Pierce. There's a reason I am not writing the story and God is. He knows how it all works out, where it all leads, what it all means.

I don't.

His eyes return, knowing the past I've lived, a bit of my nightmares. "Maybe ... I guess ... it's accepting there are things we simply don't understand. But He does."

And I see. At least a bit more. When we find ourselves groping along, famished for more, we can choose. When we are despairing, we can choose to live as Israelites gathering manna. For forty long years, God's people daily eat manna—a substance whose name literally means "What is it?" Hungry, they choose to gather up that which is baffling. They fill on that which has no meaning. More than 14,600 days they take their daily nourishment from that which they don't comprehend. They find soul-filling in the inexplicable.

They eat the mystery.

They *eat* the mystery.

And the mystery, that which made no sense, is "like wafers of honey" on the lips.

> He gave you manna to eat in the wilderness, something your ancestors had never known, to humble and test you so that in the end it might go well with you.
>
> *Deuteronomy 8:16*

A pickup drives into the lane. I watch from the window, two brothers meeting, talking, then hand gestures mirroring each other. I think of buried babies and broken, weeping fathers over graves and a world pocked with pain and all the mysteries I have refused, refused, to let nourish me. If it were my daughter, my son? Would I really choose the manna? I only tremble, wonder. With memories of gravestones, of combing fingers through tangled hair, I wonder too ... if the rent in the canvas of our life's backdrop, the losses that puncture our world, our own emptiness, might actually become places to see.

To see through to God.

Lord God, Maker of all, when You give manna moments, may I give You thanks for the mystery. Because the manna that makes no sense—You will make it my sustenance. Today, in all the "what is it?" moments, turn me to give thanks for who You are.

bread grace

For all the promises of God find their Yes in him.

2 Corinthians 1:20 ESV

I remember it right then, passing pig farms. And that God would bring that story to memory now.

How bread became a comfort when bombs fell in World War II, shattering earth and all that is within and children wept for parents, cried for food. Refugee camps offered beds to huddling, dirty frames but could not furnish rest. Blast of days haunted pitch of nights. Nothing comforted shell-shocked, gaunt children. Fear rimmed the eyes and the hearts pounded, too loud, and the sleep fled. I know how nights blinked with the saucer eyes, the vigilant, terrified eyes. But somewhere in the dark, up between each narrow row of beds, a hand came to pull up the thin sheets, a hand to touch each bony shoulder and offer the fear-chased something to seize.

A piece of bread.

Dazed child hands took the bread, tucked in with bread. They gave thanks and rested on pillows of trust. The bread hushed the fears with assurance: "The sun sets and He has provided and you've ate. Tomorrow the sun will rise and again He will provide. You will eat bread again."[25] Hands clutch bread. And finally it comes: the terrified sleep deep.

I shake the head; sleeping with bread, a strange mental image. And yet really ... isn't that what that gratitude journal on the counter is? Opening the hand to receive the moments. Trusting what is received to be grace. Taking it as bread. Recount how we laughed today. How we cried today and it too was grace. How He fed us. We ate. We filled. We swept up the crumbs. So He lays us down to sleep. Trust tucks in. He has blessed today. Will He not bless again tomorrow? Sleeping with bread may seem strange, but Jesus knew the wilder.

He knew I'd only trust, rest, when I lived with bread in hand. When I eat manna.

Eucharisteo, remembering with thanks, *this is the bread.*

We take the moments as bread and give thanks and *the thanks itself becomes bread.* The thanks itself nourishes. *Thanks feeds our trust.*

And it swells up in me and I can't stop it, this surging sense of emancipation. Over a steering wheel in a white pickup, I can't help this glorious laugh, the laugh of the unafraid and the bold, the giddy hope of the bread carriers, the manna eaters.

Until Home and Promised Land and complete clarity, I'm a wanderer crossing bridges, wanderer eating manna, eating mystery. For really, as long as I live, travel, is there ever anything else to eat? I either take the "what is it?" manna with thanks, eat the mystery of the moment with trust, and am nourished another day — or refuse it ... and die. Jesus calls me to surrender and there's nothing like releasing fears and falling into peace. It terrifies, true. But it exhilarates. This, this is what I've always wanted and never knew: this utter trust, this enlivening fall of surrender into safe hands.

There is no joy without trust!

I can feel all the sinews releasing, the opening of the heart chambers, the unfurling of a life into one reverberating, exultant yes!

For no matter how many promises God has made, they are "Yes" in Christ (2 Corinthians 1:20).

Yes in Christ!

To the enfleshed Yes who said yes to this moment and yes to last year's illness and yes to the cracks of my childhood and yes to the nail and yes to my name in the Book of Life, hear me say YES!

The power of sin and death and fear-sent-from-the-Enemy are forever ended because we can trust in the bridge even if it's caving, in God even when it's black, in manna nourishment even when we don't know what it is. The God whom we thank for fulfilling the promises of the past will fulfill His promises again.

In Christ, the answers to the questions of every moment are always *Yes!*

Lord God, Bread of Life, not only do You nourish me, but in thanking You for the nourishing, that thanks itself becomes bread. The thanks itself nourishes—because thanks is what feeds our trust. When I am soul-starved today, Lord, remind me that every feast begins with the word thanks.

wedded grace

"A man leaves his father and mother and is joined to his wife,
and the two are united into one." This is a great mystery,
but it is an illustration of the way Christ and the church are one.

Ephesians 5:31 – 32 NLT

When the back door of the sanctuary opens and she floats down the aisle under that veil of white, the groom grins giddy.

A son leans down the pew and whispers it too loud. "The guy looks like he's going to split, he's so happy."

The groom smiles like he's swallowed the canary through all three stanzas of the hymn they sing together. He beams deliriously when he tells us all from the platform, "I'm so grateful to the Lord that God let this day finally happen."

It looks like his cheeks might hurt, his happiness through the vows: "After my complete commitment to the Lord, I promise you will be first in my life."

The Farmer squeezes my hand. Murmurs it in my ear. "We should go home and recite our vows again too."

I turn to catch his eye. "All over again. In a heartbeat." He grins like he's twenty, winks, and pulls me all into him.

And when the preacher says the groom can kiss his bride, he fumbles nervous with the hem of the veil, too anxious to get to her, and the guests all chuckle embarrassed and when he finally cups her face in his hands and revels unabashedly in her, I look away to the floor. This is all theirs.

Afterward, at the reception, there's a little bottle of honey, liquid light in glass, on the plate of each guest. A son pats the Farmer's arm and tells him they found honey, still good, in the pyramids. That honey always lasts.

That they've given us a token of forever.

On Sunday morning, we sit in the pews of our chapel, and the preacher's preaching who we are in Christ.

"In Christ, you have immediate access to God and all of this is yours—joy, acceptance, completeness, rest, righteousness, access to the throne of God. You are sealed and He has pledged Himself to His people and you are His."

And I look around and it strikes me—Why aren't we all standing? Why aren't we all grinning giddy? Why aren't we all smiling like we just might split?

I keep reading the vows the preacher has on the screen, slow and captivated.

He's given all these gifts to all His children, no matter where we are—why not slow and really revel in this because what love is greater than this?

- *Joy is yours.* "Though you have not seen Him, you love Him, and though you do not see Him now, but believe in Him, you greatly rejoice with joy inexpressible and full of glory." *(1 Peter 1:8 NASB)*

- *Acceptance is yours.* "To the praise of the glory of his grace, wherein he hath made us accepted in the beloved." *(Ephesians 1:6 KJV)*

- *Completeness is yours.* "And in Him you have been made complete." *(Colossians 2:10 NASB)*

Why don't our cheeks hurt with the happiness of it all? What more could we want? How do we contain ourselves? Surely all the believers believe?

The vows of the Christ, they are covenant, and He lasts when we lose everything else and all the gifts are in Christ alone.

We could float.

On the way out of the chapel after service, I catch a glimpse of it through the stair door window, what's hanging there in the stairwell.

I step into the empty quiet of the landing, just to the read the words again, quilted there on the wall hanging.

> And I John saw the holy city, new Jerusalem, coming down from God out of heaven, prepared as a bride adorned for her husband ...
> And God shall wipe away all tears from their eyes; and there shall be no more death, neither sorrow, nor crying, neither shall there be any more pain: for the former things are passed away.
>
> *Revelation 21:2, 4 KJV*

The stairway's still. This is ours. Like honey, sweet to the soul and healing to the bones, all His covenant, a gift of forever.

When the Farmer asks me on the way home why I'm smiling, I squeeze his hand. Murmur something about how I just can't stop, the promises that won't let me go — all the light honey in the trees ...

Lord God, today, make me giddy with gratitude for Your covenanted gifts — all joy, all acceptance, all completeness, all in Christ. Never let my heart grow so cold that I get over this. Wed me to worship and woo me to praise and wake me to the Word-God who deserves my all.

love song grace

I have loved you with an everlasting love;
I have drawn you with unfailing kindness.

Jeremiah 31:3

Only as the gifts are attended does God's choosing of *us* become so utterly passionate.

It's a new voice, this endless stream of grace, one I never get over. This love song He is singing, it is the antithesis of life's theme song, that refrain of rejection I know so well. That mental soundtrack of condemnation and criticism that I've let run on continuous replay, lyrics I learned from the grade-three boys huddled on the ice, exploding laughter when my skates slid east, west, and I fell south; from the trendy city girl moved to the country who snickered at my thrift store shirts; from the critical eye of every evaluator, judge, assessment, grade. That heavy beat of failure, a pounding bass of disappointment, it has pulsed through my days and I've mouthed the words, singing it to myself, memorizing the ugly lines by heart. They become the heart.

For years, I tried medication, blade, work, escape, all attempts to drown out that incessant, reverberating drum of self-rejection. All futility, acidic emptiness.

But here, I hear it well: The only thing to rip out the tape echoing self-rejection is the song of His serenade. One thousand gifts tuned me to the beat. It really is like C. S. Lewis argued—that the most fundamental thing is not *how we think of God* but rather *what God thinks of us*: "How God thinks of us is not only more important, but infinitely more important."[26] Years of Christian discipleship, Bible study, churchgoing had been about me thinking *about* God; practicing *eucharisteo* was the very first I had really considered at length what God *thought of me*—this ridiculous and relentlessly pursuing love, so bold. Everywhere, everything, Love!

Giving thanks awakens me to a God giving Himself, God giving Himself *to me*—for me—a surrender of love.

The discipline of giving thanks, of unwrapping one thousand gifts, it unwraps God's heart bare.

I choose you. Live!

He chooses His children to *fully* live! Fully live the fullest life—the astonished gratitude, the awed joy, the flying and the free.

I hear the beat of his heart, that song crystal clear: "'I have loved you,' says the LORD" (Malachi 1:2).

In a thousand ways He woos.

In a thousand ways I fall in love.

Isn't falling in love always the fullest life?

Oh, Lord, if You sing love over me forever, could I not sing thanks to You just for today?

one-hundred-times-a-day grace

All this is for your benefit,
so that the grace that is reaching more and more people
may cause thanksgiving to overflow to the glory of God.

2 Corinthians 4:15

Out the kitchen window the sky rolls out. Apple blossoms fill the orchard. The morning dove warms her bluing hope. I can hear Him, what He is telling the whole world and even me here: this is for you. The lover's smile in the morning, the child's laughter down the slide, the elder's eyes at eventide: this is for you. And the earth under your feet, the rain over your face upturned, the stars spinning all round you in the brazen glory: this is for you, you, you. These are for you—*gifts* —these are for you—*grace*—these are for you— *God*, so count the ways He loves, a thousand, *more, never stop*, that when you wake in the morning you can't help turn humbly to the east, unfold your hand to the heavens, and though you tremble and though you wonder, though the world is ugly, it is beautiful and you can slow and you can trust and you can receive each moment as grace. *Eucharisteo. Eucharisteo. Eucharisteo.*

And the moment opens unexpectedly. I'm in the cemetery

kneeling, tracing the only five letters carved deep in that slab of granite laid down in the dirt.

"A-I-M-E-E." *Loved one.*

I remember her silken hair. I still don't know why He took her. I don't know why her children don't run free on spring days with mine, laugh with my sister's. Don't know why my parents' hearts were left to weep, eroding all away. Though I cry, this I know: *God is always good and I am always loved* and *eucharisteo* has made me my truest self, "full of grace." Doesn't *eucharisteo* rename all God's children their truest name.

"Loved one."

Me, my dad, my mama, all the children, all the broken ones, all the world, He sings us safe with the refrain of our name, "Loved one."

In the window next to the stove, the porcelain dove soars. In the sill a framed print of Rembrandt's *Supper at Emmaus* invites. How many times a day do I look at this print in my kitchen and return to that sacred moment of soul communion in a still gallery? How many times a day do I again reach to embrace Him in communion thanks? It comes again now like it does every day, what I had read after I had already counted thousands of gifts: that this discipline of counting graces is as old as God's people themselves, the seriously devout Jews of today still giving thanks to God one hundred times a day. The words of the rabbis have been impressed deep into my skin, my being, their words beckoning the way into joy:

> Blessings keep our awareness of life's holy potential ever present. *They awaken us to our lives....* With each blessing uttered we extend the boundaries of the sacred and ritualize *our love of life. One hundred times a day, everywhere we turn, everything we touch, everyone we see.* The blessings can be whispered. No one even need hear. No one but the Holy One. "*Holy One of blessing, Your presence fills the Universe. Your presence fills me.*"[27]

My gratitude journal is lying open on its permanent home on the counter, enumerating moments, making a ledger of His love. It is G. K. Chesterton who encapsulated the truth of my numbering life: "The greatest of poems is an inventory."[28] I grin happy in the midst. No, I'll never stop the counting, never cease transcribing the ballad of the world, the rhyme of His heart. He and I, a couplet. Count one thousand gifts, bless the Holy One one hundred times a day, commune with His presence filling the laundry room, the kitchen, the hospital, the graveyard, the highways and byways and workways and all the blazing starways, His presence filling me.

This is what it means to fully live.

Father God, if devout Jews thank You one hundred times a day — might I thank You one thousand times in a lifetime? Might I begin anew today? Because when we've been with You ten thousand years, we'll have no less years to sing Your thanks than when we've first begun. May my extravagant practice begin now. Bless the Lord, O my soul — because this is what blesses the soul.

numbered grace

So teach us to number our days,
That we may present to You a heart of wisdom.
Psalm 90:12 NASB

In morning light in the woods, I kneel low with a camera.

In a clearing of saplings, a friend from church smiles into the March winds. I click the shutter. She began chemo this week to contain four cancerous lumps that can't contain her mouthed thanks to God. I say, "Cheese!" and her four-year-old tilts his head and flashes his dimple. Her five children ring her like a promise.

Less than ten miles away, my sister sits in a rocking chair watching the red digits blink on an oximeter.

She's sitting there with the 24/7 monitoring of oxygen saturation levels of my niece born under heaving breath prayers. The child whose every breath reminds us to pray to YHWH, God, whose name sounds like our own breathing. For seventy-three days they have written down the numbers on the oximeter screen, high, low, of her lungs inhaling, exhaling . . . stopping.

Midafternoon in the kitchen, Hope turns at the sink and smiles at me, her with hair pulled back in a barrette and laying long down her back, her wearing my sweater but her own shoes because mine are too small now. It's only a turning, but I'm struck. Awakened to my daughter who doesn't seem a child anymore. She is twelve and she isn't. So tall and lovely. She reaches for a towel.

She's a stem of slender grass, hardly swaying in spring winds.

I murmur it. "Well, Hope—I think my days are numbered now ..."

Weren't they always? And I just don't bother keeping track?

My eyes can't leave her, taken with her so grand.

Hope dries her hands on the towel, knits her brow, confused. "Why are your days numbered?"

Numbered.

I hadn't really meant it quite like that. Not like my sister recording oxygen numbers. Not like a mother of five counting chemo days.

I half smile, only a bit tender in the upturning. "Just thinking. The days of being taller than my children are numbered now. By summer's end, you'll be looking down at your old Mama ..."

She blushes, shakes her head, that long mane of hair falling thick over her shoulders, laughing ... "Mama!"

She's elegance. Willow girl, sky eyes. I record the moment.

Numbered. Is this how He teaches?

How else to seize a heart of wisdom with your life?

Number the beats, record the blessings, enumerate the gifts, see One at the center of it all, and know there is much and it is fleeting and it is in the accounting of a life that we accumulate thanks for anything in life. This way is gone all too soon. Who keeps track to keep a heart of wisdom, to keep a perspective that keeps Him in focus?

Is it the accountants who know the full measure of His grace?

The heart of wisdom, always this accounting heart ...

Hope is bent over Shalom, Shalom with bows in her hair that Hope once wore and how much longer these ribbons of pink? I watch them and wonder if this is it:

The way to learn to number our days is to count the moments of His grace.

I don't want to miss what this all sums up to.

The children making up games about a grandmother's big toe ... and the girl-giggles shaking rocking chairs ... and the deepening laughter of teenage boys and the robin bobbing scarlet hope across the back lawn, a blaze, and the littlest in her striped leotards ... and sons with widening shoulders and a brother smiling when the other walks into this living room tumbling with jokes ... and the Farmer stealing a sideways grin my way and him saying: "Isn't it just good medicine to hear them all so happy?"

And her so long and lovely in my kitchen, turning and unfurling, her one heart beating this steady mercy.

One long certain beat after one long surrendered beat ...

Lord God, today, please make my heart an accounting heart that I may present to You a heart of wisdom. When I count the moments of Your grace, I number my days—and don't grow numb to Your grace. Or my life.

affectionate grace

And then I'll marry you for good — forever!
  I'll marry you true and proper, in love and tenderness.
Yes, I'll marry you and neither leave you nor let you go.
  You'll know me, GOD, for who I really am.

Hosea 2:19 – 20 MSG

The bride wears white.

And the day I get married I do, yet most of my life I've worn black. I know who I've been.

The first memory I ever held was the blood of my sister running, everything alive draining away. I came from here. We breathed grief. Black fears formed me.

There were years I cut myself along the thin skin of the wrists, wild for a way out of a darkness that chokes.

On a Sunday morning we sit in our country chapel. Shalom slips up on the Farmer's lap. I sit waiting, rubbing my wrist. Rubbing the edge of my black cuff. Before us are the bread and the juice of the vine. The loaf of bread that will be broken in half.

The bread will be pure white. I can never thank Him enough.

It's still in the chapel sanctuary. The piano notes begin. One woman's quavering voice begins alone.

"When I survey the wondrous cross . . ."

The nails right through. The glorious way out of everything that has been. Out of all my black ... the horror of death, the relentless prison of fear, the way pain pursued, a whole family aching endless with wounds we couldn't heal. Him the only Way out.

And when I survey, she's there too, way in the back of my past, Bible teacher Kay Arthur on a long-ago platform, her voice quaking with Calvary's love—it's hell and it's healing, and I'm not yet twenty-one, and when she tells me what love saved me, the spit and the beard plucked cruel, His ribs rising and falling hard, wild gasp for breath, the purest God-Man subjected to vilest humanity—all my hard exterior cracks right open and runs liquid and what do we know of true love?

"See from His head, His hands, His feet, sorrow and love flow mingled down ..."

And I'm sitting there before Communion, rubbing my wrist, and all I can think of is that woman in Luke 7, the one in the shadows with her alabaster jar and she's weeping in the black. She knows who she's been.

A dark storm, she cries. She wets Jesus' feet with her tears. She "rains," it reads, in the original Greek *brecho*. She rains; she's this *brecho* that breaks. She's this full rain falling. She's this heart-water let loose. Him so pure and His feet so dirty. Her so filthy and Him her only purity. Will anyone wash His feet with their love?

And that woman, she has no pitcher but she has passion—the kind no Pharisee could ever understand and she has no water but she has her heart.

She pours it out. *She pours it out.*

And with no towel but tresses, no hand cloth but her hair, she does the unthinkable, the scorned and the disgraced. When all Jewish women were required to keep their hair done up, lest they be seen as shameful and loose, she lets her locks down.

Rabbis, men of the law, said that if a woman loosed her hair in public, let her hair flow mingled down, it was grounds for divorce. Grounds to be shamed and sent away.

But there is a love far greater than law.

That Luke woman, she lets her hair loose, lets her love loose, and she looks loose and there are always Michals who will scorn David's dancing before the ark — but Jesus lets her kiss Him.

It seems shocking, appalling, too intimate, and this *kataphileo*, these kisses, this is the same word of the father kissing the prodigal son, a symbolic picture of God embracing, the father falling on the neck of his child and kissing, and doesn't the whole realm of earth need to be seized with a power of a great affection, "for we are members of his body, of his flesh, and of his bones" (Ephesians 5:30 KJV).

The Pharisee had no water for His feet but she gave her heart-water.

And the Pharisee had no towel but she laid out her loose, silken hair.

And the Pharisee gave no kiss but she couldn't stop kissing His feet, her grateful love the most expensive perfume — the kind that cost her the respect of men but earned her the pearl of great price, the acceptance of Jesus — "for she loved much" (Luke 7:47 ESV) ... "Your faith has saved you; go in peace" (Luke 7:50).

She gave her grateful love as an intimate gift.

And her heart-water and costly love are gifts fully received and accepted by Christ.

And our God is the God who whispers, "Call Me Husband." The God who says, "Yet you were naked and bare. Then I passed by you and saw you, and behold, you were at the time for love; so I spread My skirt over you and covered your nakedness ... and entered a covenant with you so that you became Mine" (Ezekiel 16:7–9 NASB).

The Savior celebrates communion with His bride, the spiritual oneness He made her for. Will anyone wash His feet with their love?

"Were the whole realm of nature mine, that were an offering far too small ..."

I'm murmuring the notes of the song before Communion and these inner dark clouds split into white, the *brecho* that breaks, and Elie Wiese had said, "No one is as capable of gratitude as one who has emerged from the kingdom of night."[29]

In the middle of the hymn, Shalom leans off the Farmer's lap, leans her face into mine that's emerged from the dark, her long hair, curling wisps, framing everything and she reaches out to touch my cheek ...

My wet cheek. I can never thank Him enough.

She who's been freed of much, freely loves, and she who knows how she's forgiven, how she gives thanks. She gives back everything. It is possible to have a form of religion and not be formed by love for Christ. And it's possible to see the law but be blind to love. And love for all, no matter what, is what never fails ...

Who feels such gratitude for their salvation in Christ that they live such affection for Christ? Who can say just this: "Lord, you know all things; you know that I love you"? Oh please, Lord—let it be said of us.

What is greater proof to the world of the power of the gospel of Christ than the world witnessing the power of profuse love for Christ?

Shalom brushes away what's running down, all my rain, and she barely whispers it. "Why you cryin', Mama ... and smiling?"

I have no words. Just shake my head. Just eyes on the words of the hymn.

Just love falling.

"Because of Jesus, Mama?"

I nod and the sanctuary fills:

Love so amazing, so divine, demands
my soul,
my life,
my all.

Lord, forgive me. It is possible to have a form of religion and not be formed by love for Christ. Lord, forgive me: It is possible to see the law but be blind to love. Lord, forgive me. You know all things and You know all the days I didn't thank You—that I have not expressed my love to You. Today, cause me to feel such gratitude for my salvation in Christ that I live such affection for Christ.

standing grace

No longer will violence be heard in your land,
    nor ruin or destruction within your borders;
but you will call your walls Salvation
    and your gates Praise.

Isaiah 60:18

God doesn't need us to praise Him but He needs us to praise.

What else keeps us from bitterness?

Down by the water's edge the boys build a sandcastle.

Caleb wields his shovel like a man with a back built for trenches, for getting to the bottom of things. Sand sprays and he piles.

The summer I got meningitis, I'd lain on a blanket, still, and he ran after seagulls on this beach, about in this same spot, just east of the lifeguard chair. He'd been three that summer and smelled of buttery popcorn and his laughter squealing after swooping gulls, it had gone down like a carbonated elixir. I had gotten well. He had gotten taller. Thirteen more summers and he had shed the boy skin and I watch now how he bends. How to grow up the man that's just under that boy's skin?

Levi hauls up pails of water from the shore and he pours. "See them standing over there, Mom?" He leans over his five-gallon pail and whispers it in my direction, a secret slipping down to me off a slope of freckles.

"I heard that boy say to his dad that our castle's big. Think they're watching us build, Mom?" He half turns and scoops out a handful of wet sand to gird up a sandy palisade. He already knows how it's best to just keep digging and not look to see who's watching.

Kai and Joshua, the sand dribbles straight from their fingers and it's the tips of them sculpting, grains pressed down into the grooves of who they are. The walls grow higher. They keep at it, building and forming. Or this happens—the sand settles, sinks. Crumbles. It's there on the beach—nothing stands still, the moments always moving in a direction.

And it is like that, the way the sand moves, every word moving either one way or the other—words raising Christ or building self higher.

Words praising Him or wrangling to be praised ourselves.

This seeping of bitterness or straight spires of blessings.

"I need more water, Levi—or it's going to fall." Joshua curves over his section of wall like a prayer. I'm not sure how my life stands. How my inner and outer walls stand, how I make a home. Unless we make it a habit to give thanks, we habitually give our family grief.

Unless we consistently speak praise, we consistently speak poison.

Unless we are intentional about giving God glory throughout the day, our days unintentionally give way to grumbling.

"Levi—it's crumbling over here!" Kai turns quick. He's looking beyond himself for help. It's only when we focus on the Christic center of everything that everything finds it center and walls stand. It's in praising a Savior in all things that we are we saved from discouragement in all things.

"Thanks, Levi." Kai murmurs what matters to Levi. Kai pats more sand in cracks and Levi tilts the pail and kneeling together, they bridge the gap.

"Thanks, Levi."

Does it always come down to just two ways to do life? Do doxology —or do destruction.

From here, I watch how they build their house.

How they look over their shoulder to see if it stands . . .

⌒

Father God, make me speak praise today, not poison; make me intentionally give You glory throughout the day, that my day doesn't unintentionally crumble in grumbling. In thanking You in all things, I am saved from discouragement in all things and this today is my earnest prayer: Make me do doxology, not destruction.

lovely grace

For his invisible attributes,
namely, his eternal power and divine nature,
have been clearly perceived,
ever since the creation of the world,
in the things that have been made.

Romans 1:19–21 ESV

So after dinner she picks coneflowers in the garden. Cradles the long stems in her apron skirt, carries them up through the picket gate. And she turns to me on the top step of the porch, holds her apron out to me, all those purple petals—art in an apron.

"Why is there all this loveliness?" She wants to know.

I almost tell her—the world is full of loveliness because it's full of His love.

Isn't that the meaning of beauty? The fundamental purpose of loveliness is to convey His love. Everywhere, wildflowers, even in cracks in concrete sidewalks. Everywhere, this fragrance, this pursuit, this passion.

But I don't know how to say that—when I know that coneflowers unfold off the porch and she stands there with an apron heavy with garden glory and the sunflowers nod yes, when 30,000 children have

starved to death in the last 90 days in the Horn of Africa famine.
That's over 330 children every single day.

Why is there all *this loveliness*?

Don't you mean—why is there famine and why is there this
shocking disparity, and what is right in a world of diets and death by
starvation?

But doesn't she really have a right to question it all—the
sunflowers sparking in sun flare, the light falling late through the
trees, all gold like this, the phlox blooming along the picket? I see that
too, on the porch. The extravagant art that makes up this world, it
does jockey for an answer.

The existence of loveliness everywhere, it begs explaining.

If I raise the problem of evil in this world—shouldn't she raise
higher the greater problem of good? If evil is seeming evidence to
eradicate God from our mental landscape, then doesn't goodness, even
in this apron, testify to the gospel truth of God?

How can we behold loveliness and say that this world looks like
it would if there were no God? I don't know if I have thought of this
before—the great problem of good on this planet.

Augustine had asked two questions of the world: "If there is no
God, why is there so much good? If there is a God, why is there so
much evil?"

I wonder if I have spent a lifetime murmuring under my breath
only the second question? But why don't I first get hung up on the
first question? The one my girl is bringing in with the flowers—why
all this loveliness and where does it come from? The great problem of
good on this planet implies that there is a Great God in heaven.

Do we not wonder at the why of good because fundamentally all
human beings presume the overspilling grace of God? That good is
our intended atmosphere—and evil is the exception? Isn't our default
to ignore the expected and focus on the unexpected?

And even our deeming anything good or evil, it betrays our deep-seated beliefs—because how can mere nature be either? Isn't it just is? To even assess events as good and evil reveals our true paradigm: We believe there is a moral center at the center of the cosmos, God at the axis of the universe.

But if there is really a God at the center of the universe, love at the core of the cosmos, love manifesting itself as loveliness in the garden —doesn't He care about the 330 children with names and dreams who lay in Somalia with flies buzzing around their listless, wasting-away limbs till they breathe their last starving breath sometime this afternoon? Yet, if I think God doesn't care about the hurting—am I not believing the chief lie of humanity? The one hissed in the Garden to Eve, the first deception that deceives us still—that God doesn't care about the needs of His children. And maybe this is why the world hemorrhages—if we think God doesn't care, why should we?

Isn't it easier to blame Him? When I believe the Edenic lie that God doesn't care—is that the excuse to turn away, to spread the lie that God doesn't care—when maybe the truth is that it's humanity that doesn't care? If we love because He first loved us ... do we now care, because we know He did first care, has always cared, will always care—and has the nail scars to definitively prove it. If all the world believed the truth of God's character—that God cares—wouldn't this world become a caring place? He cares, so we care; He loved first, so we love now. *Why is there all this loveliness?*

Do I tell her this—that there is enough loveliness, enough beauty, enough love in this world—enough food in this world—if we would just share? That the problem of evil in the world isn't a problem for proof of God—but a problem of our own turned-inward hearts? And when we turn our hearts outward, we in turn bear testimony to the loving existence of God, of the body of Christ right here ...

I pick one coneflower out of her apron, twirl it between fingers.

Do I tell her that all this loveliness does this too: All this good makes me grateful, and my own heart needs this—a filling of His great-fullness. Gratefulness is always to Someone and when I am grateful, isn't it always evidence of God—a filling with awe of His great-ness. For all this world's sureness of the benefit of gratitude, how can we then deny that there is a Benefactor?

There is never nameless gratitude, but every instance of gratitude gives away what every skeptic really believes: Every breath is a gift and if life is a gift, there is a Giver, and if there is a Giver—all's grace. When all's grace—we give, because a gift never stops being a gift to be given …

"It's God, isn't it?—All this loveliness …" She says it to me smiling, picking out one of the coneflowers to inhale deep, picking up the scent of God.

She didn't need me to say anything.

There are things that need no words. His love clearly manifest in the everywhere problem of good. In every coneflower curling itself into a megaphone of mercy.

This one long echo of evidence, a loveliness lingering …

Oh, God, in a world that faces the very real problem of evil, may I face it everywhere today—the very real proof of good. Today, fill me with gratefulness for the great-fullness of You, Great God in heaven. All this loveliness, evidence of all Your love—regardless.

kindling grace

Then they cried out to the LORD in their trouble,
and he delivered them from their distress.
He led them by a straight way
to a city where they could settle.
Let them give thanks to the LORD for his unfailing love.

Psalm 107:6 – 8

Mama has the tea ready when I get there for prayer group and Bible study first thing in the morning.

I have on the socks that the woman with the five kids and the stage-four cancer knit for me.

This is always the first thing—to go right into the throne room of God wearing nothing less than your aching prayers.

Anne's on time for our early Saturday morning study at Mama's, sitting at the end of the living room, there in the wingback, there with her Bible long open, like a woman waiting for the Coming.

I, of course, come late. Like a foolish woman straight out of a 6:00 a.m. parable, still trying to trim her lamp, trying to remember her oil, trying to stay awake. Anne, she smiles grace, as the rain pounds steady on the windows, all the leaves coming down wet and clinging, yellow and red and sad in first gray light.

I take the seat at the end of Mama's couch. Curl my red knit socks up under me. Mama, she hands me a mug of steaming tea, apple cinnamon, and tells me it's Psalm 107 this morning and could I just read the chapter right out loud?

Read it because it's manna and you've got nothing to give if you haven't gathered and you have to gather Word-manna at daybreak if you're going to gain from it the daylong.

Read it because it's your very life and why live emaciated and I open it like a woman who needs to be cured of one wild and lifelong eating disorder. I read Psalm 107: "Let them give thanks to the Lord for his unfailing love and his wonderful deeds for mankind ..." And Anne looks over and Mama looks up and Mama asks it aloud. "Well?"

I pull at my socks and there is a lone beautiful woman battling cancer with her knitting needles and chemo and mothers grieving over children gone and men broken over everything shattered and hadn't Spurgeon said it?

> There is no greater mercy that I know of on earth than good health except it be sickness; and that has often been a greater mercy to me than health ... It is a good thing to be without a trouble; but it is a better thing to have a trouble, and know how to get grace enough to bear it.[30]

Know how to get grace enough to bear it.

It is a better thing to have a trouble, and know how to get grace enough to bear it. And we get grace enough to bear it—when we run into the arms of Grace who bore it all, into Him who is more than enough.

I run my hand across the Scripture page. Gather the manna up into hands, what really is, and all that feeds. Our cries to the Lord are what give us communion with the Lord. It's the dire distress that drives us into the deep devotion. It's when all fails, His love never fails—and this is why we are a people who can always give thanks.

The lights in the early morning, lights reflecting in the window, in the dark and in the rain—those lights look like tongues of fire.

Mama murmurs the words again. "Then they cried out to the LORD in their trouble ... Let them give thanks to the LORD." The Word open before a trio of women, it burns.

What if I gave thanks in the trouble, for the trouble, because the trouble is a gift that causes me to turn? What if I loved God not for His goods but for His love itself that is goodness enough? The theologian J. R. Miller wrote:

> Christian thanksgiving is the life of Christ in the heart— transforming the disposition and the whole character. Thanksgiving must be wrought into the life as a *habit*—before it can become a fixed and permanent quality. An occasional burst of praise, in the midst of years of complaining, is not what is required. Songs on rare, sunshiny days; and no songs when skies are cloudy—will not make a life of gratitude. The heart must learn to sing *always* ... Thanksgiving has attained its rightful place in us, only when it is part of all our days and dominates all our experiences.[31]

Mama fills our cups again with tea and the steam, it rises straight up, and I can see it in the window, the rising in burning lights. The reflection of those socks tucked up under me, the grief underlying. I drink down all this heat.

It's only when grief and grace kindle us to the very same flame of gratitude to God—it's only then that our love for God ignites in a pure blaze of glory.

It's raining so hard.

We read and pray and offer up our tenacious thanks. Close our Bibles. Carry out our manna. I pull boots on, up over those socks, and cry out and into the communion. Step out into the morning storming.

Into the leaves falling in wind, the clinging in everything streaming straight down.

All these leaves, all this amber and scarlet—all this in pure flame.

God of fire, of light, of purity and holy glory, burn me with your Word. Take my distress and make it beautiful, this opportunity for deeper communion with You. May it light a purer devotion to You in all things that come today, I pray . . .

endless grace

So then, just as you received Christ Jesus as Lord,
continue to live your lives in him, rooted and built up in him,
strengthened in the faith as you were taught,
and overflowing with thankfulness . . .
and in Christ you have been brought to fullness.
Colossians 2:6 – 7, 10

Come Monday morning I forget. A child loses a book, has an exam,
is late for practice. I stress over the trite, a phone call, what's for dinner,
a deadline.

Am I living God's best for this life or am I bankrupting any legacy
of faith? What misery lurks in the next twenty-four hours and the
next? Stress can be an addiction and worry can be our lunge for
control and we forget the answer to this moment.

My baby is five. She falls asleep in my arms after the close of dinner
prayers, us still seated at table, and I hold her long after the Farmer
has put the rest of the tribe to bed, her curls damp and etching into
my skin and I don't move. Her face is turned toward mine, broad and
open, eyelashes whisper of gold. I trace her lips, gentle curve of all
things beautiful. The way her eyes danced today, soul light, the arch of
her eyebrows and that lyrical laugh, heaven's echo that entirely undoes
me. Her breath is warm on my face, all that is alive and warm and

breathing inside of her now, falling upon me, and I can't capture it, hold it, this, her life now, me in this moment. She is leaving me, she's growing up and moving away from me, and she stirs and I sweep back the crop of the golden ringlets.

Stay, Little-One, stay.

Love's a deep wound and what *is* a mother without a child and why can't I hold on to now forever and her here and me here and why does time snatch away a heart I don't think mine can beat without?

Why do we all have to grow old? Why do we have to keep saying good-bye?

He soothes His own restless child in arms with the whisper, law of the universe that He's writing deep into this heart: *eucharisteo always precedes the miracle, child.*

And the chin trembles and I stroke her cheek, her body leaning back against mine, and I tentatively open the hand to receive the gift of now ... I name the now gifts and I await miracle.

That button nose. I touch a finger to its tip and smile. I gaze long, memorizing.

That sprinkling bridge of freckles. I brush my finger across them. These, these I will remember.

The way that singular curl spirals over her ear. The way it winds like silken staircase, on and on and on. And I lean over and the lips seal the delicate spot on her forehead with a long kiss, her skin berry wine and I feel Him, His kiss of tender truth:

All fear is but the notion that God's love ends.

Did you think I end, that I will not be enough?

I am infinite, child.

I wrap a thread of her curls around a finger. I stare into that face conceived in love, reflecting love, and I feel His fall soft on me. I am child in His arms and His breath falls warm upon my face and what I feel for this daughter He feels for me, and the gifts, all these gifts

I keep counting, they are His love gifts and they're slowly waking me up to the tenderest, fiercest Love of all.

Cradling this child, her eyelashes fluttering, her breath rising and falling in sure and steady rhythm, I know it in the pulsing, real, surest kind of way: "Perfect love casts out all fear." His love had done that.

The table still needs to be cleared. The bowls washed. The bread put away. Snow falls in the dark, white on a barn roof. I can't imagine what deeper layers of my wounds *eucharisteo* will gently peel back to heal, but I take her sleeping hand and trace the lines of her skin and I keep on counting blessings to keep on remembering to keep on walking out into the unknown.

I clutch a Perfect Love that knows no end.

~

Lord God, forgive me for raging against time's snatching away—in a thousand different ways—a heart I don't think mine can beat without. Remind me that all fear is but the notion that Your love somehow ends. You never end; our God is always infinite and enough. Today, let me walk unafraid: Your endless love ends all my fears.

losing grace

Every good and perfect gift is from above,
coming down from the Father of the heavenly lights,
who does not change like shifting shadows.

James 1:17

In the middle of a stiff winter wind she asks to go to the beach.

That's where she says she wants to celebrate the turning of her calendar year, this year's birthday. To stand on the frozen snow and turn her face directly into whatever is coming this way.

Nothing can mean nothing and everything means something. Yes — everything.

We're the only ones there. We walk the long boardwalk, our footsteps echoing hollow. She will be sixty-one this year. We stand on iced sand hemmed with white snow and she says nothing, gazing out at bared waters.

I don't ask what she's thinking. The sunlight seems paled, hardly there in the numbing cold. I watch the way her hair moves in the wind, white waves of their own.

We wander down to where the waves crash on the stones, the water breaking its way onto the unwavering sand.

Doesn't her silence say this, that this was the way to live? The water lets go again and again on the granite, this oceanic surge of song, this symphonic crescendo.

Is there anything more beautiful than the wild surrender to *the Rock?*

The song is always found in the surrender.

Mama knew there'd be days like these, when I'd see.

How many more years do I have with her to walk the winter shore? Her hair is whiter than winter and are we already in this season now?

I want spring again. I feel like the child, our shoulders touching here at the sea.

There's a whole lifetime of memories here at the lake. How many Sunday picnics of fried chicken have we had right up there at the lighthouse? She'd serve extra helpings of green coleslaw and I'd pump the swing high and I could see how we might soar straight out over the lake. There's a time when you think nothing will end.

I lean into her and she leans into me, and we're warmer like this, close. Doesn't there have to be more than a decade left of this? No, there doesn't have to be anything. The waves keep breaking. Couldn't she stay until she's 117?

When you wake to losing someone, you win love. When you realize that what you have you will lose, you win real eyes. You win grateful joy.

It comes across the water and I turn to face it directly: It's only when you realize everyone you love will one day leave you that you really begin to love. I reach over for Mama's hand and she does that, she squeezes mine softly and that says more ... maybe more than anything. Maybe most.

Someday, it is possible, I could stand here on my own sixty-first. I can close my eyes and almost see that. How then she will be the memory already flown across the waters. How the song will sing on and I will hear notes that were long hers.

And the thought comes like a wave over me: *How I will miss her!*

The way to experience unlimited elation may be to imagine unexpected limitation. Imagine losing sight and open your eyes to a brighter light. No water, and the next cold glass becomes desert rain. Envision life without the loveliness of those you love—and you see how much you love.

Her half smile there in the wind, it makes me half hurt, her pure worn beauty.

There's a way to wake up and not to live numb. The way to love life is to imagine losing it. The one who loses his life finds it.

The water keeps giving away to the shore. One day all this will be gone. The sun, it seems so strong now, bright across water.

Mama, she lets the wind blow her hood right back and I don't feel numb and there is a theological term for this, all this: *Grace.*

Full-blown grace.

Standing there, she and I, we watch as it comes straight across the waters—as it comes directly this way.

Us here and alive and in awe that any of this is at all ...

This wind awaking everything.

Father God, may I wake to losing someone today—so I can win love. Cause me to realize that someday I'll lose what I have—so I can win real eyes. Let me experience unlimited elation today—by imagining unexpected limitation. Let me envision life without the loveliness of those I love—and I can see to love more.

joyous grace

Dear brothers and sisters,
when troubles come your way,
consider it an opportunity for great joy.
James 1:2 NLT

"What in the world were you thinking? How many times have we said no running? I am just ..." I'm spewing and it's ugly and the words are so frazzled with frustration they fray midstream. I can feel the slow smothering, the tight choking, and I can feel it in the throat, rising.

My knees are stiff and it's jarring, how peace can shatter faster than glass, the breakneck speeds at which I can fall—and refuse to bend the knees at all.

I look into the faces of the guilty and a son arcs his eyebrow, shrugs his shoulders, nonchalant.

I hold my head in my hands and ask it honest before God and children and my daily mess: *Can we really expect joy all the time?*

I will struggle to heed this until I am no more: "Dear brothers and sisters, when troubles come your way, consider it an opportunity for great joy" (James 1:2 NLT), and I will listen and *again* I will listen and I will wrestle to put skin on it: "Rejoice in the Lord always. I will say it again: Rejoice!" (Philippians 4:4).

I gnaw my lip. The body howls when joy is extinguished. The face shrivels pain, the voice pitches angry cry. "No man can live without joy" is what Thomas Aquinas wrote. And I confess, it is true, I have known many dead waiting to die.

The glass lies everywhere broken.

I may feel disappointment and the despair may flood high, but to *give thanks* is an action and *rejoice* is a verb and these are not mere pulsing emotions. While I may not always feel joy, God asks me to give thanks in all things because He knows that the *feeling* of joy begins in the *action* of thanksgiving.

I know it well after a day smattered with rowdiness and worn a bit ragged with bickering. Joy doesn't negate all other emotions—joy *transcends* all other emotions.

Only self can kill joy.

I'm the one doing this to me. The demanding of my own will is the singular force that smothers out joy—nothing else. Dare I ask what I think I deserve? A life with no discomfort, no inconveniences? What do I really deserve?

God does not give rights but He imparts responsibilities— response-abilities—inviting us to respond to His love-gifts. And I know and can feel it tight: I'm responding miserably to the gift of this moment. In fact, I'm refusing it. Proudly refusing to accept this moment, dismissing it as no gift at all, I refuse God. I reject God. *Why is this eucharisteo always so hard?*

I had thought joy's flame needed protecting.

My own wild desire to *protect* my joy at all costs is the exact force that *kills* my joy.

But flames need a bit of wind.

I hadn't known that joy meant dying. I can trust.

I can *let go.*

Joy—it's always obedience.

I know it deeper now: This *eucharisteo* is no game of Pollyanna but the hard edge of blade.

Only self can kill joy.

I take a long deep breath. I step from the stairs, stairs that have led all the way down into this.

I kneel down into a mess of glass.

Eucharisteo makes the knees the vantage point of a life. I bend, and the body, it says it quiet: "Thy will be done." *This* is the way a body and a mouth say thank you: *Thy will be done.* This is the way the self dies, falls into the arms of Love.

This is why. This is why the fight for joy is always so hard.

"No one who ever said to God, 'Thy will be done,' and meant it with his heart, ever failed to find joy—not just in heaven, or even down the road in the future in this world, but in this world *at that very moment*," asserts Peter Kreeft. "Every other Christian who has ever lived has found exactly the same thing in his own experience. It is an experiment that has been performed over and over again billions of times, always with the same result."[32]

I am kneeling in glass and my memories of shattered glass and Jesus comes soft— *"Thy will be done" is My own joy story, child, from beginning to end.*

And I hear it soft too, what all His life speaks: Joy is in the acquiescing.

A circle of children stand around me, watching, waiting. Long slivers of transparency, blades, lie before me, catching light.

I humbly open my hand.

Without a word, one by one, they come to the outer edges and they kneel too.

And I humbly open my hand to release my will to receive His, to accept His wind. I accept the gift of now as it is—*accept God*—for I can't be receptive to God unless I receive what He gives. Joy's light flickers, breathes, fueled by the will of God—fueled by Him.

A shaft filters through an afternoon window and the cracks of the aged wood revive in sun.

I pray.

I let go. Lay the hand open. The sun slides across old hairline scars. My palm holds light.

~

Lord God, You ask me to give thanks in all things today—because You know that the feeling of joy begins in the action of thanksgiving. Today, cause me to do Your will, not mine—and let me release my desire to protect my joy at all costs. Today, open my hand to joy in surrendered obedience.

pit grace

Praise the LORD, my soul,
  and forget not all his benefits—
who forgives all your sins
  and heals all your diseases,
who redeems your life from the pit
  and crowns you with love and compassion ...

Psalm 103:2 – 4

I am mad.

I'd like to will myself out of it but the blood is pounding loud in my ears and the sons slash at each other with the dagger eyes. *Why?* Can I just go back to the moon and the brazen glory? But there's always the descent from the mount. The meeting of the crowd, the complaining, the cursing.

How to be a contemplative here, seeing the fullness of God ...?

Why throw toast in your brother's face?

"*Why* would you throw that at him?" I'm too shrill, too gaped, too blind-white angry.

How do I fix this? Them? Me? In the messy, Jesus whispers, "What do you want?" and in the ugly, I cry, "I want to *see*—see You in these faces." He speaks soft, "Seek My face." I want to answer with David, "My heart says to you, 'Your face, LORD, do I seek'" (Psalm 27:8 ESV) but I'm desperate to grab someone, anyone, and shake hard, *"How do I have the holy vision in this mess?* How do I see grace, give thanks, find joy in this sin-stinking place?"

The moon and the geese fly high, unsullied and wide-eyed, and I'm too twisted.

A boy drives a plate hard back down the table at his brother. And God tries to gently drive timeworn words from another wrestler—from the knowing of my head to the bleeding of the heart:

> You would be very ashamed if you knew what the experiences you call setbacks, upheavals, pointless disturbances, and tedious annoyances really are. You would realize that your complaints about them are nothing more nor less than blasphemies—though that never occurs to you. Nothing happens to you except by the will of God, and yet [God's] beloved children curse it because they do not know it for what it is.[33]

A blasphemer.

I pull out a chair from the table, sink down. The sunflower heads have turned low. What compels me to name these moments upheavals and annoyances instead of grace and gift? Why deprive myself of joy's oxygen? The swiftness and starkness of the answer startle. *Because you believe in the power of the pit.*

Really? I lay my head on the table. Do I really smother my own joy because I believe that anger achieves more than love? That Satan's way is more powerful, more practical, *more fulfilling* in my daily life than Jesus' way? Why else get angry? Isn't it because I think complaining, exasperation, resentment will pound me up into the full life I really want? When I choose—and it *is* a choice—to crush joy with bitterness, am I not purposefully choosing to take the way of the Prince of Darkness? Choosing the angry way of Lucifer because I think it is more effective—*more expedient*—than giving thanks?

Blasphemer. *Blasphemer.*

I rake my fingers through my hair. Who's the real sinner at breakfast on Tuesday, the one with the stinking pig in the temple?

Senses are impaired if they don't sense the Spirit and somebody, *tell me*, how do I tear open tear-swollen eyelids to see through this for what it really is?

Can I be so audacious? To expect to see God in these faces when I am the blasphemer who complains, who doesn't acknowledge this moment for Who it is?

How did Jesus do it again? He turned His eyes. "And looking up to heaven, he gave thanks and broke the loaves. Then he gave ..." (Matthew 14:19). He looked up to heaven, to see where this moment comes from. Always first the eyes, the focus. I can't leave crowds for mountaintop, daily blur for Walden Pond — but there's always the possibility of the singular vision. I remember: Contemplative simplicity isn't a matter of circumstances; it's a matter of *focus.*

I take a deep breath, say nothing to them, but I look up to heaven and I give thanks aloud, in a whisper: "Father, thank You for these two sons. Thank You for here and now. Thank You that You don't leave us in our mess."

My heart rate slows. Something hard inside softens, opens, and this thanks aloud feels mechanical. But I can feel the heart gears working. "Thank You for toast. Thank You for Cross-grace for this anger, for the hope of forgiveness and brothers and new mercies."

I look for the *ugly-beautiful*, count it as grace, transfigure the mess into joy with thanks and *eucharisteo* leaves the paper, finds way to the eyes, the lips. This, this is what Annie Dillard meant: "Seeing is of course very much a matter of verbalization. Unless I call my attention to what passes before my eyes, I simply won't see it. It is, as Ruskin says, 'not merely unnoticed, but in the full, clear sense of the word, unseen.' "[34]

I speak the unseen into seeing and I can feel it, this steady breathing in the rhythm of grace—*give thanks (in), give thanks (out).* The eyes focus, apertures capturing Beauty in ugliness. There's a doxology of praise that splits the domestic dark.

I look over at my son tearing away at toast. Why am I a habitual reductionist? Why do I reduce God in this moment to mere annoying frustration? Why do I reduce The Greatest to the lesser instead of seeing the lesser, this mess, as reflecting The Greatest? I have to learn how to see, to look through to the Largeness behind all the smallness.

Isn't He here?

God, today, when I fall into a pit of anger—bring me face-to-face with the reality of my choice: I am choosing the way of the Prince of Darkness as more beneficial than the way of Christ. Keep my gaze on You so You can redeem even the pit moments—especially the pit moments. Let me not crush joy with bitterness or choose anger over giving You thanks.

shielding grace

Then he said to them all:
"Whoever wants to be my disciple must deny themselves
and take up their cross daily and follow me."
Luke 9:23

All the mothers around the world, around the seas rising high and the fires burning low, they all rock babies on a globe that spins on this axis of thin black letters.

We have Bibles at the table.

Pages of black letters, like long iron shafts, and around this the whole world goes around, spinning on His Story.

And I can hear it, how it turns after dinner, the children all turning Truth pages of Scripture around the table, pages skin thin, and we can see right through to the center.

This is my favorite book, Kai tells us this, clutching the Bible's leather-bound pages tight, and that smile, and he wants to read Ephesians aloud to us.

My mama turns the pages of that special edition of the Four Holy Gospels, traces the illuminated letters, the art framing the masterpiece of His expression. Mama's stilled.

After we clear the table, Levi belts his Bible right to his waist. He says this way he'll always have it close. His Bible, it looks like a shield tied to him and I want one.

Joshua, he spends Sunday afternoon reading *Unshaken*, how Haiti quaked and God never moved, and I watch how he can't stop turning the pages. Caleb says he wants to read it after Josh is done and I remember how we prayed through those days when the world seemed to implode. The Farmer calls me to come see images of Japan. I lay down my reading of Job, my book of common prayer.

I look at the pictures of Japan after the tsunami, of a curve of the planet smeared with this wave of ache, splintered wood piercing right into the earth. Women weep. Grieving can be prayer, the way we cry and know He hears.

I don't see one photo of a broken heart.

How do broken hearts mend? Do some hearts heal all wrong, all twisted and crooked and weak?

What do we make of a world that needs remaking? There's only one Crossbeam that promises a whole new world.

Only one Beam to line a heart up straight again, one Carpenter who can repair a torn-apart heart.

Levi's on the couch, reading the gospel of Matthew.

And it's here, even here, this slender pin at the center of the globe — that slides certain under the violently grinding plates and a surging ocean wall and all our fissured lives, and it's the Word of the Word-God who took the shaft and keeps His promises and names Himself the Father of the Needy.

God has done that: put the poor man on the center stage in His story of compassion for the world.

The Farmer is lingering long over this photo — a man standing with his son in the midst of a wreckage of lumber and dreams and steel.

If I am moved but choose not to respond, won't I soon harden, unable to respond?

When we are touched, we must reach out or soon we stiffen and nothing touches us and we feel nothing.

That Bible Levi is reading, it has these words, Jesus' words. "Now that you know these things ..."

Christian hands never clasp and He doesn't give gifts for gain because a gift can never stop being a gift—it is always meant to be given. When we are grateful for His gifts, we give the gifts away because a gift never stops being a gift.

How will this planet change if God's people do not become its change?

All afternoon I keep coming back to my study Bible.

I run my fingers along the Holy Writ, run my hands across the lines like groping along a ledge, looking for a crevice to grip in this world shook hard and wracked with pain.

I find it there, in His pierced-through hands ...

And I hold on.

God, no matter when or where, Your Word is our sword against the pain of this world. And as I go out in the power of Your name, comfort me today with Your reassuring whisper that I am always safe in the strong protection of Your shielding grace.

full-bodied grace

"Do you understand what I have done for you?" he asked them ...
"Now that I, your Lord and Teacher, have washed your feet,
you also should wash one another's feet."

John 13:12, 14

Jesus is about to let flesh be broken with nail, heart be broken with rejection, chains be broken with bleeding love. And in His last hours before His earthly end, He doesn't run out to buy something or catch a flight to go see something, but He wraps a towel around his waist and kneels low to take the feet of His forsakers gently in hand and wash away the grime between their toes.

This is the full-bodied *eucharisteo*, the *eucharisteo* that touches body and soul: hands and knees and feet awash in grace.

At the last, this is what will determine a fulfilling, meaningful life—a life that, behind all the facades, every one of us longs to live: gratitude for the blessings that expresses itself by *becoming the blessing*.

Eucharisteo is giving thanks for grace. But in the breaking and giving of bread, in the washing of feet, Jesus makes it clear that *eucharisteo* is, yes, more: *it is giving grace away*. *Eucharisteo* is the hand that opens to receive grace, then, with thanks, breaks the bread; that moves out into the larger circle of life and washes the feet of the world with that grace. Without the breaking and giving, without the washing of feet, *eucharisteo* isn't complete. The Communion service is only complete *in service.* Communion, by necessity, always leads us into community.

Eucharisteo means "to give thanks," and *give* is a verb, something that we do. God calls me *to do* thanks. *To give the thanks away.* That thanks-*giving* might literally become thanks-*living.* That our lives become the very blessings we have received.

I am blessed; I *can* bless. *Imagine!* I could let Him make *me* the gift! I could *be* the joy!

This is one of His miracles too—the taking of a life and making it a blessing.

Liturgy has its roots in the Greek word *leitourgia*, meaning "public work" or "public servant."

This life of washing dishes, of domestic routine, it can be something wholly different. This life of rote work, it is itself public work, a public serving—even this scrubbing of pans—and thus, if done unto God, the mundane work can become the living liturgy of the Last Supper. *I could become the blessing, live the liturgy!* I rinse pots and sing it softly, "This is my song of thanks to You ..."

In the moment of singing that one line, dedicating the work as thanks to Him, something—the miracle—happens, and every time. When service is unto people, the bones can grow weary, the frustration deep. Because, agrees Dorothy Sayers, "whenever man is made the centre of things, he becomes the storm-centre of trouble. The moment you think of serving people, you begin to have a notion that other people owe you something for your pains.... You will begin to bargain for reward, to angle for applause."[35]

When the laundry is for the dozen arms of children or the dozen legs, it's true, I think I'm due some appreciation. So comes a storm of trouble and lightning strikes joy. But when Christ is at the center, when dishes, laundry, work, is my song of thanks to Him, joy rains.

Passionately serving Christ alone makes us the loving servant to all. When the eyes of the heart focus on God, and the hands on always washing the feet of Jesus alone — the bones, they sing joy, and the work returns to its purest state: *eucharisteo*. The work becomes worship, a liturgy of thankfulness.

Father of all, make me a servant of Christ alone today, that I might be the loving servant of all, bending the knee to You to bend the knee and wash the feet of others. Today, make me know it again: eucharisteo isn't fully in my heart until I make my life about washing feet.

dark grace

In him we were also chosen,
having been predestined according to the plan
of him who works out everything in conformity
with the purpose of his will.

Ephesians 1:11

When the night sky frays to day, smudged light coming up over fields,
I wake Levi.

Today's our date with the city hospital, an operating table, a
surgeon. He's sleepy. He drags to the back door, holding his splint and
bandaged hand to his chest, and I tie his shoelaces. The Farmer leans
against the open door and takes my hand and I take Levi's other one.
We will pray for the going, the cutting, the healing. Then it comes,
this murmur, and from my lips ...

"Lord ..." All the feelings since the blade and the breaking, all my
questioning and asking, they swell, hot lava to the surface, and I choke
it back, the thick farming hand squeezing mine.

" ... that I'd day after day after day greedily take what looks like
it's good from Your hand—a child gloating over sweet candy ..." My
voice catches hard. I've been a thief, trying to hoard away all the good.

" ... but that I'd thrash wild to escape when what You give from

Your hand feels bad—like gravel in the mouth. Oh, Father, *forgive* ...
Shall I accept good from You, and not trouble?"

I pray Job's words and heat flows down liquid.

What if that which feels like trouble, gravel in the mouth, is only
that—*feeling*? What if faith says *all is* ... I think it. But do I really
mean it?

I gather up Levi and hand and the man at the door kisses us both
good-bye and we wind through the dawn dark. The radio snaps out
sound bites of presidents, celebrities. I click off the radio and flip over
to Scripture on CD. The gospel of Matthew. In the slumber of towns,
the odd kitchen light flashes by. *"Jesus said ..." "And then Jesus replied
..." "And a voice from heaven said ..."* My fingers wrap hard around the
steering wheel. At a graying intersection of two empty country roads,
I idle long, stunned. It's coming out of the same stereo speakers, like
the voices of presidents, dignitaries.

These are the words of God.

Headlights make holes in the slate morning. I nudge Levi gentle,
awed, "We're listening to *God*." And out of the speakers I hear Him
clear:

> But Jesus told him, "No! The Scriptures say,
>
> 'People do not live by bread alone,
>   but by every word that comes from the mouth of God' "
>
> *Matthew 4:4 NLT*

I listen and I live. There is only *one* way to live full and it is "by
every word that comes from the mouth of God."

It is all that Jesus used to survive in the desert, in His wrangle with
silver-tongued Lucifer, only this: "It is written." And it's the Word of
God that turns the rocks in the mouth to loaves on the tongue. That
makes the eyes see, the body fill with light.

I glance at the clock. Levi is to roll into the operating theater in three hours. The Word of God whispers through the speakers. Levi drifts back to sleep. The countryside splits open, the earth unpeeled into sun. The wheat wears gold.

I drive out of dark and into morning glory, awakened to the strange truth that all new life comes out of the dark places, and hasn't it always been? Out of darkness, God spoke forth the teeming life. That wheat round and ripe across all these fields, they swelled as hope embryos in womb of the black earth. Out of the dark, tender life unfurled. Out of my own inner pitch, six human beings emerged, new life, wet and fresh.

All new life labors out of the very bowels of darkness.

Fullest life itself dawns from nothing but Calvary darkness and tomb-cave black into the radiance of Easter morning.

And there is no other way.

Then ... yes: It is suffering that has the realest possibility to bear down and deliver grace.

And grace that chooses to bear the cross of suffering overcomes that suffering.

I need to breathe.

I roll down the window. I inhale the pungency of a passing hayfield in bloom of clover, ditches with those all together wild black-eyed Susans swaying in early air. I try to think straight, truest straight. My pain, my dark — all the world's pain, all the world's dark — it might actually taste sweet to the tongue, be the genesis of new life?

Yes. And emptiness itself can birth the fullness of grace because in the emptiness we have the opportunity to turn to God, the only Begetter of grace, and there find all the fullness of joy.

So God transfigures all the world?

Darkness transfigures into light, bad transfigures into good, grief transfigures into grace, empty transfigures into full. God wastes nothing—makes everything work out according to His plan.

We pull into the hospital parking lot, and I park across from an entrance sign that reads Oncology. I open the door for Levi.

I wear my lenses and I pray to see. Who knows when you might climb a mount of transfiguration?

God, all the world is an opportunity to behold more of Your transfiguring darkness into grace. I won't ever get over it. I'm beholden to it all my life, now and forever. I want to accept all You give and learn to see into the darkness as You do, as a place to fill with Your light. Help me, Father. Help me to see in the dark.

strained grace

I will give thanks to the LORD because of his righteousness;
I will sing the praises of the name of the LORD Most High.

Psalm 7:17

This weekend there were guitars.

There were guitars and a hymn and there were voices rising and raised hands, and who could help it? "Were the whole realm of nature mine"—even this, the raised hands, the bowed head, the murmuring of thanks—it would be "an offering far too small."

I had thought this. I had thought this standing there worshiping with the guitars and strings. The empty space filling those guitars. The empty hands, released and raised. The cries all rising.

It can startle. In the willing hands of the believing, the emptiness can sing. He means to fill our emptiness with song. The way home, I had hummed quiet.

This weekend there were wounds. Sometime before bed, I say something offhand and he says nothing. He doesn't have to. I turn and can see it in his eyes and it's so loud. Hollowness can have a language of its own.

Behind a closed bedroom door he turns his back and I shake my head. Fling hands about, confused. Ugly. Want to raise my voice. I get the irony of this—and irony, it can hurt like swung steel. What I don't get is how he's not getting me and I'm not getting him and how did we get here so fast?

The empty space, it's between us. All this dark chamber.

It was after the guitars had been put in their cases that morning that someone had said it to me, told me about strings and space, about how to make music.

Music is made in stress. A string pulled tight, it has to be plucked, it has to be stressed. Moved from its comfortable, resting position. The bending of the string induces stress. As the string bends, as the string arches in stress and then releases, it vibrates—and there is the offering.

This one clear note, high and long. Stressed and empty and stretched right out, this is the space of song.

In stress there can be song. The resonance is in the surrender.

After the lights are turned out, I lie there in the dark, in this tight silence between us, remembering how the cries can rise.

Music could be here.

I ask and he speaks and I listen and try to echo back his heart, that I have heard him, and I turn to him, bend, move out of the comfortable position, out the rest of self-protection, and I reach for his hand. This bending, it's a stretch, a stress—but where else can the songs be found?

In the dark emptiness I find his and he squeezes my hand.

The resonance is always in the surrender.

The stress, the spaces right full of emptiness, these can be song makers. God means to make song out of stress. Out of all this emptiness.

Maybe this is always how to make life-worship: He holds tight and He strums and I could surrender to the music of God.

I shift a bit closer, and I'm retuned and returned, and it's there in the shadows, like a refrain—this sonorous offering of thanks.

Father God, I bend the knee knowing: You intend to take all my stress and make it song. I bend the knee knowing: the resonance of my life happens in surrender. I bend the knee and offer You my emptiness — in You it can sing.

re-membering grace

Jesus said, "Were not ten healed? Where are the nine?
Can none be found to come back and give glory to God except
this outsider?" Then he said to him, "Get up. On your way.
Your faith has healed and saved you."

Luke 17:18 MSG

A silly little turn of my foot in a game of charades gone ridiculously wrong.

And the bones in my ankle disengage, swell my foot like a bluing balloon, and I writhe quiet and smile thin.

Because really, aren't I one of those women who comes unglued and broken only a thousand times a day?

The heart of this world is fractured and we all bear the fault lines. I ice my throbbing ankle hill with a Ziploc bag of melting snow. Hobble around with the laundry for days.

I'm lying on the couch with my foot propped high over my head, when a friend e-mails, "Pray for me? I can manage the nausea and exhaustion. It's the mouth sores that are the hardest."

She's the mother of five young children.

"I'm just not sure how I'll be able to do my job to take care of my babies while on these drugs every day."

She's on an aggressive, determined round of three chemo drugs.

"I am just thankful that such a medicine exists and there continues to be things to do that keep me living and mothering."

She's a mother with stage-three invasive breast cancer. The universe's right shattered. My heart leaks through all the cracks. And she's thankful.

I limp over piles of books. Try to get away from everything shattered. Kids argue loud and doors slam and floors shake and I sigh weary. I pick up the peels of an orange left to wither on the coffee table, a whole sphere right skinned. On the way to the garbage can, I stumble, stub my good foot on the rocking chair. I howl. Flail. Dance hobble back to the kitchen.

And I pray for the sores oozing in a mouth of a mama singing lullabies to her babies. This is one busted-up, hurting world and I want all the mothers to live. *You hear me, God? Live!*

Why can't this woman, whom I love, breathe for years more and hold her babies till they grow old and laugh at the wonder of eighteenth birthdays and lie there in the dark listening to their heavy slumber, all their lungs and life rising and filling and falling, rhythms of grace?

Why can't she grow old enough to pluck out a few gray hairs, live long enough to have hands wrinkled with memories and real love, to stand with her husband and wonder over grandbabies?

Why do I sit across the table from her and listen to her say the words—that the doctors don't expect her to see spring. *Oh God, please hear our cries!*

And the planet spins with a mother who isn't bitter but gives thanks to God for the medicine that takes her hair and her strength but keeps her living and mothering one day more, that keeps her over the sink with a cloth and over the toilet with a brush and over their pillows with prayers just one day more ...

And if she can be thankful for the chemo killing her cells to keep her alive just for today with no guarantees for tomorrow—can't I sing the lullaby of gratitude to my own moaning soul? Just for today?

And I am just thankful, Lord, for . . .

But can I remember? What am I thankful for? My foot's killing me. And it's not killing me at all.

And that's just the point . . .

This fallen world never stops dis-membering who we are. We're all breaking a bit more every day, even in small ways. And there, even as we ache, is the gentle whisper of God. With the quiet urging to give thanks anyways, to do this in re-membrance of Him. But why in the world give thanks? Why in the name of heaven?

Because when we remember how He blesses, loves us, when we recollect His goodnesses to us, we heal—we re-member.

In the remembering to give thanks, our broken places are re-membered—made whole.

When we re-member all His blessings, we re-member all our fractures, and in giving thanks in the assembly it's our very souls that re-assemble.

Is that it? That the mama with cancer giving thanks for right now— she is the one who is fully really living? *All in Him, all giving glory.*

At the table I prop up my swollen foot and murmur thanks to Him —for a chair, for a leg, me hobbling through mothering today, giving thanks to Him who let Himself be broken to make us whole, and doing this thanks in remembrance of His daily grace, it re-members and mends me and the pain eases.

The fracture lines in my heart all healing in this fusion to Him.

Lord, today, in the broken places, cause me to give thanks, to do what You ask, in re-membrance of You. So I may recollect all Your goodnesses, so I may heal—and re-member.

storm grace

Therefore, since we are receiving a kingdom that cannot be shaken,
let us be thankful, and so worship God acceptably
with reverence and awe.

Hebrew 12:28

"If God really works in everything, then why don't we thank Him for
everything?"

She asks me this straight out.

My daughter, Hope, and I, we sit in the truck on the field's hem,
waiting to give the Farmer his lunch.

The Farmer is planting bean seeds into earth's dark bed. The sky is
rising darker in the west.

He races rain.

"For every drop of rain You keep from falling on us as we plant—
thank You, Lord ..."

I had murmured the prayer, water splatting hard against the
windshield of the pickup.

We need at least one more day of dry weather to plant a year's
worth of beans, our livelihood.

"And for every drop of rain that You do let fall—thank You,
Lord ..." My daughter, Hope, whispers her strange echo.

Really? I turn, searching her face.

She looks me right in the eye.

"If God really works in everything, then why don't we thank Him for everything? Why do we accept good from His hand—and not bad?"

This is hard. Maybe the hardest of all. She is young. She has much to come.

I have held dying babies. Eaten with those who live in the town garbage heap. Wept with women who've been violated, with the bankrupt, the heart-crushed, the terminal. And this never stops being true: Neglecting to give thanks only deepens the wound of the world.

Doesn't God call His people to a nondiscriminating response in all circumstances? "Giving thanks always and for everything" (Ephesians 5:20 ESV).

If I only thank Him when the fig tree buds—is this "selective faith"? Practical atheism? What of faith in a God who wastes nothing? Who makes all into grace?

And yet, is thanking God for everything . . . thanking Him for evil?

Rivulets run down glass, blurring my husband and all our seeded prayers. What do I accurately see and know?

When we bought the Enemy's lie in the beginning and ate from the Tree of the Knowledge of Good and Evil, Satan hissed then that we'd really see and know what is good and evil.

But the Father of Lies, he'd duped us in the whole nine yards. Though we ate of that tree, we did not become like God.

We have no knowledge of good and evil apart from God. My seeing, it is not omniscient. Can I really see if a death, disaster, dilemma, is actually evil? Mine is only to faithfully see His Word and wholly obey Him in this. Therein is the Tree of Life.

Is this why He commands us to give thanks *always and for everything*? Because to thank God in all is to refuse Satan's relentless lure to be godlike in all.

To thank God in all is to bend the knee in allegiance to God, who alone knows all.

To thank God in all is to give God glory in all. Is this not our chief end?

When I only give thanks for some things, aren't I likely to miss giving God glory in most things?

Murmuring thanks doesn't deny that an event is a tragedy and neither does it deny that there's a cracking fissure straight across the heart.

Giving thanks is only this: making the canyon of pain into a megaphone to proclaim the ultimate goodness of God.

Our thanks to God is our witness to the goodness of God when Satan and all the world would sneer at us to recant.

I lay my hand on the rain-filmed windowpane and I see clearer. But this is not easy: That which I refuse to thank Christ for, I refuse to believe Christ can redeem.

The gray sky is drumming steady on the truck's tin roof.

His perfect love casts out all fears and leaves only thanks and I listen to her sing it, like a chorus with the rain: Thank You, Lord. Thank You, Lord.

Like a song from the belly of the fish, like a Jonah refrain echoing off the walls of the great fish: "But I with the voice of thanksgiving will sacrifice to you ..." (Jonah 2:9 ESV)

Like a haunting, holy answer to what she asks, the song of the saints, always thanksgiving—practicing here the only song that will be sung at the very last of time: "Praise and glory and wisdom and thanks ... be to our God for ever and ever" (Revelation 7:12 ESV).

Thank You, Lord. I lilt it soft with her, faith's brazen song facing storms ...

The rain falling hard now.

Lord God, I thank You in all things, to refuse Satan's relentless lure to be godlike in all things. I bend my knee in allegiance to You, who alone knows all. I praise You in all, to give You glory in all and make my canyon of pain into a megaphone to proclaim Your ultimate goodness. There is nothing I refuse to thank You for—because I am convinced there is nothing You won't redeem.

breathing grace

... in his grace there is life;
weeping may be for a night,
but joy comes in the morning.
Psalm 30:5 BBE

The ring Sara sent me in June, it didn't fit my middle finger.

She'd worn it on her middle finger—until its sterling silver weight had made her enflamed knuckles burn.

That's when she wound it off slow, slipped it in an envelope, and had it dropped off at the post office.

Because she knew—the fire in my bones had been about extinguished.

And if I wore it, would I feel the heat ignite?

The letter she'd tucked in with the ring read:

> *I am sending you my favorite silver ring I used to wear on my middle finger every day. I can't wear it anymore as it's too heavy on my sore fingers ... It is purposefully hammered and bent, the way I often felt—the way you are feeling—but it is beautiful and perfect in its imperfections.*

I don't know how Sara knew this season had battered hard. Don't know when I told her that fear sometimes made my teeth chatter. How to keep breathing when your bones feel a bit deadened and ash-gray?

I wrote to her one night, my first real letter to her:

> *I wish you were here tonight, Sara. The sun is setting over the snow all melting. The world is pink and glowing, warm and resting. The dishwasher is twirling, swirling, humming. Shalom is here in the rocking chair reading aloud to herself from her reader . . . little whispers . . . sounding words out.*
>
> *I wanted to share the beauty of this moment with you, Sara. Just to sit with you and share eucharisteo with you. And when I see things that make me sing and ache and give thanks for the wonder of this amazing grace, just this moment, I think of how you live what I long to.*

Sara had turned all the pages in that story of *eucharisteo* that I had stumbled to scratch awkwardly down.

Her very first letter to me had said her vocabulary had a new word: *eucharisteo*. She wasn't simply reading it; she was living it. She wrote it on her wall, painted it on canvas, pinned to her inspiration board. Her spine was fusing and her lungs ached and she smiled a bit weakly to think she might live decades with an eight on the pain scale, housebound three years because this world's air would kill her — but she was taking every moment as grace, *charis*, giving thanks for it, and finding joy, *chara*. Grace, gratitude, joy — *eucharisteo*.

Sara chose joy.

And I told her I carried her with me wherever I went — on planes, across the mountains, out to the ocean, right to the edge. Me, the woman terrified to leave her house, wearing the ring of the woman who couldn't leave hers.

When I didn't think I could walk out the door and keep breathing, I'd feel the ring. Sara would stand at the door and dance if she had this chance. I couldn't contort this blessing into a burden.

She had told me once, "I had to choose fear — or completely trust Him. One cannot exist if the other is true."

So I walked out my door and I breathed. Stepping into fears can be the first step into real faith and focusing the eyes on all the grace here keeps the focus on His all-sufficient grace.

Fear is banished in this present moment when the presence of I AM fills it. We could do that: Practice the awareness of God's filling present. Sara had written it too:

> *The pain is present and I know I'm getting slower, but this is it: to live for this moment and this moment only. I'm just thankful He's with me. That I'm never lonely for Him.*
>
> *And my gift today? There is a tree in front of another building that I can see from my window. There was a slow breeze today, and the branches drifted back and forth so slowly, like they were dancing and waving to me.*
>
> *I had to resist the urge to wave back.*

Sara chose joy and saw grace and she waved back.

I sent her photos of the flowers on the front porch, practicing the praise of God in the present, sent photos of smiling friends who choose joy with her.

And in a few weeks Sara smiles back from the screen's webcam and tells me in this gravelly voice, coughing it out, that she is saying it too: *Yes* to God. I have to turn from the screen, everything running liquid. She says it too? She knows it too: When we need peace, we only need to say yes to God's purposes.

How can she say that? Because she lives what she believes — and she scrawls it everywhere and all over my heart: eucharisteo. *Yes, God, yes!*

Grace, gratitude, joy — *eucharisteo.*

And a night in late September, after hospice is called in and she knows she's finally, thankfully, turned homeward, Sara writes:

> *I don't think I'll be able to write again as I'm getting too weak, but you need to know — when you feel weak, take a deep breath.*

I close my eyes tight, blink it all back. Sara knows what biblical scholars know, the very name of God—*YHWH*—sounds like our breathing—aspirated consonants. God Himself names Himself—and the name He chooses is the sound of our own breathing.

When you are weak, take a deep breath. That's what Sara said at the end: Breathe. Say His name. Say yes to God. *Eucharisteo.*

Her last words to me, they blink up in an e-mail: "You will never be alone or need to be afraid."

I reach out to touch the screen, touch her one last time, ring touching her last pixels and she is still breathing.

As long as she breathes, she says yes to God.

I keep my hands there on the screen, on Sara's words, on Sara—her encircling me in silver, my bones all burning love and Him and joy.

And my daughter, Hope, she's playing it in the night shadows again, playing it again tonight, "Cherry Blossoms in Rain" on the piano, the song she now calls "Sara's Song"—her fingers, all her fingers, playing the notes.

And again there's an ache, a haunting echo, and the notes like the Oriental East, like a winging or a long leaving, like standing at the edge of what once was and witnessing the losing of something pure and prayed for.

After the last high note, Hope whispers it into the stilled dark: "Mama? That whole song, it's played on the black notes."

The black notes. The black notes make music too.

Somewhere in the house, in the dark, I can hear it—how a door opens, how Sara now walks straight through into light.

When she turns and waves back to grace, I'll take a deep breath and wave to the extraordinary joy of her too, her silver ring shimmering on my hand here ...

The weight of all His sheer glory.

Lord God, my every breath is saying Your name. Even when my life seems to be playing only black notes — how can I not choose eucharisteo: grace, gratitude, joy?

amaryllis grace

"Surely, just as I have intended so it has happened,
and just as I have planned so it will stand."
Isaiah 14:24 NASB

Why in the world, everywhere I turn, every page, always death? I'd like some happy, blithe, Pollyanna words, please. For a happy, blithe, Pollyanna life.

My gratitude journal lies open on the counter. I retrieve it, flip back through pages, and run my hand over penned numbers, memories of the Pollyanna moments. And I can see it in the looking back, how this daily practice of the discipline of gratitude is the way to daily practice the delight of God and what in the spring had been #362 *suds in the sink* grew over weeks and months.

G. K. Chesterton had said it, "Joy is the gigantic secret of the Christian."[36] This counting blessings, it's the unlocking of the mystery of joy, joy hiding in gratitude. Aren't the Jesus people the most thankful?

And then it had seemed like it might be over all too soon. Come early winter, I jotted haltingly, not wanting it to end. And when I wrote the one thousandth gift, I had written careful:

1000. Resurrection bloom, an amaryllis

My mother-in-law had given us that amaryllis bulb the year before.

I had set it in the kitchen windowsill, under the porcelain dove. I had waited. A full rotation of the earth through the galaxy, I had waited. Cancer had left Mom Voskamp's remains buried deep. And then. Her bulb had trumpeted a call: *Fully live! Live fully!* My one thousandth gift. I had swallowed hard. God had used the dare to give me this; led me all the way to give me this as the thousandth gift, exactly like this, to unfurl just this: *Live fully!* Mom Voskamp spoke to me from the grave. Here are gifts worth waiting 365 days for, gifts worth counting to one thousand for, gifts that will unbelievably emerge out of the deathly dark. Joy is always worth the wait, and fully living always worth the believing. The pursuit! The bloom had trumpeted for weeks.

I had read it in Job, what makes reading God's message in every moment a form of art, a masterpiece of the fullest life: God speaks to us not in one language but two: "For God does speak — now one way, now another" (33:14). One way, His finger writing words in stars (Psalm 19:1 – 3), His eternal power written naked in all creation (Romans 1:20); and now another way, the sharp Holy Writ of Scripture that makes a careful incision into a life, blade words that kindly cut the tissue back to where soul and spirit join, tenderly laying bare the intents of the heart (Hebrews 4:12).

To read His message in all the moments, in the waiting moments, the dark moments, the moments before the blooming, I'll need to read His passion on the page; wear the lens of the Word, to read His writing in the world. Only the Word is the answer to rightly reading the world.

I had kept turning the pages. And into another year, another spring, another year of beans and corn and wheat under sun, I had kept writing it down, a free-for-all, a journal in my purse, one by my bed, another on the counter by the sink, a file on my computer, because the dare to write *one thousand* gifts becomes the dare to celebrate innumerable, *endless* gifts! That initial discipline, the daily game to count, keep counting to one thousand, it was God's necessary tool to reshape me, remake me, rename me—unfurl me.

Daily discipline is the door to full freedom and the discipline to count to one thousand gave way to the freedom of wonder and I can't imagine not staying awake to God in the moment, the joy in the now.

Was this now only the beginning of really becoming?

⟨⟩

God, all that You make is good. And all that seems to oppose Your will is but a tool to accomplish it. Change my perspective today to see beyond the shadows, above the clouds, where the light never stops shining. Plant the truth of it in me: there are gifts worth counting to one thousand for, gifts that will emerge out of the deathly dark. Unfurl amaryllis grace today through the daily discipline of counting gifts, for I believe it: Joy is always worth the wait!

happiest grace

For the sin of this one man, Adam, brought death to many.
But even greater is God's wonderful grace and his gift of forgiveness
to many through this other man, Jesus Christ.
Romans 5:15 NLT

During the hour drive it takes to get to the lake on a Sunday
afternoon, I think of that sermon we'd had in the morning. The
preacher preaching pure gospel, how to be born again.

Twenty-five years he's been preaching it in our little country
chapel, to the hog farmers, the corn croppers, the mothers with babies
in arms. How you can't work for God's love, angle for it, or jockey for
it—you can't earn God's love. *You can only turn toward God's love.*

When we all unpile at the lake, the little girls run and cousins
squeal happy at the water's edge.

My mama and I, we stand there, toes in sand and the wind blowing
back hair . . .

Our faces turned right toward the sun.

It's a gift, the preacher said. Salvation *is* the gift, the one wrapped
in God taking on skin, laying His bare love out for the world, arms
spreading to the very ends of the limbs of the tree of life.

There is their laughter. There is their running. There is my mama
smiling. There is that singular seagull writing across the sky. These are

gifts. They beg praise to Him. Holy joy lies in the habit of murmuring thanks to God for the smallest of graces. I falter, but this is the habit to wear for a lifetime.

And really? There is only one gift — the one ocean of Christ that falls as rain over us in a thousand ways.

Christ is the offering and salvation is the gift and repentance is what makes us recipients of grace. *Christ* is the gift. *Christ* is the bridge home. *Christ* is our joy. How can I forget this, ever stop giving thanks for Him alone?

Happiness is not getting something but being given to Someone.

It is the sacrifice of Christ that returns us to God and communion with Him is possible anywhere and bless the Lord, oh, my soul, bless the very Maker of my soul.

Water keeps washing up over my toes.

A whole sea rushing up to meet the feet turned.

A sea rushing up to the shore and washing the feet turned ...

And a Father catching his girl falling ... all this happiness ... just in Him, right until last light.

Oh God, my God, holy joy lies in the habit of murmuring thanks to You for the smallest of graces. Forgive my faltering and make this thanksgiving to You the habit I'll wear all of my life. Because You, my Lord and Savior, You are the one Gift, the one Bridge — the one Ocean that falls as rain over me in a thousand ways. Kindle my heart again, to know that happiness is not getting something but being given to Someone.

comforting grace

Shout for joy, you heavens;
> rejoice, you earth;
> burst into song, you mountains!
For the LORD comforts his people
> and will have compassion on his afflicted ones.

Isaiah 49:13

I hear it on Sunday, thinking our preacher's looking straight at me, me trying to look away:

> When God moves us out of our comfort zone—into places that are way bigger than us, places that are difficult, hard, painful, places that even hurt—*this is a gift.*
>
> We are being given a gift.
>
> These hard places give us the gift of intimately knowing God in ways that would never be possible in our comfort zones.

Where's the back door of the chapel? *I'd like out.*

I look out the window to snow coming down. Shift hard in my chair. Can't find any comfortable position. I've been way out of my comfort zone for months. God taking this book I'd written, my story with my bare heart, taking me way out of my comfort zone.

All the way to the Bible Study Sisters on Saturday morning, I'd told myself I wasn't opening my mouth, not saying a word, not letting anyone into how all this felt. And when the other Anne had looked up from Zechariah 8 and asked me how it was for me, I didn't say a thing, couldn't, for everything quavering, heart running all liquid. I had mouthed it to the ceiling, a murmur looking up, trying to keep it all from spilling. "How did I get here?"

When God moves us out of our comfort zone ... When God ...

We're in the God-zone when we're out of our comfort zone and the Holy Spirit, our Comforter, comforts us when we step outside our comfort zone. It's only in the uncomfortable places that we can experience the tenderness of the Comforter.

When everything opened and fell on Saturday morning, Annette had left her chair to come and hold me and Mama had reached over and squeezed my hand and I had brushed it back, smiled, believing. Knowing. Anne had prayed long and earnest and I had felt the Spirit's embrace, like the warmth of the sun laying its arm down across my shoulder. I had felt it, how the sun had shone.

We're in step with the Holy Spirit when we step out into hard things. Faith gets out of the boat. And walking in the Spirit means stepping out to walk in the waves and feeling the comfort of His grip. *Isn't this gift?*

And on Sunday morning I look across the sanctuary. Can you really say that to the girl who doesn't wear her engagement ring anymore, to the beautiful mother whose husband left and the cancer has come, to the bent widow sitting next to the empty chair? Can you really say that to them, to the world? That the greatest gift we can ever receive is the gift of losing our earthly security and comfort? So that we can unwrap the intimacy of the Savior and His heavenly comfort.

I swallow hard.

Counting one thousand gifts is about *eucharisteo*, that Greek word that expresses what Christ did at the Last Supper: take the bread of pain as grace. Give thanks for that which is hard. Endure the cross, all in view of the joy set before.

Counting one thousand gifts means counting the hard things— *otherwise I've miscounted.*

After Sunday lunch and the dishes, I sit with the kids opening up a game board and I open a book and read this: "Ecstasy comes from the Greek word *ekstasis. Ek* meaning out. And *stasis* meaning standstill. Ecstatic = out of static."

I close the book. He keeps whispering it to my trembling heart, to me who knows and then forgets: Those who fully live, who live ecstatic lives of joy, embrace moving out of comfort zones. Ecstatic joy is found outside of static comfort zones. Because it's moving out to where the Spirit moves. The Spirit is never static. Never standstill. Like the wind, the Spirit always moves.

Shalom crawls up onto my lap. I lay the book down but I hold on to the words.

"Mrs. Nagel told me at church that she'd seen flowers poking up before this snow came. Do you think they are still out there somewhere, underneath the snow, Mama?" She looks out the window.

The snow's still coming down, a mystery of white.

"There are signs of spring out there." I tuck a curl behind her ear and say it soft. "Outside, in the cold, still signs of spring. Gifts coming."

She smiles, rubs her hands happy.

Outside of comfort's warmth, gifts unfurling underneath. Signs of radical change emerging everywhere.

Winter being overturned, of *eucharisteo* in the midst of hard things —of a revolution of thanks in all things to the God over all things.

Shalom and I fill a pitcher of water for the crocuses on the table. She counts the blooms. "There are seven!"

I smile at her so ecstatic.

And I stand there watching . . .

Watching the water flow out into this ponding circle and then moving out, always farther and further out.

~

Lord, thank You for the gift of coaxing me out of my comfort zone and further into the comfort of You. I really trust You enough to say it today: Thank You for the gift of losing my earthly security and comfort — so that I can unwrap the intimacy of You and Your heavenly comfort. Today, Father God, move me out of static comfort zones so I may know the ecstatic joy of the comfort of Christ!

cycling grace

"Holy, holy, holy is the LORD Almighty;
the whole earth is full of his glory."

Isaiah 6:3

In an endless cycle of grace He gives us gifts to serve the world.
This is how to make a life great and *eucharisteo* embarks us on the
path: "Whoever wants to become great among you must be your
servant, and whoever wants to be first must be your slave" (Matthew
20:26–27).

Outside my window, the whole of creation chooses just this. The
leaves of the maple tree freely unfurl oxygen, clouds overhead grow
pregnant with rain to bless, the soil of our fields offer up yield. All His
created world throbs with the joy in *eucharisteo*: "It is more blessed to
give than to receive" (Acts 20:35).

This is the way Jesus Himself chose. "That is what the Son of Man
has done: He came to serve, not be served—and then to give away his
life in exchange for the many who are held hostage" (Matthew 20:28
MSG).

It's the astonishing truth that while I serve Christ, it is He who
serves me. Jesus Christ still lives with a towel around His waist, bent in
service to His people ... in service to me as I serve, that I need never
serve in my own strength. Jesus Christ, who came into this world "not

to be served but to serve, and to give his life as a ransom for many" (Mark 10:45), will one day come again and "put on an apron, and serve them as they sit and eat!" (Luke 12:37 NLT), and even this very day He faithfully serves that we might say, "The Lord is my helper" (Hebrews 13:6).

Every day for a month we as a family read together Isaiah 58, and we can't get over it and we come to know it in the marrow and the fiber:

> Feed the hungry,
>   and help those in trouble.
> Then your light will shine out from the darkness,
>   and the darkness around you will be as bright as noon.
> The LORD will guide you continually,
>   giving you water when you are dry
>   and restoring your strength.
> You will be like a well-watered garden,
>   like an ever-flowing spring.
>
> *Isaiah 58:10– 11 NLT*

It's the fundamental, lavish, radical nature of the upside-down economy of God.

Empty to fill.

While the Deceiver jockeys to dupe us into thinking otherwise, we who are made in the image of God, being formed into Christ's likeness, our happiness comes too, not in the having, but in the handing over. Give your life away in exchange for many lives, give away your blessings to multiply blessings, give away so that many might increase—and do it all for the love of God. I can bless, pour out, be broken and given in our home and the larger world and never fear that there won't be enough to give.

Eucharisteo has taught me to trust that there is always enough God.

He has no end. He calls us to serve, and it is Him whom we serve, but He, very God, kneels down to serve us as we serve. The servant-hearted never serve alone. Spend the whole of your one wild and beautiful life investing in many lives, and God simply will not be outdone.

God extravagantly pays back everything we give away and exactly in the currency that is not of this world but of the one we yearn for: *joy in Him.*

Father God, the glorious God from whom and through whom and to whom are all things, You reign and You rain down blessings, that my life may become a blessing. Lord God, please—pour me out in this place, my life used up in Your endless cycle of grace.

wearing grace

The LORD your God is in your midst,
a mighty one who will save;
he will rejoice over you with gladness;
he will quiet you by his love;
he will exult over you with loud singing.

Zephaniah 3:17 ESV

It'd been a bit of an everyday miracle—us leaving the farm and all those baby pigs out in the barn and traveling to Ecuador to meet children sponsored through the Christian humanitarian organization, Compassion International.

On our first day in Ecuador, on a steep mountainside under direct sun, we bent beside Rosa, a pig farmer herself, and planted potatoes into her loamy earth.

Rosa's youngest, little Liliana, she scooped up a puppy right there next to the potato patch and she just hid behind its gaping mouth, her eyes all large and laughing.

Rosa told us what Liliana had done—that Liliana had found that puppy wandering abandoned, lost, outside her classroom. That Liliana had brought the puppy home to love. That Liliana loved. And when Liliana gaped all happy, just like the puppy, I laughed right out loud.

And there it was again, words from *One Thousand Gifts*—and I could feel it again, the joy of it welling: *We receive grace.*

And through us, grace could flow on. Like a cycle of water in continuous movement, grace is meant to fall, a rain ... again, again, again. We could share the grace, multiply the joy, extend the table of the feast, enlarge the paradise of His presence.

We are blessed. We can bless. This is happiness.

We are blessed, and couldn't we bless and couldn't this fullness flow on and on and on and isn't this the realest happiness?

Liliana, living in a single-parent home, living in abject poverty, looking for a sponsorship through Compassion, Liliana with less than little, she brings a puppy home just to love, and I'm the one scooping it up, what really is—that the giving away is the getting of joy.

After a week of beautiful children and praying with families up the Amazon and serving with pastors planting churches, we fly a continent home. And a week later, and a whole half a world north of Liliana and her puppy, I wake up strangely happy. Life change is as simple as changing our choices, and transformation is fully possible when we form our decisions differently—form them into the image of Christ.

A fashion catalog comes in the mail. Models standing beside llamas in the village of some cobbled South American street. I've just seen it, the dirt floors, the dark and no sinks, behind the doors on the street where the model sways thin in her $588 dress. I think of Rosa's one bran-sack window and how she turned away when her heart rained grief. Poverty can't be airbrushed and it hides its tears and you won't see it modeled on the front covers of glossy magazines.

I like the model's shoes.

How in the world can I like her shoes?

There is this, and it unknots everything in me, smoothes me out, and it's the way the choices change: *What if we wanted to be beautiful more than we wanted to buy beautiful?*

The Enemy tempts that stuff is what makes us lovely—when the Truth is surrender makes us the loveliest and what is more lovely than love? Love, it knows no other way than to give away.

Liliana, she had mimicked puppy joy and I had laughed right out loud and so had she, and the moment, it had light all along the seams. What could be lovelier than this? Her loving a lost puppy and me loving her and Christ loving all the lost? Why not change all the choices for this? Model all that matters, the Beautiful, a life like Christ's—and imitate Christ's joy—the way He gives.

The way the happiness and healing is always in the opening of a hand, the opening a life to the largeness of God. It stays with me and I wear *this*, the joy of it—the way Liliana laughed in all her sheer loveliness.

Lord of my life, what if I wanted to be beautiful more than I wanted to buy beautiful? Though the Enemy tempts that stuff is what makes me lovely, remind me that surrender to You makes us the loveliest and what is more lovely than counting the ways You love? Change my life by changing my choices and transform me by forming my decisions into the image of the sheer loveliness of Christ.

trumpeting grace

Let the heart of those who seek the LORD be glad ...
Seek His face continually.
Remember His wonderful deeds which he has done.

1 Chronicles 16:10–12 NASB

I hadn't agreed with everything in the book I'd picked up, but right
after I read that one story, I went looking for an old horn to screw right
to the wall—because there really are things worth the proclaiming.

And when I find this one old horn, I walk around the house, horn
in hand, trying to figure if it looks best on this wall?

Or maybe on the back of this door? The Farmer raises his
eyebrows.

"A horn on a wall?" He's grinning boyish. Joshua is playing scales.
Levi's reciting Latin chants. Shalom and Malakai are arguing loud over
a game of chess.

"Because you're thinking it's not quite loud enough in here yet?"

"You!" I poke him in the shoulder, him broad like a beam that
carries half my world. "Does it look right here?"

"I think I've got a wall out in the barn it might look perfect on."
He winks, shields himself with his arm to fend off the next poke.

"But if you knew the story ..." I try to defend and he nods, knowing, smiling, "Uh-huh." And I nod, knowing stories can turn around whole hard hearts. Jesus walked back roads and spun stories and turned around lives and the axis of the cosmos.

So I tell this story at lunch.

"A man drove a stretch of highway past this tattered cardboard sign that read 'Honk if you're happy.'" I pass down the squash.

And who doesn't roll his eyes at such naïveté? As if the world is this strange hybrid of Pollyanna and Sesame Street—if you're happy and you know it, *honk, honk*—when it's really just a strange new, old world, broken and a mess. Shalom offers me her glass and I pour water.

"But there's this one day when the man drives past the sign with his little girl, and on a whim he beeps the horn. And every day when he passes the sign, his daughter begs him to do it again, and pretty soon, every time he's on this stretch of highway, this jaded man, this cynical man, is anticipating the sign. Anticipating honking his horn. And do you know what he said?"

I want to make sure I get it right. I push back my chair, to get the library book from my nightstand. Flip through the pages ... There— that one good story in the book:

> Deep inside and just for a moment, I felt a little happier than I had just seconds before—as if honking the horn made me happier ... If on a one-to-ten scale, I was feeling an emotional two, when I honked the horn, my happiness grew several points ...
>
> In time, when I turned on to Highway 544, I noticed that my emotional setpoint would begin to rise. That entire 13.4 mile stretch began to become a place of emotional rejuvenation for me.[37]

I lay the book down on the table, reach for the water pitcher.

"See what happened to him? The sign read, 'Honk if you're happy.' And he discovered that the act of honking the horn—it made him happy."

"Honk, honk!" Malakai grins at the end of the table. His mouth's full of food. I love him wild.

"So who puts up a cardboard sign beside a highway — Honk if you're happy?" I have to get to the rest of the story before the table erupts into a fest of honking Canadians.

"This man has to find out. So he finds a house on the other side of the trees that line the highway — and he goes up to the door and asks the folks if they know anything about the happy sign. And the man at the door welcomes him in and says yes, yes, he made the sign."

And this is why he made the sign: Because he was sitting there every day in his house, sitting there in a darkened bedroom with his young wife who was terminal, sitting there watching her every day as she lay there waiting to die. And one day when he really couldn't take it anymore, he painted up that sign and stuck it out by the road. Because, he said — I reach for the book again, to find the right page, to get the words right: "I just wanted people in their cars not to take this moment for granted. This special, never-again-to-be-repeated moment with the ones they care for most should be savored and they should be aware of the happiness in the moment."[38]

I look around at all their faces ringing the table, the jewel of them slipping around me in this space. Light's falling across the table. Hope's one strand of loose hair is its own gold. Something inside me trumpets loud and long.

I can only whisper the end of the story.

At first, after the man had put out the sign, there was only a honk here and there, and his dying wife asked what that was about and the husband explained how he'd put the sign out there and after a few days there was more and more honking. And the husband said that the honking ...

I look down again at the book but everything's blurring. Finally the line surfaces.

… became like medicine to her. As she lay there, she heard the horns and found great comfort in knowing that she was not isolated in a dark room dying. She was part of the happiness of the world. It was literally all around her.[39]

It was literally all around her.
So much light's falling across the table.
"I'm thinking it will look best in that doorway."
The Farmer winks.
And when the Farmer heads out to the shop after lunch, I call after him — *Remember to bring in a screwdriver so we can hang the horn!*
And he waves back to me as he runs across the farmyard. And when I'm standing in the kitchen wiping off the counters, I hear it clear, from the farm pickup parked out in the laneway, out by the shop: Honk! Honk! Honk!
I laugh. He's out there honking the horn of his truck!
I turn to the window, laughing … He's happy! *Happy* …
And I reach for my pen atop my open gratitude journal there on the counter. "Honk if you're happy" is really "to be happy, honk."
And "give thanks if you are joy-filled" is really "to be joy-filled, *give thanks.*"
And I write it down. "The Farmer honking a horn — and that grin of his."
This has become like medicine to me.
Shalom waves to the Farmer from the window. He's waving back at her. She sings the words quiet to him, "Honk if you're happy!" — and she knows he can't hear.
But all the world is heaven's clarion and even in the dark, we are surrounded by it, all the happiness of the world, and I keep the journal close, the thanks ready.
Because literally — it was all around her.

Thank You, God, for the horns You place in my life every day—the chances to honk and be happy. Show me more! And if a joy-filled heart is good medicine, then giving thanks is my daily prescription. Lord, You make all this world heaven's clarion and even in the dark I am surrounded by it and let me do it a thousand times today—offer honking thanks up to Your throne—joy ringing through all the earth and me!

becoming grace

I will bless you ... and you will be a blessing.

Genesis 12:2

I walk in our back door to candlelight still flickering, hang the keys on the hook, and look around at the steep mountain of laundry there in the mudroom, the shoes scattered, a coat dropped. The mudroom sink is grime ringed. Fingerprints smear across the mirror.

I laugh the happiest wonder.

In the afternoon's drizzle, I give happy thanks for the daily mess with a smile a mile wide because this is again my chance to wholeheartedly serve God, to do full-bodied *eucharisteo* with the hands and the heart and the lips. I can count each task a gift, pure *eucharisteo*.

Grace!

This work—the thousand endless jobs—they each give the opportunity for one to *become* the gift, *a thousand times over!* Because with every one of the thousand endless jobs, I become the gift to God and to others because this work is the public God serving, the daily liturgy of thanks, the completing of the Communion service with my service.

Eucharisteo wakens me wide-eyed and nodding to the truth that I—a mother of six—now *own* a truth bought with the practice of *eucharisteo*.

I reach out and touch the reflection in the splattered mirror over the sink and whisper into those eyes: Yes, today, *again*, yes, *you can bless!* Here you can enact *eucharisteo*; here you can become a current in a river of grace that redeems the world.

Even me. I think of my brother-in-law, John. John, who had buried his two sons, who let me into his healing through crazy grief when he said, "The way through the pain is to reach out to others in theirs." I have known ache and becoming the blessing is what deeply blesses us and this is the way He binds up our wounds.

I think back to earlier, washing each other's feet at the women's small group. How we take Communion. Then, quietly, I fill the basins with water warm and circled together as a community we *give* communion. We bare our toes, soles, and I bend with sisters in Christ, dip my hands into water, and touch shy skin. We wash feet, all around, we wash feet. We lap water across skin and I hold a woman's heel and I gently bathe and as group facilitator I ask each in the room to think about this washing of feet as symbolic of our lives on a grand scale, of how we are called to complete the Communion service in service. I tilt my head to look into her face and I ask it quiet in a quiet room: "Do you, in your day-to-day life, feel served? How might we as a community better serve you?"

And she, mother of eight, an elder's wife, children's ministry leader, one who pours her life out in unending ways, she whispers, haltingly through emotion. "But I'm the one who needs to ask if I've been a blessing."

"But you—*oh, how you have blessed*." With the tepid water, I wash her toes, these beads between fingers, and I recount the long string of ways she's intimately blessed me: "The day you took me for a walk through the woods and listened to the faint heartbeat of my faith. The countless words you have sent me, a hand of friendship." I take the cloth and wash her heel. "The way you have been real with me, transparent and authentic, and we have been mothers and we have been sisters and we have wept." And I look up into her face, her wet feet in my hands, and again the chin wobbles all feeling. In this room of women, washing feet, it overflows. With memories of the ways each has become the blessing. Unmasked, we wash our faces in tears of joy. Hands cupping dripping soles, I see how it is our very presence in each other's lives that makes us the gift. By the very function not of our doing *but of our being*, I see we are the beloved of God.

And so we *become* the love of God, blessing those He loves.

And even here, right where I am, I can become the blessing again, a little life that multiplies joy, making the larger world a better place.

God can enter into me, even me, and use these hands, these feet, to be His love, a love that goes on and on and on forever, endless cycle of grace.

I am nearing the wonder of Communion.

God, whenever the pain comes, let me know it gently: Joy and pain, they are but two arteries of the one heart that pumps through all those who don't numb themselves to really living—and the way through the pain is to reach out to others in theirs. Use me today, and let me become the gift back to You through the work before me. In thanks for all Your gifts, make me a gift, because becoming the blessing is what deeply blesses. Enter into me, even me, and use my life to be Your love. This I pray.

count 1,000 ways
He loves you . . .

1.
2.
3.
4.
5.
6.
7.
8.
9.
10.
11.
12.
13.
14.
15.
16.
17.
18.
19.
20.
21.
22.
23.
24.
25.
26.

Give thanks in all circumstances; for this is God's will for you in Christ Jesus.
—1 Thessalonians 5:18

27. _____
28. _____
29. _____
30. _____
31. _____
32. _____
33. _____
34. _____
35. _____
36. _____
37. _____
38. _____
39. _____
40. _____
41. _____
42. _____
43. _____
44. _____
45. _____
46. _____
47. _____
48. _____
49. _____
50. _____

51. _____
52. _____
53. _____
54. _____
55. _____
56. _____
57. _____
58. _____
59. _____
60. _____
61. _____
62. _____
63. _____
64. _____
65. _____
66. _____
67. _____
68. _____
69. _____
70. _____
71. _____
72. _____
73. _____
74. _____
75. _____
76. _____

When I only give thanks for some things,
aren't I likely to miss giving God glory in most things?

77. _____
78. _____
79. _____
80. _____
81. _____
82. _____
83. _____
84. _____
85. _____
86. _____
87. _____
88. _____
89. _____
90. _____
91. _____
92. _____
93. _____
94. _____
95. _____
96. _____
97. _____
98. _____
99. _____
100. _____

101. _____
102. _____
103. _____
104. _____
105. _____
106. _____
107. _____
108. _____
109. _____
110. _____
111. _____
112. _____
113. _____
114. _____
115. _____
116. _____
117. _____
118. _____
119. _____
120. _____
121. _____
122. _____
123. _____
124. _____
125. _____
126. _____

To thank God in all is to bend the knee in allegiance to God,
who alone knows all.

127. _____
128. _____
129. _____
130. _____
131. _____
132. _____
133. _____
134. _____
135. _____
136. _____
137. _____
138. _____
139. _____
140. _____
141. _____
142. _____
143. _____
144. _____
145. _____
146. _____
147. _____
148. _____
149. _____
150. _____

151. _____
152. _____
153. _____
154. _____
155. _____
156. _____
157. _____
158. _____
159. _____
160. _____
161. _____
162. _____
163. _____
164. _____
165. _____
166. _____
167. _____
168. _____
169. _____
170. _____
171. _____
172. _____
173. _____
174. _____
175. _____
176. _____

If you want to change the world, pick up your pen.
—Martin Luther

177. _____
178. _____
179. _____
180. _____
181. _____
182. _____
183. _____
184. _____
185. _____
186. _____
187. _____
188. _____
189. _____
190. _____
191. _____
192. _____
193. _____
194. _____
195. _____
196. _____
197. _____
198. _____
199. _____
200. _____

201. _____
202. _____
203. _____
204. _____
205. _____
206. _____
207. _____
208. _____
209. _____
210. _____
211. _____
212. _____
213. _____
214. _____
215. _____
216. _____
217. _____
218. _____
219. _____
220. _____
221. _____
222. _____
223. _____
224. _____
225. _____
226. _____

Our thanks to God is our witness to the goodness of God
when Satan and all world would sneer at us to recant.

227. _____
228. _____
229. _____
230. _____
231. _____
232. _____
233. _____
234. _____
235. _____
236. _____
237. _____
238. _____
239. _____
240. _____
241. _____
242. _____
243. _____
244. _____
245. _____
246. _____
247. _____
248. _____
249. _____
250. _____

251. _____

252. _____

253. _____

254. _____

255. _____

256. _____

257. _____

258. _____

259. _____

260. _____

261. _____

262. _____

263. _____

264. _____

265. _____

266. _____

267. _____

268. _____

269. _____

270. _____

271. _____

272. _____

273. _____

274. _____

275. _____

276. _____

Our perennial spiritual and psychological task is to look
at things familiar until they become unfamiliar again.
—G. K. Chesterton

277. _____
278. _____
279. _____
280. _____
281. _____
282. _____
283. _____
284. _____
285. _____
286. _____
287. _____
288. _____
289. _____
290. _____
291. _____
292. _____
293. _____
294. _____
295. _____
296. _____
297. _____
298. _____
299. _____
300. _____

301.

302.

303.

304.

305.

306.

307.

308.

309.

310.

311.

312.

313.

314.

315.

316.

317.

318.

319.

320.

321.

322.

323.

324.

325.

326.

That which I refuse to thank Christ for,
I refuse to believe Christ can redeem.

327. _____
328. _____
329. _____
330. _____
331. _____
332. _____
333. _____
334. _____
335. _____
336. _____
337. _____
338. _____
339. _____
340. _____
341. _____
342. _____
343. _____
344. _____
345. _____
346. _____
347. _____
348. _____
349. _____
350. _____

351.
352.
353.
354.
355.
356.
357.
358.
359.
360.
361.
362.
363.
364.
365.
366.
367.
368.
369.
370.
371.
372.
373.
374.
375.
376.

*Giving thanks in hard times makes the canyon of pain
into a megaphone to proclaim the ultimate goodness of God.*

377. _____
378. _____
379. _____
380. _____
381. _____
382. _____
383. _____
384. _____
385. _____
386. _____
387. _____
388. _____
389. _____
390. _____
391. _____
392. _____
393. _____
394. _____
395. _____
396. _____
397. _____
398. _____
399. _____
400. _____

401. _____
402. _____
403. _____
404. _____
405. _____
406. _____
407. _____
408. _____
409. _____
410. _____
411. _____
412. _____
413. _____
414. _____
415. _____
416. _____
417. _____
418. _____
419. _____
420. _____
421. _____
422. _____
423. _____
424. _____
425. _____
426. _____

It is in the process of being worshiped that God communicates His presence to men.
—C. S. Lewis

427. _____
428. _____
429. _____
430. _____
431. _____
432. _____
433. _____
434. _____
435. _____
436. _____
437. _____
438. _____
439. _____
440. _____
441. _____
442. _____
443. _____
444. _____
445. _____
446. _____
447. _____
448. _____
449. _____
450. _____

451. _____
452. _____
453. _____
454. _____
455. _____
456. _____
457. _____
458. _____
459. _____
460. _____
461. _____
462. _____
463. _____
464. _____
465. _____
466. _____
467. _____
468. _____
469. _____
470. _____
471. _____
472. _____
473. _____
474. _____
475. _____
476. _____

*It is suffering that has the realest possibility
to bear down and deliver grace.*

477. _____
478. _____
479. _____
480. _____
481. _____
482. _____
483. _____
484. _____
485. _____
486. _____
487. _____
488. _____
489. _____
490. _____
491. _____
492. _____
493. _____
494. _____
495. _____
496. _____
497. _____
498. _____
499. _____
500. _____

501. _____

502. _____

503. _____

504. _____

505. _____

506. _____

507. _____

508. _____

509. _____

510. _____

511. _____

512. _____

513. _____

514. _____

515. _____

516. _____

517. _____

518. _____

519. _____

520. _____

521. _____

522. _____

523. _____

524. _____

525. _____

526. _____

No gift unrecognized as coming from God is at its own best . . .
when in all gifts we find Him, then in Him we shall find all things.
—George MacDonald

527. _____
528. _____
529. _____
530. _____
531. _____
532. _____
533. _____
534. _____
535. _____
536. _____
537. _____
538. _____
539. _____
540. _____
541. _____
542. _____
543. _____
544. _____
545. _____
546. _____
547. _____
548. _____
549. _____
550. _____

551. _____
552. _____
553. _____
554. _____
555. _____
556. _____
557. _____
558. _____
559. _____
560. _____
561. _____
562. _____
563. _____
564. _____
565. _____
566. _____
567. _____
568. _____
569. _____
570. _____
571. _____
572. _____
573. _____
574. _____
575. _____
576. _____

I only deepen the wound of a hurting world
when I neglect to give thanks.

577. _____
578. _____
579. _____
580. _____
581. _____
582. _____
583. _____
584. _____
585. _____
586. _____
587. _____
588. _____
589. _____
590. _____
591. _____
592. _____
593. _____
594. _____
595. _____
596. _____
597. _____
598. _____
599. _____
600. _____

601. _____
602. _____
603. _____
604. _____
605. _____
606. _____
607. _____
608. _____
609. _____
610. _____
611. _____
612. _____
613. _____
614. _____
615. _____
616. _____
617. _____
618. _____
619. _____
620. _____
621. _____
622. _____
623. _____
624. _____
625. _____
626. _____

Who feels such gratitude for their salvation in Christ
that they feel such affection for Christ?

627. _____
628. _____
629. _____
630. _____
631. _____
632. _____
633. _____
634. _____
635. _____
636. _____
637. _____
638. _____
639. _____
640. _____
641. _____
642. _____
643. _____
644. _____
645. _____
646. _____
647. _____
648. _____
649. _____
650. _____

651. _____

652. _____

653. _____

654. _____

655. _____

656. _____

657. _____

658. _____

659. _____

660. _____

661. _____

662. _____

663. _____

664. _____

665. _____

666. _____

667. _____

668. _____

669. _____

670. _____

671. _____

672. _____

673. _____

674. _____

675. _____

676. _____

Out of his fullness we have all received grace in place of grace already given.
—John 1:16

677. _____
678. _____
679. _____
680. _____
681. _____
682. _____
683. _____
684. _____
685. _____
686. _____
687. _____
688. _____
689. _____
690. _____
691. _____
692. _____
693. _____
694. _____
695. _____
696. _____
697. _____
698. _____
699. _____
700. _____

701. _____

702. _____

703. _____

704. _____

705. _____

706. _____

707. _____

708. _____

709. _____

710. _____

711. _____

712. _____

713. _____

714. _____

715. _____

716. _____

717. _____

718. _____

719. _____

720. _____

721. _____

722. _____

723. _____

724. _____

725. _____

726. _____

Our fall is always first a failure to give thanks.

727. _____

728. _____

729. _____

730. _____

731. _____

732. _____

733. _____

734. _____

735. _____

736. _____

737. _____

738. _____

739. _____

740. _____

741. _____

742. _____

743. _____

744. _____

745. _____

746. _____

747. _____

748. _____

749. _____

750. _____

751.

752.

753.

754.

755.

756.

757.

758.

759.

760.

761.

762.

763.

764.

765.

766.

767.

768.

769.

770.

771.

772.

773.

774.

775.

776.

Gratitude bestows reverence, allowing us to encounter everyday epiphanies, those transcendent moments of awe that change forever how we experience life and the world. —Sarah Ban Breathnach

777. _____
778. _____
779. _____
780. _____
781. _____
782. _____
783. _____
784. _____
785. _____
786. _____
787. _____
788. _____
789. _____
790. _____
791. _____
792. _____
793. _____
794. _____
795. _____
796. _____
797. _____
798. _____
799. _____
800. _____

801. _____
802. _____
803. _____
804. _____
805. _____
806. _____
807. _____
808. _____
809. _____
810. _____
811. _____
812. _____
813. _____
814. _____
815. _____
816. _____
817. _____
818. _____
819. _____
820. _____
821. _____
822. _____
823. _____
824. _____
825. _____
826. _____

*In a broken world—when we remember how He blesses, loves us,
when we recollect His goodnesses to us, we heal—we re-member.*

827. _____

828. _____

829. _____

830. _____

831. _____

832. _____

833. _____

834. _____

835. _____

836. _____

837. _____

838. _____

839. _____

840. _____

841. _____

842. _____

843. _____

844. _____

845. _____

846. _____

847. _____

848. _____

849. _____

850. _____

851.

852.

853.

854.

855.

856.

857.

858.

859.

860.

861.

862.

863.

864.

865.

866.

867.

868.

869.

870.

871.

872.

873.

874.

875.

876.

The unthankful heart ... discovers no mercies; but let the thankful heart sweep through the day and, as the magnet finds the iron, so it will find, in every hour, some heavenly blessings. —Henry Ward Beecher

877. _____
878. _____
879. _____
880. _____
881. _____
882. _____
883. _____
884. _____
885. _____
886. _____
887. _____
888. _____
889. _____
890. _____
891. _____
892. _____
893. _____
894. _____
895. _____
896. _____
897. _____
898. _____
899. _____
900. _____

901. _____
902. _____
903. _____
904. _____
905. _____
906. _____
907. _____
908. _____
909. _____
910. _____
911. _____
912. _____
913. _____
914. _____
915. _____
916. _____
917. _____
918. _____
919. _____
920. _____
921. _____
922. _____
923. _____
924. _____
925. _____
926. _____

I accept this is the way to begin, and all hard things come in due time and with practice. Yet now wisps of cheese tell me gentle that this is the first secret step into eucharisteo's miracle.

927. _____

928. _____

929. _____

930. _____

931. _____

932. _____

933. _____

934. _____

935. _____

936. _____

937. _____

938. _____

939. _____

940. _____

941. _____

942. _____

943. _____

944. _____

945. _____

946. _____

947. _____

948. _____

949. _____

950. _____

951. _____
952. _____
953. _____
954. _____
955. _____
956. _____
957. _____
958. _____
959. _____
960. _____
961. _____
962. _____
963. _____
964. _____
965. _____
966. _____
967. _____
968. _____
969. _____
970. _____
971. _____
972. _____
973. _____
974. _____
975. _____
976. _____

See what great love the Father has lavished on us,
that we should be called children of God!
—1 John 3:1

977. _____

978. _____

979. _____

980. _____

981. _____

982. _____

983. _____

984. _____

985. _____

986. _____

987. _____

988. _____

989. _____

990. _____

991. _____

992. _____

993. _____

994. _____

995. _____

996. _____

997. _____

998. _____

999. _____

1000. _____

acknowledgments

Thanks be to God.

For Bill, who has stood beside me on his knees, and Mick the visionary, who chiseled relentlessly because he saw His grace in stones, and Tonia, who is an unwavering Jonathan. Your fellowship is a gift.

For Dirk, who has gently pastored every word, every encounter, like his Shepherd; for Sandy, who has marched the walls in faithful prayer, tender wisdom, and blessed friendship; for Tom and Don and Tracy and Jennifer, the dream team that has championed for His glory!

For every reader at www.aholyexperience.com — that we can do life together? That you'd take me anyway? It is one of the most humbling privileges imaginable, to do community with you. Reaching over right now and squeezing your hand and whispering, "God knows your name and your story and He cups you close and He is always good and you are always loved and may you know it right now, in your marrow and your bone, the wooing love of Christ."

For my mama, who has served and loved and given like Jesus — He's multiplied all you've offered Him and the beauty of your gift takes away my breath. Thank you, Mama — a thousand times over, thank you. For Molly, who has served and supported and is my Barnabas sister. You and Mama have been Aaron and Hur.

For Caleb and Joshua, Hope and Levi, Malakai and Shalom. Thank you for always saying, "Please — read just one more page?" But mostly, for making your lives into this story that's taken my breath away. You all have been my favorite chapters.

For Darryl, whose life whispers to all the timid, *Fly. He means for us to fly on wings of grace.* There is only one you.

For Father, Son, and Holy Spirit. We have received nothing unless it is given to us from heaven (John 3:27). For all this grace upon grace upon grace — we can only murmur:

Thanks be to God.

notes

1. Mark Buchanan, *The Holy Wild* (Colorado Springs: Multnomah, 2005), 105.

2. Ibid., 106.

3. Ibid., 108.

4. Robert Frost, "A Winter Eden," www.portitude.org/literature/frost/pt-winter_eden.php (accessed July 10, 2012).

5. Gilbert Keith Chesterton, *A Short History of England* (Teddington, Middlesex, UK: Echo Library, 2008), 30.

6. Augustine, *Confessions of Saint Augustine*, book 10, chapter 21.

7. Quoted in Belden Lane, *Ravished by Beauty: The Surprising Legacy of Reformed Spirituality* (New York: Oxford University Press, 2011), 65.

8. Ibid., 66.

9. Ibid.

10. Ibid., 69.

11. Ibid., 82.

12. Mark Buchanan, *The Rest of God: Restoring Your Soul by Restoring Your Sabbath* (Nashville: Nelson, 2007), 45, emphasis added.

13. John Piper, *When I Don't Desire God: How to Fight for Joy* (Wheaton, Ill.: Crossway, 2004), 124.

14. Desiderius Erasmus, "*Diluculum,* or The Early Rising," in *The Colloquies of Erasmus* (London: Reeves and Turner, 1878), 2:212.

15. C. S. Lewis, *God in the Dock* (Grand Rapids: Eerdmans, 1994), 52.

16. "New Letters of R. L. Stevenson," in *Harper's Monthly Magazine*, vol. 104, eds. Henry Mills Alden, Thomas Bucklin Wells, and Lee Foster Hartman (New York: Harper, 1902), 126.

17. John Piper, "From His Fullness We Have All Received, Grace Upon Grace," www.desiringgod.org/ResourceLibrary/Sermons/ByDate/2008/3394_From_His_Fullness_We_Have_All_Received_Grace_Upon_Grace/ (accessed July 10, 2012).

18. C. S. Lewis, *The Great Divorce* (New York: Macmillan, 1946), 77.

19. A. W. Tozer, *The Pursuit of God* (Camp Hill, Pa.: Christian Publications, 1982), 73.

20. C. S. Lewis, "The Weight of Glory," in *The Weight of Glory and Other Addresses* (Grand Rapids: Eerdmans, 1965), 12–13.

21. Teresa of Avila, quoted in Amy Welborn, *The Loyola Kids Book of Saints* (Chicago: Loyola, 2001), 87.

22. G. K. Chesterton, *Orthodoxy* (Rockville, Md.: Serenity, 2009), 19.

23. Quoted in G. B. F. Hallock, "The Cultivation of Humility," *Herald and Presbyter* 90 (December 24, 1919): 8.

24. Timothy Keller, "The Advent of Humility," *Christianity Today*, December 22, 2008, www.christianitytoday.com/ct/2008/december/20.51.html (accessed July 10, 2012).

25. Dennis Linn, Sheila Fabricant Linn, and Matthew Linn, *Sleeping with Bread: Holding What Gives You Life* (Mahwah N.J.: Paulist, 1995), 1.

26. Lewis, "The Weight of Glory," 10.

27. Dennis Lennon, *Fuelling the Fire: Fresh Thinking on Prayer* (Queensway, UK: Scripture Union, 2005), 43, emphasis added.

28. Chesterton, *Orthodoxy*, 55.

29. Quoted in Wilhelm Odelberg, *Les Prix Nobel 1986* (Stockholm: Nobel Foundation, 1987).

30. Charles H. Spurgeon, "The Simplicity and Sublimity of Salvation," http://articles.ochristian.com/article8386.shtml (accessed July 10, 2012).

31. J. R. Miller, "The Thanksgiving Lesson," www.gracegems.org/Miller/thanksgiving_lesson.htm (accessed July 12, 2012).

32. Peter Kreeft, "Joy," www.peterkreeft.com/topics/joy.htm (accessed July 12, 2012), emphasis added.

33. Jean-Pierre de Caussade, quoted in *A Guide to Prayer for All God's People*, Rueben Job and Norman Shawchuck, eds. (Nashville: Upper Room, 1990), 244.

34. Annie Dillard, *Pilgrim at Tinker Creek* (New York: HarperPerennial, 1998), 33.

35. Dorothy Sayers, *Letters to a Diminished Church* (Nashville: Nelson, 2004), 143.

36. Chesterton, *Orthodoxy*, 138.

37. Will Bowen, *A Complaint-Free World* (New York: Doubleday, 2007), 116, 118.

38. Ibid., 121.

39. Ibid.

Ann Voskamp is a farmer's wife, the home-educating mama to a half-dozen exuberant kids, and the author of the *New York Times* bestseller *One Thousand Gifts: A Dare to Live Fully Right Where You Are*. She tells stories. She takes pictures. She sees the whole earth full of the glory of God. A columnist with DaySpring, a contributing editor to Laity Lodge's The High Calling, and a writer of articles featured in *WORLD* magazine, *The Huffington Post*, and *Christianity Today*, Ann partners with Compassion International as a global advocate for needy children. The poor have made her rich, and telling the stories of those who need a voice has changed her own story. Ann can be found writing about messy grace and a magnificent God at her daily online journal: www.aholyexperience.com. Visit Ann's website at: www.onethousandgifts.com.

Write to Zondervan authors or their estates in care of Zondervan. Your mail will be forwarded as soon as possible, but please note that the author might not be able to respond personally. Email zauthor@zondervan.com or send postal mail to:

Ann Voskamp
c/o Zondervan
ATTN: Author Care
5300 Patterson SE
Grand Rapids, MI 49530

One Thousand Gifts

A Dare to Live Fully
Right Where You Are

Ann Voskamp

Just like you, Ann Voskamp hungers to live her one life well. Forget the bucket lists that have us escaping our everyday lives for exotic experiences. "How," Ann wondered, "do we find joy in the midst of deadlines, debt, drama, and daily duties? What does the Christ-life really look like when your days are gritty, long—and sometimes even dark? How is God even here?"

In *One Thousand Gifts*, Ann invites you to embrace everyday blessings and embark on the transformative spiritual discipline of chronicling God's gifts. It's only in this expressing of gratitude for the life we already have that we discover the life we've always wanted ... a life we can take, give thanks for, and break for others. We come to feel and know the impossible right down in our bones: we are wildly loved—by God. Let Ann's beautiful, heart-aching stories of the everyday give you a way of seeing that opens your eyes to ordinary amazing grace, a way of being present to God that makes you deeply happy, and a way of living that is finally fully alive.

Come live the best dare of all!

Selections from One Thousand Gifts

Finding Joy in What Really Matters

Ann Voskamp,
New York Times *bestselling author*

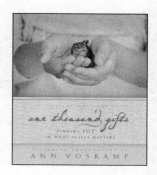

What if joy were possible — right where you are? Inspiring hundreds of thousands of readers to wake to their own wondrous lives, the *New York Times* bestseller *One Thousand Gifts: A Dare to Live Fully Right Where You Are* shares the journey of one woman facing her own hard, dark days and hidden fears, and stumbling straight into the answer of life's great riddle: How do you discover joy — right here and now?

Selections from One Thousand Gifts features powerful, life-changing passages from Voskamp's compelling story and her own exquisite photography, framing a seemingly ordinary, gritty life around true amazing grace. Because if joy is a matter of gratitude, and gratitude is a matter of perspective, then giving thanks changes not only your perspective but also your life.

Open these lyrical pages and slow down to discover the joy you've always been looking for.

Come find God in the moments!

one thousand gifts

FREE APP
iPhone • iPad • Android

ONE THOUSAND GIFTS, A THOUSAND THANKS

How do you find every day, amazing grace in the midst of deadlines, debt, drama, and daily duties?

New York Times bestselling author Ann Voskamp offers this practical, radical answer: by giving thanks for the life you already have, to find the life you've always wanted.

This exclusive mobile app will help you do just that. Capture your gifts. Count your blessings. Share your joy as it happens on the way to your own one thousand gifts.

SHARE YOUR GIFTS WHEREVER YOU ARE

The simple moments in life that bring true happiness — a high pile of freshly grated cheese, the music of your child's carefree giggles — too often pass us by without a second thought. The *One Thousand Gifts* mobile app will help you slow down and catch God in the moment.

NOW AVAILABLE

THE ONE THOUSAND GIFTS MOBILE APP FEATURES:

- Quotes on awakening to the joy-filled power of grace and gratitude...to help get you started
- Photos and texts of your gifts...to keep you going
- A one-tap option to instantly share your captured gifts on Facebook, Twitter, and Flickr...to keep your friends and your family inspired on their way to their one thousand gifts

Share Your Thoughts

With the Author: Your comments will be forwarded to the author when you send them to *zauthor@zondervan.com*.

With Zondervan: Submit your review of this book by writing to *zreview@zondervan.com*.

Free Online Resources at
www.zondervan.com

Daily Bible Verses and Devotions: Enrich your life with daily Bible verses or devotions that help you start every morning focused on God. Visit www.zondervan.com/newsletters.

Free Email Publications: Sign up for newsletters on Christian living, academic resources, church ministry, fiction, children's resources, and more. Visit www.zondervan.com/newsletters.

Zondervan Bible Search: Find and compare Bible passages in a variety of translations at www.zondervanbiblesearch.com.

Other Benefits: Register to receive online benefits like coupons and special offers, or to participate in research.